Software Architect

Software Architect

Michael Bell

WILEY

For general information on our other products and services or for technical support, please contact our Customer Care Department within the United States at (800) 762-2974, outside the United States at (317) 572-3993 or fax (317) 572-4002.

If you believe you've found a mistake in this book, please bring it to our attention by emailing our reader support team at wileysupport@wiley.com with the subject line "Possible Book Errata Submission."

Wiley also publishes its books in a variety of electronic formats. Some content that appears in print may not be available in electronic formats. For more information about Wiley products, visit our web site at www.wiley.com.

Library of Congress Control Number: 2022951780

Cover image: Courtesy of Michael Bell
Cover design: Wiley

SKY10042823_021623

About the Author

Michael Bell is an American novelist, artist, producer, and enterprise solution architect, chiefly recognized for developing the Incremental Software Architecture methodology (ISAM), Service-Oriented Modeling Framework (SOMF), Cloud Computing Modeling Notation (CCMN), and the Multidimensional Software Architecture Construction (MSAC). His innovative research and publications in the fields of software architecture, service-oriented architecture, microservices, artificial intelligence (AI), cloud computing, and big data are recognized internationally for their contribution to the software design and development communities. He has consulted for organizations including J.P. Morgan Chase, Citibank, Bank One, UBS-Paine Webber, American Express, AIG, and the U.S. government. He is the best-selling author of software architecture books, and he offers a variety of enterprise integration solutions for back-end and customer-facing systems.

About the Technical Editor

Paul C. Martello is a technical writer with more than 18 years of experience in IT. Before becoming a technical writer, he held roles ranging from elementary and business teacher in New York to history teacher for Fairfax County Public Schools in Virginia. In 2005, Paul was selected to participate in the Relief International Schools Online Teacher Exchange in Bangladesh, integrating technology in schools. He loves watching his favorite football team, the Buffalo Bills, traveling, and spending time with his family in Bristow, Virginia.

About the Contributing Editors

Noreen O'Brien has spent the better part of her life writing, editing, and creating through various mediums. From her start as a reporter to the freelance editing work she does today, she has been instrumental in the production of a multitude of papers, dissertations, and documents. She lives in Richmond, Virginia, with her son, Liam.

Monica Gagnier is an experienced editor who has worked with Michael Bell on previous books. A graduate of Syracuse University's S.I. Newhouse School of Public Communications, Gagnier is a seasoned financial journalist who has worked at such publications as BusinessWeek (now Bloomberg Businessweek), the New York Post, and the Albuquerque Journal. She lives in Santa Fe, N.M.

Contents at a Glance

Contents

Introduction: Software Architect, Who Are You?

As a software architect you've embarked on a career journey in an unchartered and unpredictable territory with no guarantee of successful technological solutions. You are employed as a software architect to participate in a corporate business, technological, and social experiment whose chief thrust is to manufacture software products deployed to virtual environments. It's also arduous to foretell the business performance quality and stability after deploying and integrating software implementations in computing ecosystems.

By no means is this a bleak portrayal of a software architecture career. On the contrary, the uncertainty of your contribution to enterprise solutions only opens the doors to business development and transformation opportunities, technological modernization, and career improvement and growth. Furthermore, your hard work and dedication can be achieved through the power of creativity, imagination, and persistence. Once you are resolved to pursue a software architecture career, or are already a devoted practitioner, you're destined for a highly successful journey.

The following sections draw a picture of an *ideal software architect* whose capability to solve organizational problems is beyond imagination. This profile represents a well-rounded software architect with close-to-perfect professional talents that organizations would most certainly employ if the need existed. However, do not fret or be discouraged. We strive to possess these outlined qualities to make a difference in people's lives by promoting business culture, strategies, mission, and vision.

Figure I.1 illustrates the ideal software architect's attributes: career-oriented, innate traits-driven, strategy-driven, culture promoter, integration-driven, leadership-oriented, solution-driven, domain-driven, and social-driven.

So, ideal software architect, who are you?

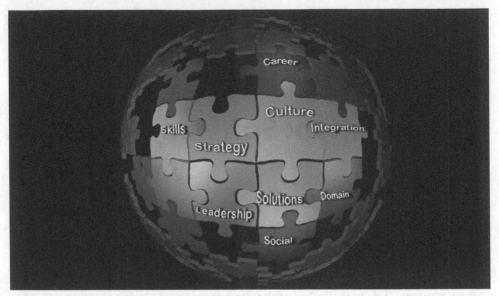

Figure I.1: An Ideal Software Architect Profile

You Promote Institutional Culture

You're hired as a software architect to inspire change, stir up enthusiasm for innovation, stimulate new ideas, affect organizational strategies, combat business and technological stagnation, and make a big difference in people's lives.

Become an Agent of Cultural Transformation

You are offered a key position to participate in transforming the *old* into the *new*. The former refers to outdated business concepts, traditional ways of doing business, archaic methods of developing software products, and waning technological solutions. The "new," on the other hand, pertains to modern technologies, creative and practical applications and systems, innovative end-to-end software architecture methodologies and life cycles, and partnerships that promote organizational dialogue to secure the business.

By partaking in such ambitious organizational metamorphosis, you're the de facto *institutional agent of cultural transformation*. You are actively engaged in a social and technological experiment that touches lives and instills change in people's behavior. This multifaceted cultural change manifests in how people communicate, interface with applications and systems, form relationships and partnerships, run their daily lives, and manage their careers.

So, how do software architects promote organizational culture? The arsenal of tools and utilities employed to impact the environment profoundly is vast.

Furthermore, the sky is the limit for technological evolution and innovation. The business and technological solutions you're being asked to provide drive the establishment of organizational *policies, best practices,* and *standards.* These rules and procedures you're advocating for promote institutional norms of behavior, foster business alliances, and forge new codes of cultural conduct.

Contribute, Do Not Follow

However, the cultural change that you're promoting does not touch only individuals. You are employed to harness the power of your talents and creativity to form a new generation of ideas and find shared values reinforced by members of your organization inspired by your innovative visions. In reality, you are a benefactor at heart, not a follower. Any organizational solution you offer contributes to the institutional knowledge base and the collective memory of your followers, who are ultimately employed to solve enterprise problems.

Further Reading

Although the topic of promoting organizational culture is discussed throughout the book, refer to these chapters to learn about the specific methods that software architects can leverage to impact institutional culture:

- Chapter 3, "Career Planning for Software Architects: A Winning Strategy" depicts four career-driven perspectives that can impact organizational culture: social-driven, technology-driven, management-driven, and strategy-driven.
- Chapter 4, "Self-Assessment for Software Architects" offers a self-scoring questionnaire that contains queries about promoting organizational culture methods.

You're an Astute Strategist

Your strategic mindset is the key to the success of your software architecture career. No matter which software architecture scope of solutions you pursue, application or enterprise level, focus on the big picture. You're a generalist by nature. Never rush into details to develop effective solutions. Having a bird's-eye view is what makes you an all-around type of person.

You're also a gifted tactician who incessantly occupies your mind with long-term and sustainable solutions to remediate business problems. The prospect of business prosperity and technological continuity motivates you to carve out complicated schedules, road maps, and product development timetables.

No matter the magnitude of your work, your strategic outlook is driven by a thorough study of business and technological events that occur on the ground. Then, by connecting the dots, you deliver superior software architecture artifacts. In this context, *connecting the dots* pertains to aggregating and utilizing all possible organizational resources, such as subject-matter experts, data, utilities, and facilities, to derive the best possible software and environment implementations.

Adopt an Effective Outside-In Strategy to Deliver Synthesized Software Architecture Solutions

You're an outside-in software architecture strategist attuned to market and industry trends, quality of organizational services, and, most important, customer imperatives. In addition, you are acquainted with advanced product development life-cycle methodologies and often follow business market developments and innovations, valuable knowledge that drives your methodological approach to meeting client requirements. Satisfying these imperatives begins with an effective business discovery and analysis process that leads to software architecture solutions.

Do not be constrained by existing technological limitations. If current organizational technologies tend to narrow the scope of your vision, you must drive change, modernization, and initiatives aligned with your software architecture vision and mission. Furthermore, you drive business and technological transformation through creativity, curiosity, and modernity synthesis. Finally, never deprive yourself of the freedom of imagination when proposing innovative software architecture implementations.

Align Software Architecture Strategies with Organizational Imperatives

As an astute software architecture strategist, you know that your technological vision and mission must align with business strategies. Remember, you're not operating in a vacuum. Your software architecture solutions, therefore, ought to promote business agendas, foster business growth, and ensure business stability and continuity.

However, aligning software architecture strategies with business vision and mission would not promote satisfactory technological solutions. Business cooperation and coordination are indeed primary and compulsory goals for software architects. Their duties, however, must go beyond business imperatives. There are accessorial software architecture strategy alignment necessities to drive a comprehensive enterprise technological balance.

Thus, software architecture strategies must also be aligned with existing deployment environments, supporting infrastructure, development platforms, data and message exchange mechanisms, architecture styles, design patterns, and integration patterns. Again, promote transformation initiatives to satisfy software architecture vision and mission if software architecture strategies cannot align with existing technologies and environments.

Figure I.2 illustrates a software architecture strategy alignment priority example chart that outlines alignment opportunities with business, technologies, environment, and infrastructure.

Figure I.2: Software Architecture Alignment Priorities

Further Reading

The topic of software architecture strategy alignment with business strategy, vision, and mission to propel technological initiatives across the organization is discussed largely in Chapter 2, "Types of Software Architects." It introduces three business needs for software architecture to foster organizational transformation and modernization: strategic collaboration, technological mediation, and technological implementation

You're a Gifted Leader

You're a leader, not necessarily a manager. You possess noteworthy interpersonal traits. You're a person of integrity who instills trust in your co-workers, managers, corporate executives, and partners. You promote institutional social harmony to foster consensus on software architecture strategies, technologies, best practices, standards, and policies. You're trusting and trustworthy because you have a positive perspective of humankind.

Your natural leadership traits inspire followers. These devoted fans respect your perspectives and are committed to collaborating with you on software architecture projects and business initiatives. As a gifted technological leader and team player, you prefer to collaborate with others. You encourage diversity of ideas and solutions by fostering the collective creativity of enthusiastic technologists. You never impose your views on others—in contrast, you're an advisor, a mentor who offers viable guidance to those who seek professional direction.

> **TIP**   Remember, you're a leader. You're not a manager or administrator who signs timesheets and reprimands staff for wrongdoing.

Tolerate Errors and Stay Open to Technological Experiences

Your innate problem-solving and decision-making skills paint a realistic view of your organization's business and technological contribution. In other words, nothing is perfect! You understand the difficulties and constraints of any proposed software architecture solution. And you're aware of the impact your technical recommendations have on your organization. You're wise to understand that ill-designed applications and systems can cause operational chaos, disrupt business continuity, negatively impact productivity, and harm your company's bottom line.

With all these potential risks to the enterprise, you're still a natural optimist and idealist, a risk-taker willing to surrender short-term gains in favor of strategic long-term technological success. These traits define a person who tolerates design errors, software implementation mishaps, and software deployment and integration flaws. In reality, you're not afraid of failure. In your mind, the design experiment journey you're willing to embark on can only promote successful technological modernization.

Build a Circle of Trustful Followers by Uplifting Their Spirits

As a software architect, you must inspire others and galvanize positive energy among your co-workers and work teams. You're here to foster creativity—the failure of imagination is not an option. You are here to usher intelligent followers who trust your software architecture judgment and good taste, and who are not afraid of making design mistakes or expressing silly opinions.

> **TIP**   Remember, you're an experimentalist whose leadership traits galvanize enthusiasm for collaborative teamwork to offer superb technological solutions for sustaining and accelerating business success.

Further Reading

Take the self-evaluation questionnaire provided in Chapter 4, "Self-Assessment for Software Architects," to find out if you possess the proper software architecture leadership talents that can galvanize enthusiasm for business innovation and technological modernization.

You're an Instrumental Solution Provider

At heart, you are a solution provider. Deep inside you, there is a veiled desire to mitigate risks, resolve social conflicts, and provide guidance to tackle organizational challenges. You always rise to the occasion to remediate business shortfalls. Furthermore, you go the extra mile to seek pragmatic technological solutions.

Promote Business Growth Through Modern Technological Solutions

You are committed to implementing potent strategic foundations for sustainable and viable business growth through technological modernization. You're a risk-taker and venture to support business transformation by leveraging the best-of-breed technical capabilities. Furthermore, you believe that technology is not just a mechanical mean for implementing temporary solutions or for offering Band-Aid remedies that do not withstand time. Simply put, you're a solution provider with technological, strategic agendas that tolerate occasional failures to achieve novel goals.

Provide Solutions Within the Boundaries of Your Software Architecture Expertise

As a software architect, you focus on design solutions—software-oriented remedies, *not hardware*. This is because you understand the boundaries of your occupation. You're aware that the solutions you provide are within the margins of software architecture practices—the field in which you excel. You may collaborate with co-workers specializing in physical infrastructure, hardware servers, and network devices. However, your chief responsibility is to design applications, services, systems, and deployment environments within your software architecture expertise.

Know the boundaries of your responsibilities. Be aware of your software architecture level of contribution. You're wise to understand that the reach of your technical solutions depends on the boundaries of your position. Namely, the job you're holding as a software architect has restricted outreaching responsibilities. This is not because you cannot accomplish tasks beyond your job description. It's simply due to the software architecture duties you're commissioned to pursue.

Understand the Scope of Your Technological Solutions

So, what would be the scope of your technological solutions?

Nowadays, common organizational practice calls for founding a hierarchical structure of software architecture roles. They are established to address three different levels of solutions. Affiliated with the top layer of a pyramid, enterprise software architects and their technological solutions must meet enterprise-level business imperatives. Then, solutions architects are related to the second layer, just beneath the enterprise architects' level. They are commissioned not only to promote enterprise software architecture strategies, but also to oversee application-level design initiatives. Finally, application architecture roles are the nucleus of any organizational software design initiative. They are positioned at the very bottom of the structural employment hierarchy, assigned to offer solutions for the narrowest range of problems. Figure I.3 illustrates the hierarchical structure of software architecture roles and their solution scope and dependencies within an enterprise.

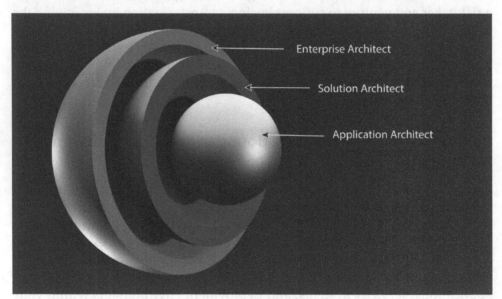

Figure I.3: Software Architecture Roles And Their Organizational Solution Scope

Further Reading

To learn more about how to scope technological solutions and set boundaries for your professional expertise visit these two chapters:

- Chapter 1, "Software Architect Capability Model," discusses a method to help scoping technological solutions and setting boundaries to a professional occupation by creating a capability model with five driving sections:

specifications, architecture practices, architecture disciplines, architecture deliverables, and quantification of skill competencies.

- Chapter 2, "Types of Software Architects," elaborates on two types of software architect roles: leading software architects and domain software architects. Each of these roles are commissioned to focus on specific solution scopes.

You're an Integrator Par Excellence

Integration duties are the bedrock foundation of your occupation. It's an integral part of your professional daily practice. No matter what level of software architecture contribution to the enterprise you provide, you're well aware that integration is a compulsory responsibility that you cannot avoid. It's a software design capability you possess, leverage, and exhibit to satisfy a broad range of business and technological imperatives. Furthermore, integration is a technological, social, and business competence you consistently demonstrate to provide large-scale business remedies. And it's a software architecture aptitude you employ to aggregate solutions mutually provided by a community of software implementations.

Connect the Dots

You're dubbed a "software integrator" because every design scheme you devise proves effective partnerships and communications between software implementations. Any design blueprint you provide presents logical views of interaction and collaboration between applications, services, and systems. And it's starkly apparent that any software architecture environment you design maintains a pragmatic alliance between distributed software assets.

You do not take the term *connecting the dots* lightly in regard to software integration. Namely, you do not sneeze at opportunities to utilize diverse sources of information, combine people's ideas, and aggregate technological fountains of knowledge to devise powerful software architecture integration solutions. In essence, you're wise to connect the dots to foster software reuse and optimize the redundancy of business functionality.

Integrate Software in a Three-Dimensional Software Architecture Environment

As a software architect, you're keenly aware that integration is not only about connecting the dots and not merely about enabling software entities to talk to each other and exchange information. Indeed, these are vital software architecture tasks that ensure business continuity, ensuing viable organizational solutions.

However, you're also mindful that software implementations do not operate in a vacuum and are deployed to a topological, geometrical, and three-dimensional landscape that offers them adequate architectural conditions to survive in. In Chapter 6, "Software Architecture Environment Construction," and Chapter 7, "Structural Construction of Software Implementations in Multidimensional Environments," this ecosystem is labeled the *software architecture environment*. As illustrated in Figure I.4, this landscape constantly undergoes structural deformation due to the behavior of the hosted software entities.

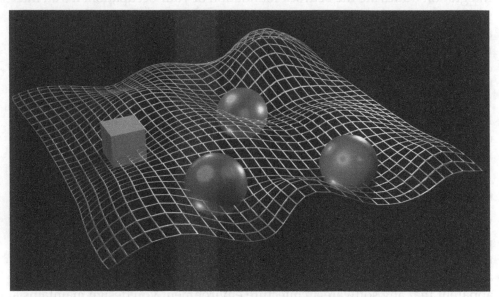

Figure I.4: Structural Deformation Of A Software Architecture Environment

Mitigate Risks in a Quantum Software Architecture Ecosystem

Your design outcomes consistently demonstrate a compromise between radical software architecture solutions. These negotiated solutions between extreme design approaches contribute vastly to the mitigation of the risks of an unpredictable deployment environment that can negatively impact business execution. Also, you're compelled to adhere to integration best practices, standards, and policies to foster a balanced software architecture environment. Your instrumental integration talents promote a sensible environment balance to minimize the erratic behavior of software. And your surpassing software integration capabilities alleviate the risks of business interruptions.

Further Reading

The book's Part 3, "Software Architecture Toolbox," represents the Multidimensional Software Architecture Construction (MSAC) methodology. This design approach offers use cases, best practices, and construction laws for software implementations and their affiliated environments:

- Chapter 6, "Software Architecture Environment Construction," is all about integration of software in a multidimensional software architecture environment hosted in production.

- Chapter 7, "Structural Construction of Software Implementations in Multidimensional Environments," represent the 3D structural composition of software entities that are deployed and integrated in a software architecture space.

You're Domain-Driven

You're well prepared to tackle business and technological problems by employing your software architecture talents. There is nothing that can swerve your focus from fulfilling your goals. Furthermore, your uncompromising devotion to offering effective and sustainable software architecture solutions is immeasurable to your organization. Your steadfast resolve to tackle business challenges is attributed to your laser-beam focus on critical problems while avoiding personal agendas and evading trivial issues.

Simply put, the secret of your unwavering commitment to providing best-of-breed software architecture solutions is rooted in your ability to concentrate on what matters. More specifically, your solutions align with corporate business and technological strategies; software architecture vision and mission; leadership directives; and institutional best practices, standards, and policies.

> **TIP** In a nutshell, you're a domain-driven software architect familiar with the business environment, the industry, the customers, and the supporting technology.

Align the Orbit of Your Software Architecture Solutions with Organizational Domains

The alignment of software architecture solutions with business imperatives characteristically yields robust technological solutions. In this context, *business imperatives* refers to different types of requirements. As a pragmatic software architect you can tailor technological solutions to specific business needs. More explicitly, your solutions to business problems may be affiliated with a specific business sector, business industry, business product, business portfolio, line of business, or business division. These particular business domains drive the technical remedies you propose.

However, business needs do not always drive the domain alignment process. Equally significant is the alignment *of software architecture strategies with business strategies*. The chief reason is that business strategies are the empirical driving forces in the enterprise. Therefore, technological solutions should foster and support long-term business plans, business models, business vision and mission, and business policies.

Moreover, from a domain alignment perspective, you're most certainly aware that the existing technological capabilities of your organization (such as infrastructure, platforms, and networks) must support software architecture solutions. In some cases, the existing technological capacity may not be advanced enough to deliver your proposed design. Therefore, promote technological modernization and transformation initiatives to improve the alignment with your architectural vision and mission.

Delineate the Scope of Your Software Architecture Solutions

Your devotion to providing software architecture solutions to specific organizational imperatives accelerates time-to-market and ensures business and technological continuity. Pinpointing the sources of business obstacles, devising feasible solutions, and mitigating domain-related issues are prescriptions for software architecture success.

TIP   By accomplishing this, you're essentially accredited as a domain-driven software architect who is business-driven, strategy-driven, technology-driven, solution-driven, and leadership-driven. Leverage these capabilities to respond to business and technological necessities.

Again, aligning your technological solutions with organizational domains promotes pragmatic software architecture. Therefore, it's highly advisable to create a solution-focused domain diagram similar to the one shown in Figure I.5. Such a depiction will demonstrate the various opportunities for software architecture success. Focus on your organizational domains that require attention. Leverage your leadership talents to focus on particular business and technological problems. Finally, focus only on domain challenges that require solutions.

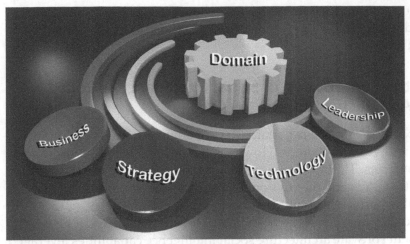

Figure I.5: Domain-Driven Software Architecture Solution Scope

Further Reading

As a domain-driven software architect whose duty is to deliver a balanced software architecture, focus on the software architecture construction life cycles, governing laws, and best practices covered in Chapter 6, "Software Architecture Environment Construction" and Chapter 7, "Structural Construction of Software Implementations in Multidimensional Environments."

Furthermore, to foster a software architecture environment equilibrium, employ your *domain-driven design skills* to meet business, strategy, technology, solution, and leadership imperatives.

You're Socially Driven

As a software architect, you're mindful that social collaboration and partnership with co-workers, industry alliances, customers, and stakeholders yields compelling technological solutions. Technical solutions have never been successful without teamwork and cooperation with subject-matter experts (SMEs). Individuals promoting personal agendas can never deliver substantial software architecture strategies.

In conclusion, software architects should fulfill their duties through the power of social intelligence. Moreover, architects who snub social skills to better accomplish the tasks they were hired for often find that their software architecture solutions ultimately fail to live up to organizational expectations. Simply put, the respectful and productive interrelationship between technologists and business leaders always demonstrates social capabilities that deliver perceptive technological solutions.

Leverage the Contribution of Social Intelligence to Your Software Architecture Career

In this context, *social intelligence* pertains to your ability to understand yourself, your needs, and your limitations. However, it's not only about your imperatives or boundaries. This self-acumen is about the capability to know others, the aptitude to understand the environment, and the faculty to develop trustful and sustainable partnerships in the workplace.

Have a look at the chief social intelligence tokens presented in Figure I.6. These represent software architecture social intelligence capabilities leveraged to drive powerful business and technology transformation solutions: *agility*, *adaptability*, and *awareness*.

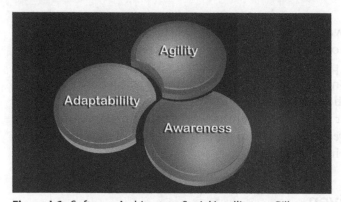

Figure I.6: Software Architecture Social Intelligence Pillars

Awareness is a unique social talent that can be leveraged to cope with complex social, business, and technological changes and challenges thrown your way. The term *adaptability* stands for versatility—an attribute that describes a skillful person with multiple talents for tackling organizational problems. Moreover, *agility* is a personal quality of a software architect who knows how to negotiate and compromise on technological solutions, resolve social conflicts, and collaborate with others in good faith.

Follow a Simple Process to Leverage Your Software Architecture Social Intelligence Skills

Your social intelligence skills can be instrumental in establishing working-related partnerships and alliances. To build a coalition of supporters and collaborators, consider these simple roadmap milestones: *search*, *connect*, *integrate*, and *cooperate*.

At the onset of this exertion, begin searching for candidates who understand your language and objectives and are willing to work together to achieve software architecture goals. While these individuals are typically found in close vicinities, such as in your organization, others can be spotted on social media and at technological conferences.

Once potential social partners are found, devote your time to connecting, raising their interest, and spurring enthusiasm for contributing to the organization and industry. Then share your knowledge. Learn from others. Interface and cooperate on strategies. *And always remember: you're not alone!*

Further Reading

The topic of software architecture social intelligence skills is covered chiefly in these two chapters:

- Chapter 4, "Self-Assessment for Software Architects," includes queries to evaluate an individual's communication, collaboration, and partnership formation skills required to promote software architecture strategies and contribute to technological transformation and innovation.

- Chapter 9, "An Outline for Software Architecture Job Interview Questions," introduces potential interview behavioral questions, preparing candidates to demonstrate communication, interpersonal relationship, and leadership capabilities.

You're Career-Driven

It's critical to carve out a long-term plan, a strategy that reflects your talents and capabilities. Equally important, stay attuned to your individual preferences, such as the types of duties that you'd like to fulfill and contribute to a specific sector and industry. However, focusing merely on your career agenda or promoting individual interests would never contribute to solving organizational problems or boosting your software architecture performance.

Remember that your preliminary duty is to collaborate with co-workers and partners to support business objectives—a vision greater than your aspirations. In software architecture, there is nothing nobler than teaming up with stakeholders to promote organizational culture, influence the outcome of business transformation, and accelerate technological modernization.

Carve Out a Software Architecture Career Strategy

A software architecture career strategy is a long-term plan that spells out incremental steps to achieving professional milestones and goals. Each milestone is an important landmark, a checkpoint for evaluating your professional progress and achievements. A career milestone can also mark a turning point, perhaps a change in direction or adjustment to your software architecture employment strategy.

The software architecture career strategy's goal should not be considered your last professional occupation. On the contrary, in a long-term career time span, there may be multiple goals to pursue. Again, each milestone assessment should determine the next career step to conquer.

Moreover, a software architecture career strategy ought to be realistic. And professional development in the field must be gradual and feasible. The journey to achieving career goals should be devoted to knowledge acquisition, self-improvement, and delivering best-of-class software products and the architecture of their hosting environments.

Knowledge acquisition refers to the incremental learning and practice of software architecture disciplines during career employment. Specifically, business and technical knowledge are acquired through years of hard work, research, and studies. *Self-improvement* is related to the knowledge acquisition process. But it is affiliated chiefly with self-motivation and the individual appetite for improving software architecture capabilities.

> **TIP** Bottom line: a software architecture career strategy encompasses a gradual and self-challenging agenda that should be reevaluated at every milestone.

Software Architecture Career Strategy Perspectives

Throughout the years, the software architecture field has grown immensely in scope. Professionals choose to focus on different architectural practices and disciplines. Some individuals pursue the leadership and governance route, while others focus merely on the technological aspects of software architecture roles. As illustrated in Figure I.7, this book centers on four chief software architecture career planning perspectives: social, technology, strategy, and leadership.

Social-Driven Career Perspective Consider this employment avenue if you seek to promote your professional objectives by forming productive alliances with collaborating partners and executives to provide business and technological solutions.

Technology-Driven Career Perspective If you focus merely on your technical skills, pursue this career path by applying software architecture capabilities and experience to provide business and technological solutions.

Leadership-Driven Career Perspective Choose this career path if you possess management skills and seek to focus on promoting enterprise culture, steering technological transformation, and establishing institutional best practices, standards, and policies.

Strategy-Driven Career Perspective This role is for you if you look to influence enterprise business and technological evolution, foster digital transformation, develop organization-wide road maps, and align business strategies with software architecture strategies.

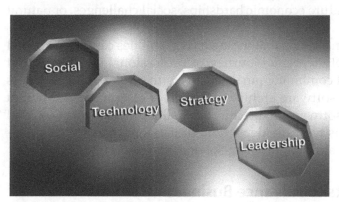

Figure I.7: Software Architecture Career Strategy Perspectives

Further Reading

A well-planned career path is a roadmap for a successful software architecture journey. But a career strategy is not the only ingredient for a flourishing occupation. Knowledge acquisition and carving out a winning strategy for software architecture interviews can indeed yield a lifetime of prosperous employment.

- Chapter 3, "Career Planning for Software Architects: A Winning Strategy," depicts the four career-driven perspectives that can impact organizational culture: social, technology, management, and strategy.

- Chapter 8, "Preparing for a Software Architecture Interview: A Winning Strategy," introduces a job interview preparation model that includes two different strategies to consider: interview defense and attack plans.

- Chapter 9, "An Outline for Software Architecture Job Interview Questions," presents potential software architecture questions that can increase the odds of acing an interview. They are grouped into ten different categories, such as technical, behavioral, social, problem-solving and decision-making, software architecture life cycle, and more.

You Trust Your Innate Talents

You undoubtedly bring a slew of talents instrumental in providing effective software architecture solutions to organizational problems. Moreover, you know that these personal traits successfully contribute to your employment duties. You may have wondered if these individual aptitudes were with you at birth, or perhaps you've learned them on the job.

Numerous scientific studies submit that the talents you have been carrying since birth are recognized as innate traits—skills not necessarily learned through experience. These are affiliated with primal instincts—natural survival abilities such as endurance, social bonding, adaptability, enthusiasm, and more. We often employ them to endure economic hardships, social challenges, or natural calamities.

However, there is no indication that these survival abilities cannot be learned and honed during a lifetime, career journey, or professional training. And it has become evident that combining innate talents with on-the-job experiences improves the ability of software architects to deliver pragmatic and potent solutions. For example, software architecture capabilities to construct powerful applications and systems typically depend on professional traits such as balanced decision-making, effective problem-solving, and good taste.

Employ Innate Traits to Advance Business and Technological Missions

It is no secret that tempestuous organizational issues often challenge software architects. Some are affiliated with the struggle to advance software architecture roadmaps, visions, missions, and strategies. Fostering and maintaining technological leadership is another difficulty that software architects wrestle with. Facing stiff resistance to business change or technological modernization initiatives is another predicament that must be tackled.

Employ your communication, patience, and self-discipline capacities to alleviate unnecessary conflicts. Respect the diversity of ideas, concepts, and solutions your co-workers, managers, and partners propose. Consider their diverse approaches to solving software development and integration problems. Most importantly, stay tuned with the four innate talents that can enhance your decision-making capabilities (as illustrated in Figure I.8): *creativity*, *imagination*, *software design aesthetic*, and *curiosity*.

Avoid Self-Induced Software Architecture Blindness

Ignoring your innate skills when you need them the most promotes business stagnation, delays technological standardization, and stalls applications and systems modernization. There is nothing riskier to business development than the underutilization of fundamental innate skills, such as creativity and imagination.

Creativity and imagination are all about the enablement of business opportunities. They are the bedrock of every software architecture implementation that allows the business to flourish and win the competition. On the other hand, curiosity is an essential innate gift that galvanizes research and studies and ultimately encourages perfection. Finally, the design aesthetic is an innate skill that entices consumers to buy goods, acquire services, and look forward to the next line of innovative products.

Figure I.8: Four Leading Innate Talents

TIP   Do not engage in self-induced software architecture blindness by overlooking your innate traits.

Further Reading

Refer to Chapter 5, "Employing Innate Talents to Provide Potent Organizational Solutions," to learn more about the chief innate gifts that software architects should leverage to mitigate enterprise challenges and successfully promote software architecture agendas. This chapter also elaborates on a variety of methods to boost software architecture creativity, imagination, good design taste and aesthetics, and curiosity.

Software Architect Capability Model

In This Part

Software Architect Capability Model

Many information technology (IT) and business professionals often fail to provide clear answers to these three fundamental questions: What do software architects do? What artifacts[1] do they deliver? How should architecture skills be assessed, quantified, and vetted?

At a first glance, these sound like easy queries to address. The conventional notion that a software architect fulfills the same duties as a building or landscape architect is utterly incorrect. There is no parallel between these two occupations, because they exercise different practices in distinct fields of expertise. Furthermore, they are commissioned to achieve dissimilar goals.

A software architect is required to perform a vast number of activities, typically handled by more than one professional. So, is it possible to deduce from these tasks what architects actually do or what they deliver?

In the context of this chapter, the simplest answer we offer to such challenging questions is this:

A software architect does what a specific organization needs—nothing more!

---

[1] Software architecture artifacts are various deliverables produced during a product development life cycle. They describe the internal and external architecture of software. They typically include strategy documents, technical specifications, design blueprints, data models, security models, deployment and integration charts and diagrams, best practices and standards documents, and more.

This assertion is deliberately too broad. This concept affirms, however, that a software architect must respond to *business and technological requirements* of a particular organization. In other words, architecture tasks and deliverables vary from one institution to another. Moreover, while working for different lines of business, architects seldom tackle the same challenges, nor do they always provide solutions for similar problems.

This chapter, therefore, offers a simple architect capability model with step-by-step instructions—assisting individuals and organizations to answer these three important questions:

Occupation   What does a software architect do?

Deliverables   What should a software architect deliver to provide potent organizational solutions?

Capabilities   How should software architecture talents be vetted, assessed, and quantified to ensure successful facilitation of enterprise projects?

Software Architect Capability Model: Benefits

The software architect capability model can be leveraged by organizations and individuals to promote business and personal professional agendas. When it comes to fostering enterprise business strategies and missions, the offered architect capability model will provide limitless opportunities for business growth. The model will become a potent platform for project improvement and a tool for recruiting exceptional architecture talents, subsequently minimizing enterprise expenditure.

Individuals who aspire to become software architects will find the capability model a powerful tool for career change and professional promotion. For those already actively pursuing the architecture practice, the model can boost their aptitude to provide robust remedies for organizational challenges.

How Should Organizations Utilize the Software Architect Capability Model?

Onboarding IT personnel is utterly costly. Not only does the interviewing process consume human resources, but also candidate vetting typically puts strain on employees whose daily schedules get disrupted. But the chief challenge is even harder: many organizations do not utilize any methods to evaluate candidates' skill sets. Moreover, there is no benchmark or assessment methodology in place to quantify interviewees' knowledge of and capability to perform the jobs they are applying for.

Furthermore, to a large extent there is no industry-wide model that organizations can leverage to ensure that a software architect talent will indeed contribute to a specific enterprise project. Put differently, there is no method in place to map a software architect's capability to facilitate enterprise imperatives. The consequences of screening failures are typically dire: allocated budgets evaporate quickly, and returns on investment never materialize. Another concern to contemplate is dwindling or inadequate institutional technical knowledge. This can hinder the fulfillment of organizational strategy, vision, and mission.

To address these enterprise concerns, consider the following list. It summarizes the organizational benefits when constructing software architect capability models.

Hiring process Improving the vetting mechanisms of candidates to enable hiring the best possible talent in the marketplace

Project management Delivering powerful business solutions by assigning adequate architecture skills to a project or any other enterprise initiative

Organizational knowledge base Maintaining a robust organizational knowledge pool by retaining the most experienced workforce

Why Create a Personal Software Architect Capability Model?

It's not just enterprise managers who are hiring who should figure out how software architects ought to promote organizational business goals and strategies. Architects, too, should individually be motivated to ascertain what their personal contributions should be to an organization or an industry.

By creating a personal software architect capability model, individuals will be able to *assess* their competence strengths and weaknesses in the space of software architecture. Then they can further leverage the model's findings to *augment* their knowledge for the purpose of honing the craft of their occupation.

Another compelling reason for creating an individual architect capability model rests upon the fact that useful organizational solutions are always delivered by software architects who are fully aware of their professional capabilities.

The list that follows, then, reflects the notion that *personal goals should be intertwined with organizational imperatives—neither could survive without the other*.

Ascertaining personal knowledge gap Revealing what additional skills a software architect would need to become more instrumental when providing solutions to organizational problems

Preparing for job interviews Constructing a personal architect capability model would divulge what type of technical and/or business skills are necessary to obtain certain architecture positions

Planning for career opportunities and job promotion Assisting with establishing a sound career path for pursuing higher-level positions in organizations

Rudimentary Guiding Principles

While constructing the software architect capability model, as guided in this chapter, either for personal or enterprise needs, adhere to these essential principles:

It's all about the "what" and the "how."   As mentioned in the introduction of this chapter, an architect capability model addresses these simple questions: *What do software architects do? What do they deliver? How should their skills be vetted and assessed?*

It's all about delivering solutions.   Software architects are hired to provide *solutions* to organizational problems.

It's all about teamwork.   Architects do not operate in a vacuum, nor are they employed to pursue their personal agendas without benefiting the enterprise's strategies and vision. They must collaborate with business and IT professionals to deliver potent remedies for arising organizational challenges.

Software Architect Capability Model Creation Process

The list that follows summarizes the process for creating a software architect capability model. For each of the items in the list, a corresponding section in this chapter meticulously discusses the building block of every step of the way.

Step 1: Provide requirements and specifications.   This section offers insight about the necessary requirements and the role they play in driving architecture solutions.

Step 2: Identify software architecture practices.   This section elaborates on the practices segment of the capability model. It conveys how vital architecture occupations are for meeting business requirements and technical specifications.

Step 3: Establish software architecture disciplines.   The architecture disciplines portion of the capability model defines areas of knowledge, fields of expertise, and specialties that a software architect must possess to provide effective solutions for business and technological imperatives.

Step 4: Add software architecture deliverables.   The deliverables segment of the capability model identifies the required architecture artifacts associated with each discipline.

Step 5: Quantify skill competencies.   This part of the capability model depicts an architect's level of aptitude to deliver valuable artifacts for a project or any other enterprise initiative.

Requirements Drive Architecture Solutions

Deeply rooted in almost every product development life-cycle methodology, requirements are being delivered in response to organizational imperatives. Some requirements aim to fulfill business vision, mission, strategies, and even marketing endeavors. Others are designed to address business challenges related to market competition and survival.

The software design work that an architect provides has a staunch correlation to particular problems that requirements seek to address. Therefore, architects must meet requirements to provide tangible organizational solutions.

A software architect capability model must be driven by requirements. *Without requirements, solutions could not be provided. Lack of solutions, consequently, may expose a business to inordinate risks.*

The sections that follow, therefore, address three fundamental questions:

Events　What are the chief events that trigger the issuance of requirements?

Entities　What are the organizational entities chartered to deliver requirements?

Requirements　What type of requirements are necessary for constructing useful architect capability models?

Requirements Issued by Problem and Solution Domain Entities

In almost every corporation there are two different subject-matter expert (SME) groups, responsible for addressing internal and external organizational challenges and unforeseen events that can hamper business operations.

Problem domain　Typically affiliated with the business unit, performing a variety of tasks, such as risk analysis, business analysis, product management, business requirements, business strategy, business architecture, marketing, etc.

Solution domain　Characteristically a part of an IT organization that employs architects, developers, technical writers, operation personnel, cybersecurity experts, and others

How Do the Problem and Solution Domains Collaborate?

There are innumerable business adversities that an organization must tackle—for example, loss of revenue, increased market competition, or marketing challenges. The problem domain group (the business), therefore, must confront these issues by pursuing appropriate actions. In many cases, the business advocates the construction of innovative applications and the launch of new projects.

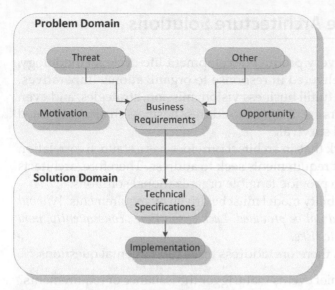

Figure 1.1: Problem and Solution Domains

So, how do business (problem domain) and IT organization (solution domain) collaborate in such cases to provide viable solutions? Figure 1.1 depicts an example of cooperation between these two domains.

The problem domain carves out business requirements to address one or more of the following issues:

Threats   Internal or external threats to the business, such as security attacks and industrial espionage of trade secrets

Motivation   Motivations to promote the business, such as growing market competition

Opportunities   Business opportunities to gain market share, such as sponsoring new products and acquiring companies

Others   Other incentives

Then the solution domain responds to the business requirements by tasking IT professionals with two chief deliverables:

■ Issuing technical specifications, also known as technical requirements

■ Driving technical specifications and tangible solutions, such as designing, coding, testing, deployment, and integration, to address the business problems

It must be noted that the scenario in Figure 1.1 is for demonstration purposes. It is an example that may not apply to all organizations. The business group that issues business requirements is not always the prime mover for launching projects in the enterprise.

In other words, requirements for new projects may also be delivered by IT personnel concerned with different issues. These may include security attacks, performance degradation, insufficient computing capacity, or even technological innovation initiatives.

Recall that other divisions or departments not affiliated with the problem or solution domains may also issue requirements for a variety of projects.

Important Facts to Remember

The following list summarizes the chief takeaways of this section:

Software architects   Architects are commissioned to provide software solutions, and therefore they are chiefly affiliated with the solution domain unit of an organization.

Business requirements   These types of requirements are characteristically provided by problem domain professionals—in many organizations by the business department.

Technical requirements   Also known as technical specifications, these types of requirements are delivered by the solution domain (IT personnel).

Project requirements issued by IT   There are instances when the solution domain provides requirements for technical projects.

Other requirements   Other divisions or departments within the enterprise may also be able to issue requirements for specific projects.

Scope of requirements   The architect capability model requirements could support small-scale projects or large organizational initiatives.

Create a Software Architect Capability Model in Five Steps

The sections that follow elaborate on the construction process of the software architect capability model, as illustrated in Figure 1.2. The following list identifies five steps that summarize chief activities to create an efficient skill competency model:

Step 1: Provide requirements and specifications.   We start creating the model from the requirements section. It includes the business requirements and technical specifications, issued by the problem and solution domain organizational entities, respectively.

Step 2: Identify software architecture practices.   The next step is all about establishing the software architecture practices. They are driven by business requirements and technical specifications.

Step 3: Establish software architecture disciplines.   Under each practice we then add the corresponding disciplines.

Step 4: Add software architecture deliverables.   Then architecture deliverables are added to interrelated disciplines.

Step 5: Quantify skill competencies.   Last, the skill competency section is created to specify the expertise level of each architect.

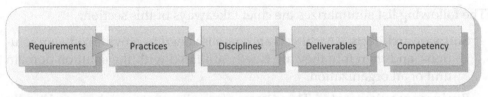

Figure 1.2: Software Architect Capability Model Creation Process

Step 1: Provide Requirements and Specifications

As indicated at the beginning of the section "Requirements Drive Architecture Deliverables," we must start with requirements to build the software architect capability model.

Before moving on, remember there is no need to be consumed by detailed requirements; they should be depicted in broad strokes. They must be abbreviated to simplify the capability model construction process. In addition, it's always a good practice to abridge the capability model rather than creating a complex and unmanageable one.

Business Requirements

As illustrated in Figure 1.3, under the problem domain section on the left side, the business requirements statement is simple and to the point. This example captures a business initiative that must be implemented: constructing a retirement planning application. Create a similar one that applies to a specific environment. It must be concise and easy to understand.

So, what might be behind the requirement statement shown in the figure? Requirement managers would probably expand on the implementation details of the retirement application. Perhaps such requirements could be laid out on umpteen pages. They may elaborate on myriad features and capabilities, such as user interfaces, instructions, retirement literature, retirement calculators, menus, pages, business rules, storage, and more.

Technical Specifications

Now, let's take a look at the solution domain, apparent on the right side of Figure 1.3. Here the technical specifications dominate the section. Again, in a software architect capability model there is no need to specify what the technical implementation details are. As shown, a short statement is enough.

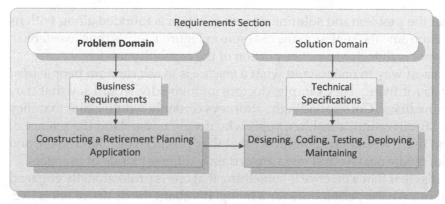

Figure 1.3: Example of Software Architect Capability Model Requirements

A longer version of the technical specifications shown might depict implementation mechanisms, technologies, and requirements for the retirement application and its commercial off-the-shelf products. Moreover, the technical specifications might include development tools and platforms, languages, scripts, storage facilities, application and integration patterns, deployment methods, configuration management, and much more.

Ensure Clear Requirements

If the software architect capability model is constructed for a project, for example, then managers are typically those who determine which talents are needed to carry out the software design duties. But such a decision, obviously, should not take place before understanding the requirements.

The peril would be that unclear requirements would most likely render confusing or ambiguous software architecture solutions.

To avoid requirements misinterpretation, in many cases, business and/or technical analysts come to aid—serving as liaisons between the organizational problem and solution domain groups. It is the duty of analysts, therefore, to construe the requirements, ensuring they are digestible and understood by managers and architects.

But if the software architect capability model is created for personal use, simply ensure that the requirements are short and easy to understand. By doing so, you eliminate the need for requirements interpretation.

Step 2: Identify Software Architecture Practices

Now that the problem and solution domains section is founded along with its issued requirements (similar to the example in Figure 1.3), it's time to establish the software architecture practice portion of the capability model.

The easiest way to understand what a *practice* is to ask random people *what* do they *do* for living. For example, doctors undoubtedly would say that they practice medicine. Correspondingly, attorneys certainly would claim that they practice law. In a similar fashion, yogis who deeply understand the science of body and mind would say delightedly that they practice yoga. And so on, and so on. So, medicine, law, and yoga are certainly different kinds of practices.

Now it's clear that a practice is something that one is professionally engaged in. It's about what a person does for a living. It's about the duties of one's livelihood. We then accordingly conclude that a software architect is an *occupation* that one pursues.

At this point comes the question that should be answered when constructing a software architect capability model: which software architecture practices are required to *meet the given requirements and technical specifications*?

Obviously, the answer is always subjective, because it depends on which software architecture practices would best provide the solutions to solve the organizational problems. And these decisions typically vary from one institution to another.

Establish Architecture Practices

Now we're ready to follow the example illustrated in Figure 1.4. It depicts two architecture practices: application architecture and data architecture. The rationale behind such a determination is based on the notion that these selected practices will offer the best solutions for the indicated requirement: constructing a retirement planning application.

This requirement insinuates that the scope of such a project will be limited to an application-level implementation—not a larger scope, such as system level. An application architect will then be the best candidate to facilitate the design and development efforts. Additionally, as discussed in Chapter 2, "Types of Software Architects," application architect tasks are confined to a narrower scope of an overall organizational solution.

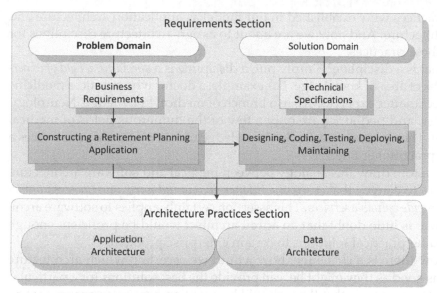

Figure 1.4: Architecture Practices

To elucidate the term *limited scope*, consider this example: a web portal that hosts retirement planning business functionality may also include reverse mortgage calculators and investment portfolio management for retirees. Consequently, the retirement planning application may be only a small part of enterprise financial offerings.

But even for such a narrow solution scope, an application architect practice calls for delivering a wide range of design artifacts. These typically include (but are not limited to) architecture blueprints—diagrams and documents depicting different application design perspectives.

By contrast, a data architect is characteristically employed to deliver different types of design artifacts. These may include data models, database schemas, table layouts, and more. Depending on how the data is designed, data architects may also insert triggers and store procedures to further manipulate the data at runtime or on different schedules.

Remember, now we're merely being asked to establish which software architecture practices will facilitate the construction of the retirement planning application. At the present time there is no need to specify the deliverables or the architecture activities required for the capability model. These will be determined later in the sections that follow.

Step 3: Establish Software Architecture Disciplines

So far, we have identified the business requirements and technical specifications. Then software architecture practices were added to the capability model.

These practices were established in our model as application architecture and data architecture. And now we are about to assign architecture disciplines for each of these practices.

So, what is a discipline? Simply put, a discipline is a *specialty*, a *field of expertise*, a subject area of knowledge. For example, a doctor who practices medicine is a subject matter expert (SME) in a branch of medical knowledge. Neurology, psychiatry, and pediatrics are only a few of the numerous fields of medical expertise. These areas of particular knowledge reveal what kinds of services a medical practitioner offers.

We therefore draw this analogy between medical and software architecture disciplines to convey that *every practitioner, in any industry, must possess proper skills to provide valuable services*. This assertion certainly applies to software architects. There is little doubt that an adroit architect would be proficient enough in providing practical solutions to certain enterprise problems.

But now there is a challenge: how would we ascertain which architecture talents, as good as they might be, can provide the best solutions for a particular project? The answer is that there should be a vetting process to ensure that an architect indeed masters the proper disciplines to facilitate a specific development initiative. Simply put, *when assessing an architect's competency, architecture disciplines then become job prerequisites*.

Apply Architecture Disciplines to Architecture Practices

Presently we are back at the same key question raised at the onset of this chapter: what do software architects do? The answer argued that not only may architects possess different skill sets, but even projects require different architecture talents. Therefore, it was impossible to provide a conclusive response. But now we've arrived at a point where we can revise this fundamental query. So, let's ask a more specific one: in what fields do architects *practice*, and what *disciplines* do they master? The sections that follow not only answer this question but also explain how to associate architecture disciplines with architecture practices.

To figure that out, let's follow the same logic demonstrated in the example in Figure 1.5. As is apparent, the business requirements and technical specifications defined earlier were driving the establishment of the application architecture and data architecture practices. Next, we're about to apply disciplines to these specific practices.

Applying Disciplines to the Application Architecture Practice

Even with the narrow solution scope of an application an architect is commissioned to deliver design artifacts prior to the development process. On one hand, an architect must fulfill business requirements and technical specifications and, on the other, adhere to design best practices. Generally, a common architect responsibility is to break down an application into modules, components, and services. Another duty that many architects provide is to technically mentor and guide development teams.

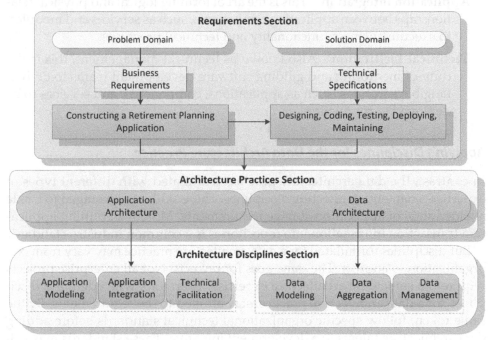

Figure 1.5: Architecture Disciplines

But in the context of the business requirements presented, the architect ought to focus only on the task at hand: constructing a retirement planning application. This example shows the three disciplines that are applied to the specific application architecture practice: application modeling, application integration, and technical facilitation.

You may wonder why the project manager opted for these particular architecture disciplines and not others. Keep in mind that every organization's software development life cycle calls for different disciplines when building products. Furthermore, it depends on how each production environment is laid out and what the integration requirements are for the specific organization.

Remember, disciplines typically vary in each organization even for the same application architecture practice.

The following list summarizes the disciplines shown in Figure 1.5 for the application architecture practice:

Application modeling   This is the discipline of delivering design artifacts, visually or textually, specifying application structure, modules, components, objects, and services using an artificial modeling language.

Application integration   This is the art of forming logical and physical relationships between application components, such as services and modules, to execute business functionality and technical processes.

Technical facilitation   Also known as technical management, this is the duty of mentoring and guiding software development teams to deliver tangible solutions, such as applications, components, and services to be deployed to production.

Applying Disciplines for the Data Architecture Practice

In contrast, the data architecture practice is affiliated with different types of expertise—namely, architecture disciplines. These skills are leveraged to tackle a wide range of application storage requirements. Moreover, putting application transaction information into repositories is a common industry standard.

But disciplines formulated for a data architecture practice may vary from one organization to another. The same goes for projects. Not all enterprise projects require the same data architecture expertise. Therefore, when defining disciplines for a data architecture practice, stay attuned to the requirements. By the same token, follow specific organizational technical standards before adding data architecture talents to a development initiative. These standards may call for different data architecture skills.

Find in Figure 1.5 the three disciplines related to the data architecture practice. The areas of expertise in this example are required to handle the storage business requirements and technical specifications for the retirement planning application. Consider the following data architecture disciplines:

Data modeling   Using their modeling skills, data architects deliver a diversity of design artifacts, such as conceptual, logical, and physical schemas. These blueprints will facilitate the construction of the retirement planning database.

Data aggregation   This architecture discipline facilitates the collection of retirement rules and regulation data from distributed data sources across the organization. The retirement planning application then will be able to leverage this information for its retirement calculators.

Data management   Once the retiree's data is stored in the application repository, the data management discipline becomes handy to establish a data recovery strategy, devise backup mechanisms, and even maintain data integrity.

Step 4: Add Software Architecture Deliverables

Time to work on the next piece of the puzzle: the deliverables section of the software architect capability model.

There are countless deliverables expected from each software architect during the development life cycle. It's also widely known that deliverables are expected not only at the conclusion of any enterprise initiative or project. An architect may also be chartered to provide design artifacts at a project's milestones.

So, how should these deliverables be manifested in our software architect capability model? The most logical placement for deliverables would be under the various architecture disciplines defined so far.

About Software Architecture Deliverables

But what are software architecture deliverables? Deliverables are the work of every practitioner in any field of expertise. In other words:

Deliverables are renderings of software architecture discipline activities, devised to foster organizational solutions and facilitate development goals.

For example, a software architect who is adept in the application modeling discipline would more likely be required to produce conceptual, logical, and physical design models. Similarly, a security architect who is skillful in the security modeling discipline may be asked to deliver best practices for implementing security policies.

Then who would be on the deliverables' receiving end? Remember that a deliverable must have a target audience and must facilitate stakeholders who participate in the product development life cycle. These individuals may be managers, developers, engineers, database architects, operation personnel, and more.

So, what type of deliverables should we expect from software architects? As anticipated, the answers to these questions are subjective because there is no industry-wide standard to support every single organization on the market. Companies typically develop their own sets of architecture deliverables, derived from business models, business requirements, technical imperatives, and other necessities.

Moreover, there are recognized bodies of knowledge, organizations, and publications that offer architecture life-cycle guidance and frameworks,[2] which also recommend and classify deliverables for projects. But in the context of

---

[2] For architecture life-cycle guidance and framework examples, refer to the Open Group Architecture Framework (TOGAF) at www.opengroup.org/togaf and to the Architecture Development Method (ADM) at www.opengroup.org/public/arch/p2/p2_intro.htm.

constructing a software architect capability model, it is crucial to adhere to deliverables requirements devised by specific organizational best practices.

If a capability model is developed for personal use, here is some all-purpose guidance for adding deliverables to the software architect capability model:

Leverage experience.   Remember what the architecture deliverables were for previous projects.

Conduct research.   If the personal experience is not rich enough, read articles, books, and case studies.

Consult professionals.   Ask co-workers, software architects, managers, and analysts.

Add the Deliverables Section

Let's take a look at the example in Figure 1.6 to understand how the software architecture deliverables section is linked to the requirements, practices, and, finally, disciplines. To accomplish this, we simply start from the top:

1. The requirements section for the retirement planning application leads down the path to the architecture practices.

2. From there, the track downward meets the architecture disciplines section.

3. Finally, as is apparent, we find three deliverables for each of these disciplines.

The list that follows elaborates on the application architect deliverables affiliated with their three corresponding disciplines, as illustrated in Figure 1.6:

1. Application Modeling Discipline

    a. **Conceptual Architecture Model**. This is typically an application decomposition diagram depicting components and services and their relationships.

    b. **Logical Architecture Model**. An architect delivers a presentation of message flows, interfaces, and dependencies of application components, modules, and services.

    c. **Physical Architecture Model**. This pertains to diagrams illustrating the application's component deployment scheme in production, such as servers, network configuration, and routers.

2. Application Integration Discipline

    a. **Message Flow Diagrams**. These are illustrations depicting interactions and message exchanges between the application and other distributed entities in a production environment. The entities may be services, middleware, and remote data sources.

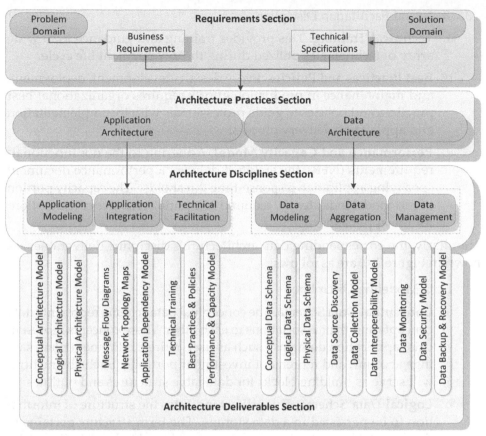

Figure 1.6: Software Architecture Deliverables Section

b. **Network Topology Maps**. These pertain to physical or logical placement of network components in a deployment environment. The logical presentation shows network connections between nodes, each of which typically represents a device. The physical topology map illustrates links between actual network devices, such as switches, routers, hubs, and modems.

c. **Application Dependency Model**. When integrating an application with other entities in production, a dependency model[3] reveals which peer applications, services, servers, and network resources it depends on. This model is also used to assess the complexity of the architecture of an application landscape.

---

[3] Software architects' common practice is to employ application discovery and dependency mapping (ADDM) tools to map dependencies between applications and production environment entities, such as distributed software implementations and infrastructure.

3. Technical Facilitation Discipline

  a. **Technical Training**. This provides training and guidance for a wide array of technologies utilized during the development life cycle.

  b. **Best Practices and Policies**. Every design, development, deployment, and maintenance in production efforts requires organizational best practices and policies to guide professionals with the implementation and application delivery process.

  c. **Performance and Capacity Model**. Adhering to the nonfunctional[4] requirements (NFR), the architect delivers a performance document specifying application response-time thresholds.[5] The capacity portion of this model indicates the required computing resource consumption[6] for the application.

Similarly, the corresponding data architecture's discipline deliverables, as shown in Figure 1.6, are as follows:

1. Data Modeling Discipline

  a. **Conceptual Data Schema**. The conceptual data schema represents data concepts and their associations to each other. These concepts represent chief application domains,[7] such as user, retiree, retirement plan, savings account, and retirement investment portfolio. Such abstractions will serve as building blocks for data table structures and outlines.

  b. **Logical Data Schema**. This artifact indicates the structure of information to be persisted in a data storage. The term *structure* pertains to database tables and columns, primary and foreign keys, indices, triggers, store procedures, database objects, and more.

  c. **Physical Data Schema**. This deliverable depicts the physical aspects that enable data persistence. It elaborates on how the data should be presented to the user and stored in databases. In addition, this physical perspective provides guidance for database deployment and configuration, data integration, ensuring computer capacity for data storage, and more.

---

[4] Nonfunctional requirements are specifications that describe the operational attributes and behavior of an application or system. These characteristics may include requirements such as maintainability, scalability, reusability, durability, data integrity, and fault tolerance.

[5] Performance thresholds are the maximum acceptable variances for specific metrics you can use to assess an individual project or group of projects, such as a portfolio. They are the upper-limit parameter values you can set for performance, earned value, and index calculations.

[6] *Computing resource consumption* refers to application and system utilization of deployment environment resources, such as memory, disk space, network bandwidth, and capacity of data.

[7] Application domains chiefly pertain to business applications and services.

2. Data Aggregation Discipline

   a. **Data Source Discovery.** This delivery specifies a list of data sources, third-party information providers, and repositories that the application utilizes to provide retirement planning services.

   b. **Data Collection Model**. This delivery specifies the method and when the data should be collected. The collection method pertains to network protocols, security, and interface mechanisms to ensure data integrity and acceptable transmission rates.

   c. **Data Interoperability Model**. The application architect is also chartered to ensure compatibility between the data sets collected from different data sources. This model typically specifies mechanisms for data format conversions, data filtering, and data cleansing to standardize data structures and models during transactions and message exchange.

3. Data Management Discipline

   a. **Data Monitoring**. This discipline is about employing monitoring tools to observe information exchange between the application and its environment entities, such as data repositories, consuming applications, and users. The chief reasons are to detect performance and data integrity issues and breaches to data security.

   b. **Data Security Model**. This deliverable identifies the security controls[8] that should be established to maintain data integrity and prevent internal or external attacks.

   c. **Data Backup and Recovery Model**. The application architect is responsible for guaranteeing maximum data availability. Simply put, this model elaborates on the mechanisms to replicate, store, archive, and recover data when needed.

Step 5: Quantify Skill Competencies

The last portion of the architect capability model is the skill competency section. The intention here is to evaluate the capability of an architect to deliver effectual solutions by delivering pragmatic artifacts. Put differently, this section proposes to specify the required expertise level of architects before they are recruited for any development initiative.

---

[8] Security control is defined by the National Institute of Standards and Technology (NIST) as "A safeguard or countermeasure prescribed for an information system or an organization designed to protect the confidentiality, integrity, and availability of its information and to meet a set of defined security requirements" (csrc.nist.gov/glossary/term/security_control).

In some cases, however, this skill evaluation method could also take place during an ongoing architecture engagement. The aim is to weigh in on the performance level of architects to discover the quality of their provided solutions.

This skill measurement exercise may be pursued because of these three chief reasons:

Self-assessment   If the software architect capability model is constructed for personal use, the skill competency section will reveal the aptitude level of an individual to deliver effective solutions for certain projects or even wider development initiatives.

Architecture skill vetting   The skill competency section will assist an organization in hiring the best possible software architecture talents for a project or any other broad scope initiative.

Assessing quality of solutions   Architecture solutions should always be evaluated during and after projects or organizational initiatives. Therefore, we assert that architects' performance is directly tied to the quality of their deliverables.

Quantifying Architecture Skills

As illustrated in Figure 1.7, the capability of architects to provide effective deliverables can be measured by grading their competency on a scale from 0 to 100. Moreover, this talent scoring method can provide better architecture fitness assessment to understand the architects' ability to accomplish tasks for the corresponding architecture disciplines.

Measuring the Application Architect Skill Levels

Consider Table 1.1. It's created for identifying the skill levels of the application architect in the context of the business requirements and technical specifications. This table corresponds to the illustration in Figure 1.7 for the purpose of simplifying the information. The table demonstrates the correlation between the architecture disciplines, deliverables, and competency levels.

Table 1.1: Application Architect Competency Example

DISCIPLINE	DELIVERABLE	COMPETENCY LEVEL %
Application Modeling	Conceptual Architecture Model	100
	Logical Architecture Model	100
	Physical Architecture Model	100

DISCIPLINE	DELIVERABLE	COMPETENCY LEVEL %
Application Integration	Message Flow Diagrams	100
	Network Topology Maps	70
	Application Dependency Model	85
Technical Facilitation	Technical Training	90
	Best Practices and Policies	100
	Performance and Capacity Model	80

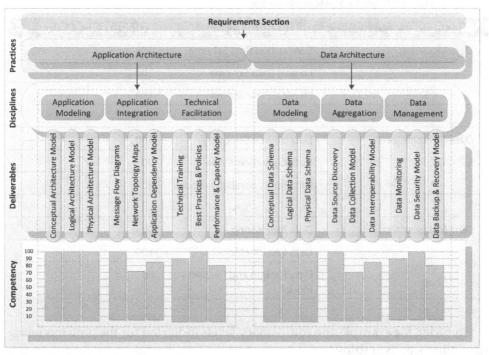

Figure 1.7: Architect Skill Competency

As shown in the table, the application modeling discipline calls for three deliverables: conceptual architecture model, logical architecture model, and physical architecture model. Note that the competency level column indicates that the skill level required for an architect to deliver these artifacts is 100 percent. This measurement could also be used for assessing the competency level of an architect to provide solutions during an ongoing project or any organizational initiative.

Furthermore, the competency levels for the application integration discipline show different scale levels for each of the corresponding deliverables, and similarly different skill competency measurements are indicated for the deliverables affiliated with the technical facilitation discipline.

Measuring Data Architect Skill Levels

In the same fashion, consider Table 1.2. It's provided here for depicting the skill level of the data architect related to the requirements and specifications. This table corresponds to the illustration in Figure 1.7. Moreover, the table demonstrates the association between the architecture disciplines, deliverables, and competency levels.

Table 1.2: Data Architect Competency Example

DISCIPLINE	DELIVERABLE	COMPETENCY LEVEL %
Data Modeling	Conceptual Data Schema	100
	Logical Data Schema	100
	Physical Data Shema	100
Data Aggregation	Data Source Discovery	100
	Data Collection Model	70
	Data Interoperability Model	85
Data Management	Data Monitoring	90
	Data Security Model	100
	Data Backup and Recovery Model	80

Consider, for example, the competency levels indicated for the data modeling discipline's deliverables:

- Conceptual data schema: 100 percent
- Logical data schema: 100 percent
- Physical data schema: 100 percent

This architect's professional capability assessment method can also be applied during an ongoing project.

Moreover, the same goes for the data aggregation discipline—note the competency levels indicated for the corresponding deliverables—and for the deliverables related to the data management discipline.

Skill Competency Patterns for Architects

The discussion about being able to assess or quantify an architect's capability to provide solutions leads to the *skill competency pattern* idea discussed in this section. In this context, therefore, the term *pattern* pertains to a *graphical representation* of an architect's ability to solve organizational challenges.

The pattern concept is not so much about the quantification of skill competency levels. It's about *visual representations* of architects' capabilities to deliver artifacts for projects. Such visual representations are typically easier to compare to each other and as a result discover gaps in knowledge and aptitude. Then later, you can draw quick conclusions about collective or individual efforts to provide solutions.

To understand better what a competency pattern is, let's take a look at the example in Figure 1.8. For the sake of simplicity, only the application architecture practice and its related disciplines, deliverables, and skill competency scale are presented.

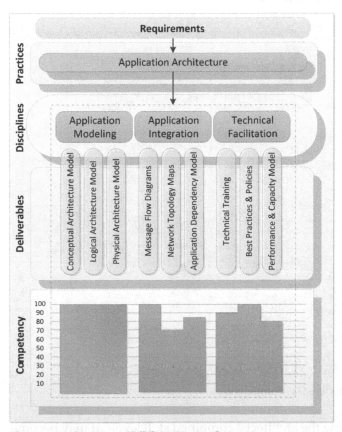

Figure 1.8: Creating a Skill Competency Pattern

As is apparent, the pattern is shown in the competency section on the bottom of this illustration. This pattern obviously signifies the architect's capability to deliver several artifacts for three software architecture disciplines: application modeling, application integration, and technical facilitation. Note that the discussed pattern still adheres to the skill competency measurements. The only difference is that the bars were united to show area patterns.

The sections that follow elaborate on the different ways individuals and organizations can utilize the competency pattern to fulfill different goals.

How Can Organizations Utilize the Skill Competency Pattern?

One of the most compelling reasons for utilizing the skill competency pattern is when architecture solutions are required for a project. Such an initiative, for example, may call for migrating legacy applications to the cloud. Apparently, the scope of such work may require a couple of architecture talents. The example in Figure 1.9 depicts the skill competency pattern of these architects: application architect 1 and application architect 2.

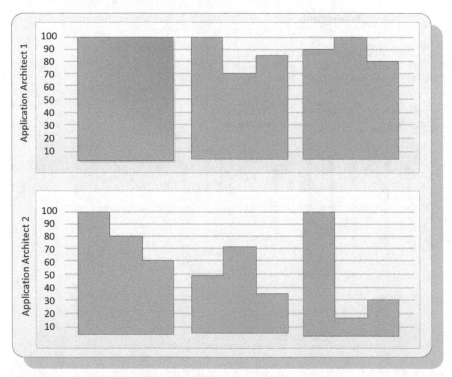

Figure 1.9: Comparing Architecture Skill Competencies

Just by visually assessing the architects' combined skill levels, it may become clear that their collective architecture capabilities might not meet the cloud migration project requirements. The skill competency pattern then can assist management to visually assess their combined architect capability to provide solutions. Proper measures should then be taken if concerns arise. Filling in the *knowledge gap* by training or adding more architecture talents to the project will certainly boost the capability of the team to deliver effective artifacts.

The skill competency pattern, therefore, is a valuable tool for organizations to ascertain the capacity of architects to deliver effective solutions. Here is the summary of the benefits:

Discovering individual contribution   Assessing and quantifying the capacity of an architect to contribute to a common enterprise effort

Comparing skill levels   Comparing the competency levels of architects assigned to the same project

Revealing the collective competency gap   Discovering gaps in the knowledge and capabilities of architects who participate in the same project

How an Individual Can Utilize the Skill Competency Pattern

When it comes to an individual's usage of the skill competency pattern, the promise of benefiting from it is limitless. Here are several examples:

The competency level of an ambitious and hard-working architect characteristically increases as time goes by. This proficiency progress can be reflected in the skill competency pattern created at each career milestone. In other words, an architect would be able to monitor the personal competency level progress, draw conclusions, and take proper measures to address career challenges when needed. The individual pattern would then become a personal visual representation tool to trace professional accomplishments.

An individual skill competency pattern can also be compared to other patterns that belong to co-worker architects, for example, who perform similar duties. If after such comparison gaps in skill levels are found, individuals would likely be motivated to augment their knowledge.

Moreover, it's possible to create a skill competency pattern for a job requirement if there is intimate knowledge available about the required skills. In this case, an individual skill competency pattern could be compared to the job competency pattern to reveal if there is a good match.

Consider these benefits of the individual skill competency pattern:

Tracing career progress   By comparing personal skill competency patterns assessed at different career checkpoints, an individual can monitor personal growth in architecture capabilities.

Industry comparisons   Individuals can assess architecture skill capabilities against common market job requirements.

Preparing for interviews   It's never a bad idea to show up for an interview with an individual skill competency pattern to demonstrate strengths in particular disciplines.

Interview Questions

Interviewers will always ask questions about the role of an architect in the enterprise. These types of questions are never taken off the table. Prepare for the hardest queries and hope for the best outcomes. Therefore, the interview questions presented in the list that follows should be rigorously studied and researched until satisfactory answers are obtained. Furthermore, before an interview, use all means to acquire vast knowledge affiliated with seven fundamental questions about the architecture life cycle[9] and deliverables:

- Why do business requirements and technical specifications drive architecture deliverables?
- What is an architecture practice?
- What is an architecture discipline?
- How are architecture disciplines correlated to architecture practices?
- What are architecture deliverables?
- How should architecture deliverables be associated with architecture disciplines?
- How can architecture skills be assessed?

It's common to struggle with strategic questions, such as architecture roles and solutions. Therefore, remember to provide examples with each answer. Do not confuse an interviewer with complex or blurred definitions. State the facts clearly and keep the answers as short as possible.

And again—be prepared!

---

[9] The architecture life cycle depicts the activities and goals that software architects ought to fulfill during the software development life cycle. Refer to the software architecture life-cycle questions in Chapter 9, "An Outline for Software Architecture Job Interview Questions."

Software Architecture Career Planning

In This Part

Types of Software Architects

It's not unusual to run across software architects who collectively possess diverse capabilities in different fields of expertise. The gain in their technological knowledge is attributed to the paths they chose to ultimately pursue before their software architecture careers. Some emerged from software development. For others, software architecture has been their all-time goal while serving years as software engineers in operations. And various individuals have been maintaining applications and systems in production since immediately after college.

Because of these diverse experiences, organizations often establish classes of architects, ranking them based on their potential contributions and talents. It's not a secret that this categorization is frequently administrative, with the purpose of determining payroll ranks, compensation, and benefits. The common industry practice of establishing levels of architecture roles within an enterprise, nevertheless, must go far beyond bureaucratic purposes. Astute executives understand this notion. Their chief purpose is to align software architecture talents with organizational strategy and vision. This can promote business growth and goals immensely.

In contrast to the common industry practice that advocates ranking architects, the software architect capability model (discussed in Chapter 1, "Software Architect Capability Model") proposes to match architecture talents with business strategies, project requirements, and other technological needs. Furthermore, the architect capability model answers three fundamental questions about software architecture practices and disciplines:

- What do software architects do?
- What artifacts do they deliver?
- How should architecture skills be assessed, quantified, and vetted?

Business Needs for Technological Solutions

The effort to categorize architecture roles in the enterprise emanates from business imperatives. Put differently, the business typically drives the need for technological solutions. Software architects, therefore, should provide adequate remedies to address organizational problems.

So, what are these business needs that must be tackled by software architects? Figure 2.1 answers this question. It illustrates the three levels of business imperatives that require technological solutions: *strategy*, *mediation*, and *implementation*.

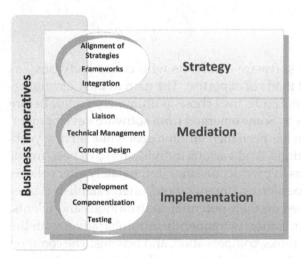

Figure 2.1: Business Imperatives

Business Needs for Software Architecture: Strategic Collaboration

Every business must recognize that it would be impossible to apply effective remedies to its problems without proper collaboration with the technological arm of the organization. Neither entity could exist without the other. For that reason, the coordination between business initiatives and software architecture projects is vital. Consequently, only strategic collaboration between the two entities can yield business progress and advance technological development.

CONCEPT   The rule of thumb suggests that an enterprise architecture strategy must be aligned with business strategy. And the former should propel technological undertaking across the organization, such as application and system development.

How Does Software Architecture Respond to Business Needs?

Figure 2.1 illustrates the idea that business imperatives require strategic software architecture cooperation. So how can organizational software architecture practices promote business strategies?

Alignment of strategies: Align software architecture strategies with business strategies, vision, and mission.   To be able to provide technological leadership in an organization, architecture strategic efforts must be aligned with business processes and then translated into technical capabilities.

Frameworks: Foster compliance with software architecture frameworks.   The transformation of business processes into software implementations also requires the adoption of software architecture frameworks to promote development policies, best practices, and standards.

Integration: Oversee integration of organizational assets in production environments.   Once the software implementation is successfully completed, architecture efforts should focus on integration of applications and systems in production.

Business Needs for Software Architecture: Technological Mediation

Business and software architecture strategic goals typically fail without a technical mediator. The term *technical mediator* refers to a "middleman" who on one hand understands business objectives and, on the other, is capable of promoting software architecture best practices, policies, and standards.

Furthermore, the technical mediator is commissioned to perform additional duties that are no less important. These may include translating business requirements into technical specifications, assisting with integration of applications and systems, and providing software design blueprints.

CONCEPT   Business and software architecture strategic goals call for technical mediation to formulate tangible solutions that are ultimately deployed to production.

How Could Technological Mediation Efforts Be Utilized?

As stated, business and software architecture imperatives typically utilize technical mediation services to facilitate the development and integration of business products to production. So, what are the actual duties of such a technical mediator? Take a look again at Figure 2.1 that illustrates three common industry mediation responsibilities frequently performed to promote business and technological goals.

Liaison   Tightens the relationship between business leads and software architects to facilitate technological solutions

Technical management   Offers technical guidance and supervision for software development activities

Concept design   Provides software architecture blueprints to drive technological solutions

Business Needs for Software Architecture: Technological Implementation

The development of applications and systems tends to consume enormous budgets and human resources. Therefore, there is nothing more anticipated by the business organization than to obtain production-ready software products. This is the ultimate goal of every business unit that sponsors technological implementations. Moreover, without tangible and timely delivered applications and/or systems, business products cannot be offered to potential consumers. And without customers, organizations are doomed to fail.

How Does the Implementation of Software Products Meet Business Needs?

The business need for technological implementations is typically carried out by project managers, team leads, and software developers who are attuned to business requirements. As illustrated in Figure 2.1, the list that follows reiterates these chief software construction activities:

Development   The software development life cycle (SDLC) is mostly driven by software architecture artifacts that propel the creation of business products.

Componentization   The decomposition of business functionalities is a software design best practice that renders manageable and maintainable components and services to avoid tightly coupled implementations.

Testing   Functional and nonfunctional testing is a common industry practice to ensure operational continuity of applications and systems in production.

Organizational Leading Software Architect Levels

In the last few decades, a considerable number of technical occupations have sprung up from the general practice of software architecture. Application architecture, enterprise architecture, data architecture, and solution architecture, for example, are branches of software architecture.

CONCEPT In other words, *software architecture* is a principal term that encompasses software design duties during the SDLC.

Various organizations have established corresponding software architecture roles, commissioned to carry out these software design obligations. By way of illustration, an application architect is able to handle application architecture duties. In the same fashion, an enterprise architect would certainly be able to provide enterprise architecture strategies and integration solutions. Again, they are all considered software architects who provide solutions to business problems in their unique areas of expertise.

But merely founding organizational software architecture roles would not entirely meet the mission to address business problems. Namely, the pursuit of technological solutions to tackle business imperatives would require a diversity of software architects who possess different competency levels of software design. They must also collaborate to provide effective solutions. Their software architecture capabilities then should be mapped to the business and technological needs that are discussed in the previous section: strategic, mediation, and implementation.

So how do organizations rank the software architecture talents to meet these particular business and technological needs? The sections that follow discuss the levels and roles of software architects required to provide solutions predicated upon their capabilities.

Ranking Leading Software Architects

Enterprise architects, solution architects, and application architects are the most common leading architecture roles that organizations hire. These combined architectural talents are referred to as "the first line of technological defense," since they are employed to provide effective solutions for existing business challenges. Clearly, their chief charter is not only to promote and shield the business but also to lessen enterprise operation vulnerabilities when it comes to ill-designed applications and systems.

As illustrated in Figure 2.2, each of these three leading roles is ranked at a different organizational architect level.

Architect role level I: Enterprise architect   Commissioned to provide technological strategies that adhere to business vision and mission

Architect role level II: Solution architect   Employed to help promote enterprise architecture strategies and provide software design blueprints to address business problems

Architect role level III: Application architect   Responsible for application-level design and development activities

Table 2.1: Levels of Organizational Leading Software Architects and Their Responsibilities

ARCHITECT LEVEL	ARCHITECTURE TYPE	ROLE	CHIEF RESPONSIBILITIES	SATISFYING
I	Enterprise architect	Strategic	Strategy alignment	Business requirements
			Frameworks	
			Integration	
II	Solution architect	Mediation	Liaison	Business requirements and technical specifications
			Technical management	
			Concept design	
III	Application architect	Implementation	Development	Business requirements
			Componentization	
			Testing	

As is apparent in Figure 2.2 this illustration, each of these leading software architect levels is assigned to satisfy one of the three business and technological needs: strategic, mediation, and implementation.

Consider Table 2.1. It summarizes in a tabular format the ideas that are illustrated in Figure 2.2. This table can be used for architecture role ranking in the enterprise to present a simple outline of responsibilities that correspond to each software architect type. These three architect levels are discussed in detail in the sections that follow.

Collaboration Hierarchy of Leading Software Architects

There is always a hierarchical layer structure when it comes to the collaboration between the leading software architecture roles in an organization. This concept is illustrated in Figure 2.3.

Enterprise architecture layer   Enterprise architects typically devise technological strategies, promote software architecture frameworks, and devise integration schemes. Their duties most certainly affect solution architecture and application architecture duties.

Solution architecture layer   As is apparent, solution architects are located on the next tier in the collaboration hierarchy. Their charter is not only about promoting enterprise architecture strategies but also about facilitating the application development process.

Application architecture layer   Application architects, for one thing, are obliged to comply with enterprise architecture strategies and also to adhere to the solution architects' design blueprints.

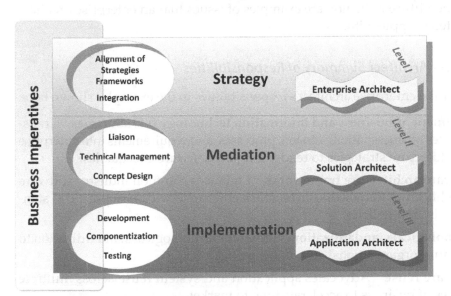

Figure 2.2: Leading Software Architect Levels

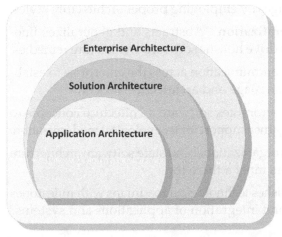

Figure 2.3: Collaboration Hierarchy of Leading Software Architects

Level I: Enterprise Architect Responsibilities

As one of the chief key players in an organization, an enterprise architect provides holistic solutions to meet demanding business needs. To accomplish this, the enterprise architect must possess broad technological horizons and superb social skills. This role also calls for effective communication capabilities to obtain firm-wide consensus for mitigating pressing business issues. Often strategic challenges, these organizational hurdles must be addressed in a timely manner to maintain the business's competitive edge. Technological modernization, technological standardization, software design best practices and standards, and even expenditure reduction are examples of issues that an enterprise architect must often grapple with.

Enterprise Architect Summary of Responsibilities

Consider the enterprise architect's responsibilities in the examples shown here:

Alignment of business and information technology (IT) strategies Transmutes business vision, mission, processes, and requirements into enterprise architecture strategies to render tangible software executables.

Software architecture frameworks Embraces common industry software architecture frameworks to establish enterprise-wide best practices, standards, and policies.

Technological standardization Promotes technological standardization to reduce organizational cost of ownership.

Software reuse Advocates application and system reuse across multiple lines of business to accelerate time to market.

Architecture repeatable solutions Formulates enterprise repeatable solutions for common business challenges by employing proper architecture styles.

Problem abstraction and generalization Abstracts and generalizes fine-grained business problems to drive holistic software architecture remedies.

Communication Encourages communication across the enterprise to establish technological common language and architecture lexicon.

Technological modernization Promotes software architecture concepts to organizational key players to garner support for technological modernization.

End-state architecture Devises organizational end state software architecture that architects and developers must adhere to.

Technological roadmap Establishes technological roadmaps with milestones and goals for development and integration of applications and systems.

Engagement of solution architects   Engages solution architects to provide tangible and detailed implementations to meet business requirements (the next section elaborates on the responsibilities of solution architects).

Integration   In charge of integration of organizational concepts and ideas. Responsible for integration of technological solutions. Accountable for conceptual, logical, and physical integration of applications and systems in production.

Architectural styles   Demonstrates superb leadership and decision-making capabilities by devising enterprise architecture styles.

Enterprise Architect Responsibility Table

Table 2.2 shows the three chief aspects of the enterprise architecture roles: collaboration, benefits, and beneficiaries. This implies that enterprise architects do not operate in a vacuum. They must form partnerships with business and IT representatives and ought to understand the benefits of their contribution to their organization and which lines of business or technological groups would benefit the most from their tasks.

Table 2.2: Enterprise Architect Responsibility Table

RESPONSIBILITY	COLLABORATES WITH	CONTRIBUTES TO	CHIEF ORGANIZATION BENEFICIARIES
Alignment of business and IT strategies	Business representatives, business architects	Focus on business and IT agendas and goals	Business and IT
Software architecture frameworks	Project managers, software architects, developers	Software development and integration best practices, standards, and policies	SDLC management and teams
Technological standardization	Executives, managers, software architects	Time to market, expenditure reduction	Business and IT
Software reuse	Software architects and developers	Time to market, expenditure reduction	Business and IT
Architecture repeatable solutions	Software architects	Software reuse, time to market, budget optimization, return on investment	Business and IT

Continues

Table 2.2 (*continued*)

RESPONSIBILITY	COLLABORATES WITH	CONTRIBUTES TO	CHIEF ORGANIZATION BENEFICIARIES
Problem abstraction and generalization	Software architects and developers	Software reuse	Software development community
Communication	Business representatives, development community	Dissemination of critical business and IT information, security awareness, technical training	Business and IT
Technological modernization	IT organization	Business efficiency, asset security, workplace productivity	Business and IT
End-state architecture	Project managers, software architects, and developers	Enterprise architecture reference architecture blueprints	IT
Technological roadmap	Members of the IT organization	Establishment of technological milestones and goals	IT
Engagement of solution architects	Solution architects	Augmentation of enterprise architecture tasks	Business and IT
Integration	IT and operation organizations	Simplification and enhancement of enterprise architecture	Business and IT
Architecture styles	IT and operation organizations	Standardization of architecture and design patterns	IT

Level II: Solution Architect Responsibilities

As illustrated in Figure 2.3, a solution architect (depicted in the middle layer) fulfills the software architecture mediation role in the enterprise. This occupation is all about brokering, aligning, organizing, facilitating, coordinating, and marshaling technological solutions. Typically referred to as the "technological middleman," the solution architect is the one who must devise tangible[1] solutions to business problems that must be identified and validated by an enterprise architect.

Moreover, serving as a technical liaison between enterprise architects and application architects, the solution architect ought to interpret enterprise technological concepts into design blueprints. This software architecture interpretation, expressed by design deliverables, is vital to application architects since design artifacts are in essence the language of choice for software developers.

A solution architect must be goal-oriented and possess a breadth of knowledge about the organization's lines of business and its corresponding business processes. This practice is also about aligning palpable software architecture solutions to satisfy business requirements that are not always easily understood by development teams.

To actualize the software architecture integration concepts devised by the enterprise architects, solution architects must be well-versed in architecture styles, architecture patterns, and design patterns. (Read more about styles and patterns in Chapter 9, "An Outline for Software Architecture Job Interview Questions.")

Solution Architect Summary of Responsibilities

The list that follows summarizes the solution architect's responsibilities and courses of action to tackle business and technological problems in the enterprise:

Software architecture vision and mission   Helps promote software architecture vision and mission devised by enterprise architects.

Transformation of architecture concepts   Transforms enterprise architecture concepts into technological solutions.

Design blueprints   Provides design blueprints for the software development and operations teams.

Interpretation of business requirements   Interprets business requirements into technical specifications.

Communication of solutions   Communicates software architecture solutions to project stakeholders to garner organizational agreement with technological directions.

Technical management   Provides technical consultation and management services to development teams.

---

[1] "Tangible solutions" implies that the solution architect is required to provide concrete remedies that are beyond the conceptual phase of the software development life cycle.

Integration   Takes part in integration efforts of business products in production.

Innovation   Promotes technological innovation and advances modern software architecture approaches.

Risk and feasibility assessments   Conducts software architecture risk and feasibility assessments for current and future application and system implementations.

Coordination of technical activities   Coordinates technical activities between development and operation teams. This includes deployment, change management, and configurations of assets in production environments. In addition, the solution architect brings together technical teams to discuss a wider range of solutions that pertain to software implementations.

Production facilitation   Offers maintenance assistance for applications and systems in production. This includes facilitation of operations related to monitoring, security, capacity planning, performance, and disaster recovery (DR).

Product evaluation and selection   Drives the selection and evaluation process for commercial off-the-shelf products that are candidates for technological adoption.

Solution Architect Responsibility Table

Table 2.3 summarizes the array of duties solutions architects are employed to pursue. This table identifies the potential partners that they typically collaborate with, the chief benefits of the solution architects' tasks, and the organizational entities that benefit the most from solution architecture activities.

Table 2.3: Solution Architect Responsibility Table

RESPONSIBILITY	COLLABORATES WITH	CONTRIBUTES TO	CHIEF ORGANIZATION BENEFICIARIES
Promote software architecture vision and mission	Enterprise architects	Establishment of software architecture milestones and goals	IT
Transformation of architecture concepts	Enterprise architects	Technological solutions	IT
Design blueprints	Application architects, developers, operations	Facilitation of the SDLC	IT

RESPONSIBILITY	COLLABORATES WITH	CONTRIBUTES TO	CHIEF ORGANIZATION BENEFICIARIES
Interpretation of business requirements	Business representatives, enterprise architects, application architects	Simplification of the SDLC	Business and IT
Communication of solutions	Business representatives, IT representatives	Organizational technological consensus	Business and IT
Technical management	Development teams	Software development productivity	Software development teams
Integration	Development teams, operation teams	Quality of services in production	Business and IT
Innovation	Solution architects, application architects, developers	Technological modernization	Business and IT
Risk and feasibility assessments	Business management, IT management	Business and operation continuity	Business and IT
Coordination of technical activities	Enterprise architects, application architects, development teams, operations teams	Partnership between architects, developers, and operations during the SDLC	IT
Production facilitation	Operations team	Software architecture consistency[2] in production	IT
Product evaluation and selection	IT representatives	Shorten the software development curve, time to market	Business and IT

[2] Software architecture consistency pertains to the verification process, during which an analysis is conducted to assess if a software implementation adheres to design artifact blueprints and devised architecture best practices, policies, and standards.

Level III: Application Architect Responsibilities

Typically confined to a single implementation framework, such as an application or services, the application architect devotes time to translating business processes into fine-grained components, programming modules, and layers. This describes the effort, therefore, is dedicated to decomposing software into concerns to promote loosely coupled implementations. The term *concerns* pertains to common application parts, such as business logic, data handling, message exchange and marshaling, and user interfaces (UIs).

Furthermore, software architects typically advocate breaking down applications into smaller segments of functionality, adhering to software architecture industry best practices. This architecture decomposition contributes to application and services performance, agility, maintainability, scalability, elasticity, and other traits required to maintain software reliance and durability in production.

> **CONCEPT**   Recall that decomposition of an application, as discussed thus far, forms loosely coupled architecture to avoid monolithic software implementations that are not nimble enough to be reused and effectively maintained in production.

To promote such an industry best practice, application architects provide design blueprints. These design artifacts are in essence the language of communication that describes the loosely coupled structural composition of an end-state architecture to the development teams. Subsequently, the software construction team must then adhere to the software architecture principles devised by the application architects.

In addition, application architects must demonstrate technological leadership and offer expertise in the software development field. They must be well-versed in application integration and deployment. They must understand production environments, networking, and infrastructure. They must know how to integrate applications with middleware. They must be familiar with programming frameworks. And they must be engaged in product selection and evaluation to boost enterprise technological modernization.

Application Architect Summary of Responsibilities

Consider the variety of the application architect's responsibilities in the list that follows:

Application-level design   Provides application-level design blueprints to the development teams.

Development scope   Scopes the software development efforts to a particular domain, project, application, system, or business initiative.

Programming frameworks   Promotes programming frameworks that are embraced by enterprise architects and solution architects. These specific frameworks devise software development best practices, standards, and policies.

Application decomposition   Responsible for application decomposition efforts to break down applications into programming modules, components, layers, and tiers.

Development guidance   Facilitates, guides, and often leads the software development process. These efforts may include the supervision of source code construction, debugging, and adoption of programming tools.

Application interfaces   Designs and publishes application interfaces for the community of software consumers.

Integration of components   Devises integration of application components.

Testing   Facilitates functional and nonfunctional testing activities in pre-production and production environments. Often provides testing scripts for quality assurance teams.

Prototyping   Supervises prototyping of programming algorithms and solution approaches to prove application viability in production.

Documentation support   Creates and updates application design artifacts during and after the software development phase.

Production facilitation   Collaborates with operation teams to deploy, integrate,[3] configure, and monitor applications in production environments.

Source code integration   Responsible for integration of programming modules developed by various team members to maintain source code integrity.

Selection and evaluation of development platforms   Leads the selection and evaluation of application development platforms.

Source code review   Conducts periodic source code reviews to ensure programming quality and source code integrity.

Architecture verification   Leads software architecture verification sessions to guarantee the compliance of source code with application design, solution architecture blueprints, and enterprise architecture strategies.

Application capacity planning   Responsible for capacity planning efforts to ensure compliance with nonfunctional requirements that tackle adequate computing resource consumption. Data, central processing unit (CPU), network bandwidth, and memory utilization are typically the chief concerns identified in capacity planning documents.

Defect tracking   Maintains an authoritative list of software defects.

---

[3] Assists with continuous integration (CI) and continuous deployment activities (CD).

Application Architect Responsibilities Table

Table 2.4 summarizes the primary duties of architects who are assigned to facilitate the SDLC. The table identifies the parties with whom their collaboration is necessary, the chief benefits, and the intended beneficiaries.

Table 2.4: Application Architect Responsibilities

RESPONSIBILITY	COLLABORATES WITH	CONTRIBUTES TO	CHIEF ORGANIZATION BENEFICIARIES
Application-level design	Solution architects, software developers	Alignment of business requirements with technological solutions, establishment of software development road-maps, promotion of best practices and standards	IT
Scopes software development efforts	Solution architects, software development teams	Streamlining and optimization of software development efforts	Development teams
Promotes programming frameworks	Enterprise architects, solution architects, development teams	Development of best practices, standards, and policies	Development teams
Application decomposition	Solution architects, development teams	Adherence to organizational software architecture best practices, compliance with non-functional requirements	IT
Development guidance	Development teams	SDLC	Development teams
Designs application interfaces	Solution architects, development teams, operation teams	Promotion of production environment interoperability	IT

RESPONSIBILITY	COLLABORATES WITH	CONTRIBUTES TO	CHIEF ORGANIZATION BENEFICIARIES
Integration of application components	Development teams	Improvement of application component reuse	Development teams
Application testing	Development teams, operation teams	Quality of services enhancement	Business and IT
Prototyping	Development teams	Feasibility of technological concepts and solutions	Development teams
Development guidance	Development teams	SDLC	IT
Documentation support	Solution architects, development teams	Documentation of software solutions, development of organizational technical knowledge base	IT
Production facilitation	Operation teams	Business and technical continuity	Business and IT
Source code integration	Development teams	Source code integrity	IT
Development platforms selection and evaluation	Development teams	Standardization of software development process, tools, utilities, and languages	IT
Source code review	Development teams	Adherence to software development best practices, standards, and policies	IT
Architecture verification	Enterprise architects, solution architects, development teams	Alignment of enterprise architecture, solution architecture, and application architecture strategies	Business and IT

Continues

Table 2.4 (*continued*)

RESPONSIBILITY	COLLABORATES WITH	CONTRIBUTES TO	CHIEF ORGANIZATION BENEFICIARIES
Application capacity planning	Development teams, operation teams	Adequate computing resources for application operations	Business and IT
Defect tracking	Development teams	Quality of application and services	Business and IT

Comparing Responsibilities of Leading Software Architects

This section introduces a comparison between the three leading organizational software architects. Table 2.5 shows the key differences between these principal architecture practitioners: enterprise architect, solution architect, and application architect. The three columns in the table drive this comparison. They answer the questions that follow:

Driven strategies   Which strategy drives each software architecture role? For example, an organizational business strategy drives the enterprise architecture practice.

Scope of responsibility   What is the range of responsibilities for each software architecture role? The application architect role, for instance, is chartered to design software solutions that execute business processes.

Design scale   What is the design boundary for each software architect? The solution architect, in particular, is commissioned to provide enterprise-level and application-level design blueprints.

Table 2.5: Types of Enterprise Leading Architects

ARCHITECT LEVEL	TYPE	DRIVEN STRATEGIES	SCOPE OF RESPONSIBILITY	DESIGN SCALE
I	Enterprise architect	Business strategy, enterprise architecture strategy	Enterprise level	Coarse-grained
II	Solution architect	Technological solution strategy	Enterprise and Application levels	Coarse-grained and fine-grained
III	Application architect	Business service strategy	Business process level	Fine-grained

Types of Domain Software Architects

In this day and age, the leading software architecture roles discussed thus far (enterprise architect, solution architect, and application architect) are the most desired talents that organizations tend to hire. Business transformation and technological evolution, however, call for a shift in current hiring goals and practices. This change requires additional software architecture talents to augment the technical capabilities of the leading software architecture roles.

The rapid changes in technology, for example, require *domain experts* in cloud computing. Progress in software security methodologies and mechanisms demands advanced cybersecurity talents. And the adoption of modern databases asks for cutting-edge data modeling skills.

Currently, the leading software architects are incapable of providing solutions for the ever-expanding business and technological requirements. Otherwise stated, leading software architecture practices must include additional expertise to meet growing business imperatives. And this in itself calls for bringing aboard a different type of software architect—called a *domain software architect*.

The sections that follow introduce examples of domain software architects who are employed to supplement the capabilities of the *leading software architecture roles* discussed thus far.

Data Architect

Data governance and management are organizational imperatives that require unique data architecture skills. Data governance is all about embracing data-related frameworks that promote best practices, standards, and policies for information sharing and exchange across an organization or even beyond the boundaries of a single enterprise. Furthermore, the driving principles of data governance are related to the identity and utilization of data within an organization. By contrast, data management addresses the operational and consumption methods affiliated with data utilization, storage, security, recovery, aggregation, and more.

Data governance imperatives typically answer the "what" and "where" type of questions as indicated in the list that follows"

Data analysis   The ability to *discover*, *understand*, and *classify* institutional data. This answers the question, "What type of data do we own?"

Data discovery   The capability to physically *locate* organizational data. Data discovery responds to the question, "Where is our data located?"

Data repurposing   The capacity to *repurpose* the data for a variety of information-sharing activities. Information repurposing typically answers the question, "For what purposes can we reutilize our data?"

Data management, on the other hand, answers the fundamental "how" type of questions. Note the examples in the list that follows:

Data access   The mechanisms that enable secure and effective access to information. How should data be accessed in the most secure manner?

Data storage   The technologies that facilitate storage of data. How should data be deposited in various data storage facilities?

Data collection, aggregation, and integration   The techniques that enable data collection and aggregation. How should data be discovered, retrieved, and gathered from various data sources?

Data utilization   The methods by which data is consumed. How should institutional data be utilized?

Data security   The means by which data is protected to foster privacy. How should an organization secure information and promote data integrity?

Data recovery and availability   The approaches that ensure data-sharing continuity. How should an organization ensure timely recovery from data server outages?

Data Architect Summary of Responsibilities

Note the examples of the data architect responsibilities outlined in the following list:

Data strategy   Leads the establishment of an organizational data strategy to provide support for data governance and management as elaborated on so far.

Data analysis   Evaluates whether existing organizational data and its utilization satisfy business requirements that call for improvement to data quality, security, integrity, and other vital institutional imperatives.

Data modeling   Delivers data models that include conceptual, logical, and physical design artifacts. These data architecture blueprints devise structural and contextual composition of information.

Data governance   Promotes data-related frameworks that devise best practices, standards, and policies for data sharing, exchange, distribution, and information flow across an organization.

Data management   Offers methods and solutions to address common organizational data operational challenges such as data access, data distribution, data security, data aggregation, and data integration.

Data migration   Introduces methods, roadmap, goals, and milestones for data migration initiatives.

Business intelligence   Data architects should promote data analytics and related reporting tasks by recommending the utilization of data warehouses that host references to historical data.

Data security   Data privacy, protection against attacks on data vulnerabilities, and data integrity are among the chief security concerns that data architects must address. In addition, data architecture must employ security platforms and detective monitoring utilities to reduce security risks.

Data integration   Employs data integration patterns to address application and system needs for data sources. These patterns offer data architecture solutions that are supported by message exchange brokers, such as data hubs, data access layers, data aggregators, data collectors, mining platforms, API gateways, and a variety of other middleware products.

Capacity planning   Devises capacity planning for data utilization to ensure adequate computing resources for data storage and network bandwidth.

Data acquisition   Recommends acquisition of data to fill in the information-sharing capability gap of an organization.

Nonfunctional requirements   Provides nonfunctional requirements to accommodate data operations needs in production. These particular imperatives are associated with performance of information exchange, availability, reliability, scalability, redundancy, integrity, recovery, and more.

Data archiving and redundancy   Introduces data backup, availability, DR, and archiving mechanisms to ensure business continuity and flawless distribution of information across an enterprise.

Data Architect Responsibilities Table

Table 2.6 shows the data architects' chief tasks, their potential partners, major contributions of their activities, and chief beneficiaries of their tasks.

Cloud Architect

A cloud architect is at the forefront of organizational modernization efforts. Technological innovation calls for a fundamental diversion from the old ways of conducting business. On the ground, this change manifests in the physical migration of enterprise applications and systems to the cloud.

But it's not only about the relocation of products from one place to another. Now, more than ever, enterprise information is stored, shared, and manipulated in a virtual environment hidden and protected from users. This cloud

Table 2.6: Data Architect Responsibilities

RESPONSIBILITY	COLLABORATES WITH	CONTRIBUTES TO	CHIEF ORGANIZATION BENEFICIARIES
Carves out organizational data strategy	Business representatives, enterprise architects, solution architects, application architects, software developers	Organizational data governance and management tasks	Business and IT
Data analysis	Business representatives, enterprise architects, solution architects, application architects, business analysts, software developers	Data quality, security, and integrity to satisfy business requirements	Business and IT
Data modeling	Application architects, software developers, solution architects	Data design represented in three views: conceptual, logical, and physical	IT
Data governance	Enterprise architects, solution architects, application architects, software developers, operation teams	Adoption of data frameworks to promote best practices, standards, and policies	IT
Data administration	Enterprise architects, solution architects, application architects, operation teams, software developers	Data solutions to address chief organizational concerns such as data access, security, and integration	IT
Data migration	Business representatives, enterprise architects, solution architects, application architects, operation teams, software developers	Methods and roadmaps for data migration	Business and IT

RESPONSIBILITY	COLLABORATES WITH	CONTRIBUTES TO	CHIEF ORGANIZATION BENEFICIARIES
Business intelligence	Business representatives, enterprise architects	Data analytics and utilization of historical data	Business
Data security	Business representatives, solution architects, application architects, software developers	Data privacy, data integrity, data quality	Business and IT
Data Integration	Enterprise architect, solution architect, application architect, development teams, operation teams	Adoption of data architecture patterns to enable efficient applications and systems integration	IT
Capacity planning	Operation teams, application architects	Optimize data utilization	Operations
Data acquisition	Business representatives, enterprise architects, solutions architects, application architects	Data acquisition initiatives to fill in the information-sharing capability gap	Business and IT
Provides data-driven non-functional requirements	Business representatives, enterprise architects, solution architects, application architects, software developers, operation teams	Performance of data exchange, data availability, data reliability, data recovery, data security, data integrity	Business and IT
Data archiving and redundancy	Business representatives, enterprise architects, solution architects, operation teams	Data availability, DR, analytics	Business and IT

migration brings changes to employees' communication styles and social behavior, management practices and direction, and modification to work environments.

In the midst of it all, cloud architects have their hands full with business and technological initiatives that are vital to the existence of their organizations. The mission is vast. And the social, business, and technological challenges pile up as time goes by. There is no limit to the variety of problems that must be solved. Cloud architects are commissioned not only to provide cloud migration and adoption strategies; they need to embrace best practices, standards, and policies for cloud operations and security as well.

Cloud Architect Summary of Responsibilities

Consider the examples of a cloud architect's responsibilities in the list that follows:

Cloud solutions   Provides solutions to meet business goals by employing cloud computing technologies.

Cultural change   Leads cultural transformation for cloud adoption in the enterprise.

Cloud architecture   Devises organizational end-state architecture to address distribution of cloud services across various geographical locations, increase software architecture elasticity and scalability, and advance integration strategies.

Cloud migration strategy   Devises strategies and methodologies for migrating organizational assets from on-premises[4] to cloud ecosystems. This technological innovation is enabled by native cloud services.

Cloud adoption strategy   Embraces a cloud adoption framework that offers best practices, standards, and policies to facilitate and expedite smooth technological transformation.

Cloud operating model[5]   Develops an organizational cloud operating model to support the cloud migration and adoption strategies and facilitate the shift in technological innovation.

Cloud governance framework   Advocates standards, best practices, and policies for service development, configuration, integration, operations, monitoring, and other aspects of cloud-related infrastructure maintenance.

---

[4] On-premise refers to a computing environment that is not located in a virtual cloud.

Cloud cost management Provides expenditure estimates and recommends cost optimization for cloud service operations and maintenance of infrastructure.

Cloud service evaluation and selection Oversees the evaluation and selection of cloud development platforms, deployment and maintenance tools, and infrastructure products.

Cloud capacity planning Delivers cloud capacity plans to ensure adequate computing resources for applications and systems. Capacity planning for the cloud can assist cloud architects in optimizing cloud environments.

Testing Supervises cloud resource utilization testing by employing native cloud services to assess applications and systems performance, data architecture elasticity, computing resource utilization for data storage, memory, CPU, and network bandwidth.

Cloud-related on-premise services Running cloud technologies on-premises (typically cloud agents that are installed externally to cloud space) is another field of expertise that a cloud architect should be familiar with. For example, such cloud utilities can provide a variety of services, such as on-premise performance metric collection, data migration, and data transformation.

Cloud security and compliance Fosters organizational policies to facilitate automated cloud security detection of threats and vulnerabilities and verification of security compliance with policies to maintain privacy and integrity of data in the cloud.

Cloud Architect Responsibilities Table

Table 2.7 identifies the chief responsibilities, partnerships, contribution, and beneficiaries of a cloud architect. Note that this talent is employed to collaborate with business and IT organizations and chartered to support organizational strategies and technological transformation. The chief responsibilities are affiliated with strategies that facilitate application, system, and data migration to the cloud.

---

[5] A "cloud operating model" is a strategy that includes best practices, standards, and policies that not only drives the migration of legacy systems to cloud computing but also establishes a business and technological framework pertaining to service operations cost and efficiency.

Table 2.7: Cloud Architect Responsibilities

RESPONSIBILITIES	COLLABORATES WITH	CONTRIBUTES TO	CHIEF ORGANIZATION BENEFICIARIES
Provides cloud solutions	Business representatives, enterprise architects, solution architects, development teams, operation teams	Utilization of cloud services to accelerate technological modernization	Business and IT
Leads cultural change	Business and IT representatives	Organizational cloud adoption	Business and IT
Devises cloud end-state architecture	Business and IT representatives	Distribution of cloud services, software architecture elasticity and scalability	Business and IT
Leads cloud migration strategy	Business and IT representatives	Technological innovation	Business and IT
Cloud adoption strategy	Enterprise architects, solution architects, software developers, operation teams	Cloud adoption framework to promote best practices, standards, and policies for technological transformation	IT
Develops cloud operating model	IT	Cloud migration and adoption strategies to facilitate technological transformation	IT
Adopts a cloud governance framework	Enterprise architects, solution architects, application architects, software development teams, operation teams	Best practices, standards, and policies for cloud service development, integration, and monitoring	IT

RESPONSIBILITIES	COLLABORATES WITH	CONTRIBUTES TO	CHIEF ORGANIZATION BENEFICIARIES
Manages cloud costs	Business representatives, IT	Cost optimization of cloud service operations	Business and IT
Evaluates and selects cloud services	Enterprise architects, solution architects, application architects, development teams, operation teams	Evaluation and selection of cloud products and services	IT
Delivers cloud capacity planning	Operation teams	Optimization of computing resources in cloud environments	Business and IT
Testing	Operation teams	Assessment of adequate cloud computing resources for applications and systems	Business and IT
Supports cloud-related on-premise services	Operation teams	Execution of cloud services that facilitate data migration from on-premise (noncloud) environments	Operation teams
Detects cloud security threats and verifies compliance with enterprise policies	Operation teams	Maintain privacy and integrity of data in the cloud	Operation teams

Security Architect

One of the most critical disciplines of the software architecture practice is driven by the need to secure applications, systems, and information. That is, security management and governance policies ensure business continuity, shield organizational assets (software and hardware) from malicious attacks, and contribute immensely to workplace productivity.

Every security architect ought to be fully aware that the protection of organizational data is led by the three traditional principles of security controls known as *confidentiality, integrity, and availability*—in short, the CIA triad.[6] These are the paramount goals of every security implementation in the enterprise:

Confidentiality   Organizational pursuit that ensures data privacy

Integrity   Refers to maintaining data quality and reliability by shielding it from unauthorized access that could damage its authenticity

Availability   The capability of organizational applications and systems to continuously authorize access to organizational data

But information protection is not the only concern of an organization. What about the harmful attacks on networks, hardware, and applications? What about the damaging consequences of attacks on infrastructure in production? To tackle a wide range of vulnerabilities, therefore, a security architect must understand the organizational technology and its driving business imperatives. The architect must also embrace security frameworks that offer security best practices, standards, and policies to safeguard business products and the technological platforms that empower them.

Security Architect Summary of Responsibilities

Consider the following list that presents examples of the security architect's responsibilities:

Security architecture   Employs frameworks that offer security principles, best practices, standards, policies, patterns, and methodologies to support organizational data confidentiality, integrity, and availability. The Health Insurance Portability and Accountability Act (HIPAA),[7] National Institute of Standards and Technology (NIST), [8] and International Organization for Standardization (ISO) 27001 and 27002,[9] are examples of such cybersecurity frameworks.

Security strategy alignment   Aligns organizational security strategies with technological strategies.

---

[6] www.f5.com/labs/articles/education/what-is-the-cia-triad
[7] HIPAA is an American framework that mandates that institutions develop security control mechanisms to protect the privacy of electronic health records.
[8] NIST is the U.S. national standard devised to foster cybersecurity standards to protect infrastructure and organizational assets. It mandates that public and private sectors adhere to cybersecurity regulations, develop policies to assess security threats, and apply cybersecurity controls.
[9] ISO 27001 and 27002 are international certifications for evaluating cybersecurity policies and controls across business and technological institutions.

Malware analysis and prevention   Recommends tools, security platforms, and security controls to protect organizational software and hardware assets. Attacks on these assets are typically inflicted by malicious software (malware), such as ransomware, adware, worms, spyware, trojan viruses, and other types of viruses.

Security risk management   Develops security risk detection, analysis, and prevention protocols to prevent the exploitation of software and hardware vulnerabilities by internal and external attacks.

Penetration testing and risk assessment   Manages penetration testing, a simulated security attack on organizational applications and systems to discover their vulnerabilities. This activity typically renders risk assessment documents distributed to development and operation teams.

Threat prevention   It's the security architect's duty to reinforce their organization's defense against cyberattacks by founding security best practices, standards, and policies.

Security awareness   Launches security awareness training programs to instill awareness about the risks of cybersecurity attacks.

Identity and access management (IAM)   Promotes security frameworks that offer technologies and policies used for controlling user access to vital enterprise data.

Incident management   Leads discovery and analysis activities devised to repair damages caused by internal and external cybersecurity attacks. In addition, security architects ought to recommend technologies and approaches designed to prevent such harmful occurrences in the future.

Public key infrastructure (PKI)   Devises processes and policies to manage organizational digital certificates. These measures pertain to creating, encrypting, storing, and distributing public key certificates.

Security controls[10]   Security architects should lead the application of security controls to safeguard organizational assets from threats designed to exploit vulnerabilities of data, processes, and hardware.

System development life cycle   Offers guidance and best practices to enforce security controls during software product development, deployment, installation, integration, and operations. The controls are typically applied to a variety of organizational assets, such as applications, systems, network devices, firewalls, and servers.

---

[10] https://purplesec.us/security-controls

Security audits A security architect leads reviews of software and hardware assets to ensure that the organization complies with cybersecurity policies and regulations and that the processes and data are shielded from security attacks.

Cybercrime investigations Conducts cybercrime investigations to assess the severity of an attack and collects forensic data from the affected organizational assets to determine the intention of the perpetrators.

Security Architect Responsibilities Table

As stated, the chief focus of the security architect is to protect organizational data from security attacks. But applying security measures must be a collaborative effort that characteristically includes the three leading architecture roles: enterprise architect, solution architect, and application architect. Obviously, when it comes to applying security controls, the operation teams are involved to enable access to infrastructure and network environments.

Table 2.8 identifies the responsibilities, partnerships, contribution, and beneficiaries of the security architect tasks and goals.

Table 2.8: Security Architect Responsibilities

RESPONSIBILITIES	COLLABORATE WITH	CONTRIBUTES TO	CHIEF ORGANIZATION BENEFICIARIES
Employs security architecture	Enterprise architects, solution architects, application architects, development teams, operation teams	Adoption of security frameworks to support data confidentiality, data integrity, and data availability	IT
Security strategy alignment	Enterprise architects, solution architects, application architects	Alignment of security strategy with technological strategy	IT
Malware analysis and prevention	Enterprise architects, solution architects, application architects, operation teams	Protection of organizational assets against malware	IT

RESPONSIBILITIES	COLLABORATE WITH	CONTRIBUTES TO	CHIEF ORGANIZATION BENEFICIARIES
Security risk management	IT representatives	Prevention of internal and external security attacks	IT
Penetration testing and risk assessment	Development teams, operation teams	Discovery of organizational asset vulnerabilities	IT
Threat prevention	Operation teams	Reinforcement of defense against cyberattacks	IT
Launches security awareness training programs	Enterprise-wide audience	Organizational awareness about cybersecurity attacks	Business and IT
IAM	Operation teams	Control user access privilege to vital enterprise data	Business and IT
Incident management	Operation teams	Mending damages caused by internal and external cybersecurity attacks	Business and IT
Manages PKI	IT representatives	Management of organizational digital certificates	IT
Security controls	Operation teams	Protection of applications and systems from security threats	IT
Facilitates SDLC	Solution architects, application architects, development teams, operation teams	Protection of organizational assets by applying security controls during the SDLC	IT
Security audits	Operation teams	Verification of organizational compliance with security policies and regulations	IT
Cybercrime investigations	Operation teams	Damage assessment of security attacks	IT

Business Architect

Business architects are typically commissioned to assimilate, interpret, and simplify business strategies. Their duties encompass a wide range of responsibilities that chiefly call for bridging the strategies devised by business leaders and enterprise architects. Claiming that a business architect's role also involves software architecture tasks would be moderately true. In most cases it depends on how an organization perceives such an occupation. Some firms charter business architects to be actively involved in software development efforts. Others consider business architecture an instrumental practice employed to lead business modeling[11] activities and even oversee the creation of business requirements.

On the business decision-making front, business architects play a pragmatic role in assessing the feasibility of business investments in software products. They are also commissioned to prioritize business solutions and ensure that organizations stay focused on their vital imperatives. Moreover, business architects often advise executives to avoid trivial projects with projected negligible returns on investment. Weeding out impractical business solutions typically contributes to the optimization of budgets and the reduction of enterprise expenditure. By pursuing these activities, business architects in essence provide valuable business investment models to safeguard against frivolous waste and promote organizational goals.

So how do business architects provide vital value to the software architecture practice? Their interpretation of business strategies ultimately manifests an immense contribution to enterprise architecture solutions. Without clear business direction and mission, enterprise architects would not be able to deliver technological strategies. Without clarification of business solutions, enterprise architects would not be able to pursue the integration of applications and systems in production. And without business requirements, enterprise architects would not be able to offer potent end-state architectures. All of these are the substantial contributions of business architects to software architecture strategies.

Business Architect Summary of Responsibilities

The list that follows represents examples of the business architect's duties:

Business strategies   Simplifies business strategies to the level that enterprise architects can understand business vision and mission

Business strategy assessment   Leads analyses to assess the feasibility of business strategies and their overall contribution to organizational solutions

---

[11] Business modeling is a business architecture discipline, devised to promote business strategies, vision, mission, and goals.

Strategy success measurement Measures the success of business strategies by utilizing business evaluation scorecards[12]

Business solutions Interprets business solutions to simplify complex business missions and facilitates the foundation of the enterprise architecture roadmap

Business capability assessment Assesses the business capabilities to provide effective remedies for organizational problems

Business investment model[13] Devises business investment models to promote business vision and goals

Strategy alignment Contributes to the alignment of business and enterprise architecture strategies to avoid uncoordinated agendas and influence technological goals

Strategy alignment verification Ensures that business and enterprise architecture strategies are aligned to guarantee that technological initiatives ultimately meet business imperatives

Business opportunities Identifies investment opportunities to promote enterprise commerce goals and contribute to business growth

Business knowledge Disseminates business knowledge across an organization to reduce operational silos and foster better collaboration between lines of business

Business process management (BPM) Leads business process modeling activities that render workflows of business functions to simplify complex enterprise activities (see `https://bpm.com/`)

Business risk assessment Provides periodic business risk assessments to alert executives about looming perils to organizational performance and earnings

Business and IT partnership Develops business and IT collaboration plans and serves as an equal partner on software architecture projects

Business solution orchestration Plans, coordinates, and orchestrates business solutions by collaborating with influential decision-makers to deliver valuable and practical business requirements

Business Architect Responsibilities Table

The responsibilities of business architects call for collaborating with business executives, managers, and analysts to promote organizational strategies. Once

---

[12] The balanced scorecard (BSC), for example, is a performance reporting card that organizations employ to assess business progress and improve performance.

[13] Business investment model is commonly devised by business architects to strengthen business strategies, promote economic growth, and foster fiscal discipline.

the strategies are finalized, business architects must collaborate with enterprise architects to influence software architecture strategies and direction. And this partnership will obviously impact technological investments and transformation. Table 2.9 reflects this notion. As is apparent, business architects are required not only to streamline business expenditure, they are also engaged to influence business investment strategies.

Table 2.9: Business Architect Responsibilities

RESPONSIBILITIES	COLLABORATES WITH	CONTRIBUTES TO	CHIEF ORGANIZATION BENEFICIARIES
Interprets business strategies	Enterprise architects	Better understanding of business vision and mission	IT
Business strategy assessment	Business representatives	Assessment of business strategies to promote organizational solutions	Business and IT
Strategy success measurement	Business representatives	Feasibility assessment of business strategy	Business
Interprets business solutions	Enterprise architect	Simplification of complex business missions to help found effective enterprise architecture roadmaps	IT
Business capability assessment	Business representatives	Evaluation of business ability to provide solutions for enterprise problems	Business
Devises business investment models	Business representatives	Establishment of approaches and processes to foster business growth through prudent investments	Business
Contributes to the alignment of business and enterprise architecture strategies	Business representatives, enterprise architects	Influence the direction of software architecture strategies	Business and IT
Business and enterprise strategies alignment verification	Business representatives, enterprise architects	Assurance that technological initiatives satisfy business needs	Business and IT

RESPONSIBILITIES	COLLABORATES WITH	CONTRIBUTES TO	CHIEF ORGANIZATION BENEFICIARIES
Discovers business opportunities	Business representatives	Identification of pragmatic business opportunities to maximize return on investment	Business
Promotes business knowledge	Business and IT representatives	Reduce silos and encourage collaboration between lines of business	Business and IT
Business process modeling	Business representatives	Discovery and documentation of business processes to reduce investment redundancy, increase asset reuse, and minimize expenditure	Business
Business risk assessment	Business representatives	Mechanisms to alert executives about risks to business performance	Business
Supports business and IT partnership	Business representatives, enterprise architects, solution architects	Coordination of business and IT activities to meet organizational goals	Business and IT
Business solution orchestration	Business representatives	Coordination of the delivery of feasible business requirements	Business

Collaboration Between Leading Software Architects and Domain Software Architects

Software architects never work in a vacuum without collaborating with peer architects. In fact, software development projects often require combined architecture skills to deliver solutions for complex business problems. Today's common recruiting practices, therefore, call for utilizing diverse talents to augment organizational software architecture knowledge. For example, an application architect who possesses strong software design skills may be lacking in cybersecurity knowledge. Similarly, an enterprise architect may need the assistance of a data architect to help design an organizational data hub.

The idea of engaging complementary software architecture talents to tackle complex business problems is picking up steam among program and project managers. This rationale propels the need for utilizing combined software design skills to facilitate the development life cycle from its inception through the testing, deployment, configuration, and integration phases.

The sections that follow then introduce common industry use case examples, illustrating the necessity for combining the forces of lead software architects and domain software architects. Before moving on, though, it would be beneficial to revisit Chapter 1, "Software Architect Capability Model." Chapter 1 is all about discovering the gaps in the knowledge and capabilities of software architects or architecture teams in order to offer effective solutions to business challenges. By discovering the gaps in talent, project managers may be compelled to augment software architecture expertise.

Use Case I: Collaboration Between an Application Architect and a Data Architect

A common partnership comes into play when an application architect is in need of a data architect. This happens not only because an application architect may lack data modeling skills, but also a project's time constraints may call for additional talent to help shorten the software development curve. Other considerations may be attributed to the well-known "separation of concerns" best practice, which requires breaking down an application into distinct programming modules that typically call for different design skillsets.

For example, this logical decomposition may render three modules: business logic, data, and UI. Developing each of these modules typically requires different types of software architects. A data architect would certainly be commissioned to design the data module. In the same fashion, a UI developer would undoubtedly be assigned to build the application's front end. And so on. . ..

The need for data design skills then calls for close collaboration between an application architect and a data architect. This partnership is essential to the success of application software development projects.

Application Architect and Data Architect Collaboration Table

Table 2.10 shows the vital support that a data architect offers the application development team. This partnership and cooperation on chief application development life-cycle activities is characteristically driven by the application architect.

Table 2.10: Application Architect and Data Architect Collaboration

APPLICATION ARCHITECT TASK	DATA ARCHITECT TASK	MUTUAL RESPONSIBILITIES
Embraces industry software development frameworks	Adopts industry data architecture frameworks	Promote application development and data modeling frameworks that offer corresponding best practices, standards, and policies
Scopes the software development efforts	Focuses on specific application data architecture tasks	Integrate application development efforts with data architecture deliverables
Decomposes an application into programming modules, components, layers, and tiers	Develops data concepts, identifies data entities and their attributes, and discovers relationships between these entities	Identify data architecture needs for application modules, components, layers, and tiers
Orchestrates and guides software development efforts	Provides data architecture support for application business functionality	Collaborate during the SDLC to accommodate the needs for utilization of data
Provides architecture blueprints for integrating application components	Ensures that the data scheme satisfies the data consumption requirements of application components	Ensure that the integration of application components drive proper data distribution
Validates the compliance of the programming source code with application architecture blueprints	Verifies if the programming source code complies with the data architecture, best practices, standards, and policies	Confirm if the data architecture satisfies the needs of the application architecture
Facilitates application functional and nonfunctional testing	Conducts data integrity and security testing for transactions between applications and their consumers	Guarantee business continuity in production
Supports application deployment, configuration, integration, security, and monitoring in production	Supports production operations associated with data distribution, integration, security, monitoring, and management of data sources	Monitor and facilitate the integration of applications with data sources in production

But the full collaboration between an application architect and data architect is not always needed. In many circumstances, data architects may operate independently to accommodate the needs for data protection, storage, formatting, and distribution across an organization. And these independent data architecture duties may take place despite the close partnership with an application architect.

Use Case II: Solution Architect and Security Architect

Collaboration between a solution architect and a security architect is common. This partnership is driven by the critical need for security frameworks that offer best practices, standards, and policies to facilitate solution architecture tasks. Note that in addition to security architecture talents, solution architects may also require data architects, infrastructure architects, and cloud architects to accomplish business and technological tasks.

Furthermore, on one hand, security architects are chartered to facilitate enterprise architecture imperatives, and on the other, they also needed to meet application-level requirements. Simply put, they are being asked to provide solutions on both levels: the enterprise level and the application level. Therefore, since solution architects act as mediators between these two levels, their partnership with security architects is valuable to all levels of organizational projects.

Solution Architect and Security Architect Collaboration Table

Time to inspect Table 2.11. It seems that this partnership is driven by solution architecture requirements. However, there is not always a direct correlation between solution architecture and security architecture implementations. In other words, security architects must not necessarily react to solution architecture activities. In fact, in most circumstances security architecture frameworks are adopted by the solutions architects themselves to shield organizational assets from internal and external attacks. And these solution architecture activities may take place without direct interaction with security architects.

The heart of the matter is that solution architects must apply security architectures to technological implementations. Consequently, the mutual responsibility of solution architects and security architects is to verify if security controls are indeed effective measures of protection.

Table 2.11: Solution Architect and Security Architect Collaboration

SOLUTION ARCHITECT TASK	SECURITY ARCHITECT TASK	MUTUAL RESPONSIBILITIES
Promotes enterprise software architecture vision and mission	Embraces organizational security architecture frameworks to support enterprise software architecture strategies	Ensure that security architecture is aligned with enterprise architecture vision and mission
Fosters organizational technological innovation	Contributes security architecture perspectives to strengthen and safeguard technological modernization	Identify and protect security vulnerabilities with the adoption of advanced technologies
Transforms enterprise architecture concepts into technological solutions	Identifies opportunities to boost the security of technological solutions	Apply security architecture standards, best practices, and policies to organizational technological solutions
Interprets business requirements into technical specifications	Augments technical specifications with security policies	Verify if technical specifications include security controls
Provides design blueprints for enterprise-level and application-level architectures	Devises security architectures for enterprise and application implementations	Embed security architecture in application-level and enterprise-level design blueprints
Mentors and guides software development teams	Conducts security awareness training to protect processes, data, and hardware	Adopt software development and security frameworks to facilitate the system development and operation life cycle
Devises integration schemes for business products in production	Applies security architecture implementations and controls to product integration efforts in production	Ensure that application and system integration patterns comply with security policies
Coordinates collaboration activities between development and operation teams	Raises the awareness of potential malicious attacks against organizational assets during the collaboration activities between software development and operation teams	Conduct security risk assessment to discover application and system vulnerabilities in production
Supports applications and systems operations in production. These activities may include deployment, configuration, integration, and performance monitoring	Establishes security architecture standards and policies for production operations	Assure that production operations adhere to security policies and standards

Use Case III: Business Architect and Enterprise Architect Collaboration

Bridging the gap between the business and IT organizations calls for architecture talents that on one hand understand organizational strategies and on the other are well-versed in technology. Both sides of the aisle, for that matter—business architects and enterprise architects—are commissioned to maintain strong communication and to collaboratively offer tangible solutions to business problems. This partnership must endure the conflicts of departmental or personal agendas. Put differently, business architects and enterprise architects must work together to promote a joint technological strategy.

Business Architect and Enterprise Architect Collaboration Table

This collaboration use case example is shown in Table 2.12. As depicted, the business architect is chartered not only to drive vital business initiatives but is also required to influence technological deliverables. This table compares the individual tasks of the business architect with the enterprise architect. Ultimately, both must be equally responsible for the outcome of their collaboration. The mutual responsibilities column represents this idea.

Table 2.12: Business Architect and Enterprise Architect Collaboration

BUSINESS ARCHITECT TASK	ENTERPRISE ARCHITECT TASK	MUTUAL RESPONSIBILITIES
Contributes to business strategies, vision, and mission	Drives technological strategies, vision, and mission	Verify the alignment of business and technology strategies
Devises business investment models	Offers roadmap for organizational technological innovation initiatives	Promote business solutions by optimizing business and technological expenditure
Locates business opportunities	Conducts research and development activities to foster technological modernization	Support enterprise-wide technological innovation initiatives to promote business goals
Identifies business problem domains	Explores potential technological solutions to address business problems	Propose technological solutions that are driven by business imperatives
Conducts business risk assessments	Delivers technical risk assessments that may affect the performance of applications and systems	Assess business performance and continuity in production

BUSINESS ARCHITECT TASK	ENTERPRISE ARCHITECT TASK	MUTUAL RESPONSIBILITIES
Delivers business requirements	Drives enterprise-wide technical specifications	Assure that technological specifications meet business requirements
Interprets business solutions	Devises technological solutions	Validate the compliance of technological solutions with business solutions
Contributes to organizational business knowledgebase	Contributes to organizational technical knowledgebase	Support firm-wide educational and training activities to increase business and technical knowledge

CHAPTER 3

Career Planning for Software Architects: A Winning Strategy

There is nothing more important than a career strategy that outlines personal milestones and goals. There is nothing more consequential than a career path that illustrates a coherent road map to fulfill professional objectives. And there is nothing more essential than a pragmatic approach to promote professional growth. These are cardinal prerequisites that every aspiring, beginning, or experienced software architect must be cognizant of. Without a meticulous career plan, business and information technology (IT) professionals are prone to embark on muddled journeys that yield negligible outcomes.

It's impossible to carve out a successful career strategy without a self-discovery process. Although we tend to recognize our strengths and weaknesses to a certain extent, when it comes to assessing our competencies to fulfill business or IT duties, we may discover uncharted traits that can be employed to provide potent solutions to business and technological challenges. The self-discovery process is not only about assessing technical capabilities. It's about finding a better match between our personal preferences and career goals.

So now our work is cut out for us. Let's roll up our sleeves and prepare to ponder new career choices. Plan a meaningful professional journey that galvanizes workplace collaborations and partnerships. Devise a career path that is fused with exciting employment opportunities. And never be afraid to ask hard questions that most likely will bring clarity to a promised future.

CONCEPT   And just before we start, consider this: there is nothing wrong about being naïve, silly, and inexperienced at the outset or during a career journey. Meet professional goals by using imagination—Not even the sky is the limit.

Software Architecture Career Planning Process

A long-lasting professional career must be driven by a plan—often referred to as a *career strategy*. And every career development plan must be steered by milestones and goals. Aspiring, beginning, and even experienced software architects who do not make the effort to carve out a personal career strategy may flub job interviews, miss promotion opportunities, and introduce unnecessary confusion to their career journey.

Bear in mind that a software architecture career strategy may run its course because of unforeseen business and technological trends. Industry changes typically impact organizational hiring priorities, budgets, and even the scope and types of projects. Therefore, when a career strategy turns out to be irrelevant, the time comes to revamp the career road map and reset goals. Put differently, a career plan must be periodically updated to reflect business and technological evolutions.

When either carving out a new software architecture career plan or updating an existing one, follow a step-by-step process that defines clear and tangible goals.

CONCEPT   The career planning process must take a pragmatic approach. It should be driven by realistic milestones and goals to circumvent an unachievable career road map.

As illustrated in Figure 3.1, the sections that follow elaborate on the career planning process, which consists of four steps.

1. **Conduct self-discovery.** Reveal personal traits and technological capabilities that can be employed to provide solutions to organizational challenges.

2. **Pursue research.** Identify particular industries, companies, business models, and lines of business that personal traits and technological capabilities can contribute the most to.

3. **Devise an approach.** Employ a method to facilitate a successful software architecture career.

4. **Plan career execution.** Devise a plan to effectively execute the software architecture career plan.

Figure 3.1: Career Planning Process

Career Planning Step 1: Conduct Self-Discovery

The career development process calls for self-discovery activities that shed light on an individual's ability to fulfill software architecture duties. A big part of the discovery exercise is to find out if an aspiring, beginning, or experienced software architect possesses adequate qualifications to tackle business and technological challenges. The discovery process then must focus on at least two chief self-discovery perspectives: technological and social. Note that Chapter 4, "Self-Assessment for Software Architects," includes additional perspectives.

Discovery of Technological and Social Talents

From a technological viewpoint, the discovery efforts should center on revealing professional talents associated with software architecture practices. Among other technical aptitudes, these discovered skills may include the ability to embrace frameworks, master software modeling, provide design blueprints, utilize architecture styles, employ integration patterns, and offer security models.

By contrast, the self-discovery of social skills may consist of a wide range of communication capabilities. These typically include the ability to explain complex design schemes to managers and collaborating teams, persuade executives and sponsors to allocate software development budgets, encourage teamwork, and foster business and IT partnerships.

> **CONCEPT**   To enhance technological and social skills, pursue a continuous self-improvement effort. It must take place before applying for any software architecture job. This educational task should be a vital part of any career planning.

Table 3.1: Career Planning Self-Discovery

DISCOVERY SUBJECT	PERSONAL TRAITS AND CAPABILITIES EXAMPLES TO EXPLORE
Technological capabilities	Embrace architecture frameworks, software modeling, deliver design blueprints, employ architecture styles, use integration patterns, devise security models
Social capabilities	Explain complex architecture, encourage teamwork, foster IT and business partnerships
Personal traits	Behavior strengths and weaknesses, moral values, individual commitment to pursue career goals
Personal preferences	Career preferences, personal goals, dreams, ambitions

Along with the technological and social self-discovery process, aspiring or even seasoned software architects ought to consider their preferences, interests, personal career goals, and even their moral values. These personal traits and occupation vision should be a vital part of career planning.

Career Planning Self-Discovery Subjects

Table 3.1 summarizes the chief subjects that should be explored. They should be the initial part of the career planning initiative. As I mentioned earlier, the self-assessment questionnaire provided in Chapter 4 is designed to discover and evaluate personal traits, technical skills, and social skills.

Career Planning Step 2: Pursue Research

One of the most common career planning activities calls for identifying software architecture niche markets. A *software architecture niche market* refers to a specific business and/or technical field that an individual can favorably contribute to. This would be a field where novice and experienced software architects could find a great deal of success by offering effective business and technological solutions.

A software architecture niche market could also be viewed as a particular industry that employs unique software products to execute specific business activities. Moreover, since a niche market could also pertain to a distinct type of business model or line of business, career planning research activities should identify which companies are affiliated with a certain industry and software products.

CONCEPT   Put differently, a software architecture niche market is an industry segment that software architects understand and are able to offer effective solutions to business and technological challenges. In essence, searching for a software architecture niche market is about the alignment of personal traits and technical specialties with particular lines of business.

Formal Education, Training, and Certification

To adequately prepare for a career journey in software architecture, formal education, such as earning a computer science degree, should be considered. But this is not mandatory, since experience in the computer field could be considered by employers as a substitute for a college degree. Other educational avenues might be more appropriate for some. For example, pursuing continuing education training or taking certification exams would be steps in the right direction. The planning process, therefore, calls for exploring these formal education and training options for formulating a successful career path.

Employment Opportunities and Interviews

The career planning research effort should also spur individuals to explore employment opportunities with hiring organizations. Again, this effort should center on companies in the software architecture niche market. For instance, home equity loans, boat mortgages, car parts, and even email marketing firms may fall under the niche market category. While searching for such companies, a good idea would be to identify their customers and the demand for their products and services. From a software architecture perspective, this would also shed light on the type of applications and systems the hiring organizations are using.

Finally, software architecture niche market companies tend to seek talents that are capable of providing technological solutions in their product lines. Thus, the interviews they conduct are typically affiliated with specific industries and lines of business. Applicants then should be prepared to answer questions that are affiliated with these particular niche markets.

Subjects of Research

Table 3.2 identifies the chief items to explore for carving out an effective career strategy. The shown examples depict areas of study and investigation. This research could be expanded to include subjects that are affiliated with employment compensation and benefits. Additional subjects could include companies' locations and their remote work policies.

Table 3.2: Subjects of Research for Career Planning Process

RESEARCH SUBJECT	EXAMPLES
Niche market	Market needs, industry, products
Formal education, training, and certification	Computer science degree, professional certifications and training, continuing education, software architecture boot camps
Hiring companies	Company culture, technologies, business imperatives, required talents, products, services, lines of business, employee compensation and benefits
Consumers	Consumer segmentation, consumer service demand, consumer demographic, consumer service requirements
Interviews	Type of interview questions and potential queries

Career Planning Step 3: Devise an Approach

Here is where the strategy is carved out during the career planning effort. The strategy spells out the approach and the main tasks to facilitate the successful fruition of a software architecture career. An unplanned and ill-conceived software architecture career may veer off the track to achieving professional goals. But this is not the only impediment. During a lifelong career journey, time must be wisely spent to avoid delays in career growth or pursuing unintended occupations that are not in line with personal preferences.

Every career plan should include the four key steps to formulate a firm approach for pursuing a software architecture career. These are explained in the sections that follow:

- "Setting Software Architecture Career Goals"
- "Setting Software Architecture Career Milestones"
- "Decision-Making"
- "Action Planning"

Setting Software Architecture Career Goals

The eventual achievement of a career goal signifies a major turning point in every professional journey. Therefore, a software architecture career strategy cannot survive if personal goals are not set. Without clear goals, a career plan won't be practical. To establish a feasible plan, attend to these career goal characteristics:

Pragmatic   Avoid setting unrealistic career goals that are impossible to fulfill. Goals must be aligned with personal preferences and software architecture capabilities.

Quantifiable   The journey to achieving career goals must be measurable and traceable to monitor professional progress.

Explicit   A career goal must be clear and unambiguous to avoid confusion and misinterpretation. This would set the focus on specific personal preferences.

Well-timed   Ensure that a timetable for achieving a goal is not unrealistic.

CONCEPT   Note that career goals are subject to change and may be revised in future career stages to reflect professional growth and earned achievements.

To establish effective career goals, craft a list similar to Table 3.3. Enterprise architect is the target occupation in this example. Note that the preferred duties for this goal are affiliated with common industry enterprise architecture roles and deliverables. In this example, banking is the chosen industry, and New York City is the favorite workplace.

Table 3.3: Software Architecture Career Goals Setting

	TARGET OCCUPATION/ GOAL	PREFERRED DUTIES	PREFERRED INDUSTRY	PREFERRED WORKPLACE
My Career Goal	Enterprise architect	Support technological modernization	Banking	New York City
		Embrace common industry software architecture frameworks to establish enterprise-wide best practices, standards, and policies		
		Devise firm-wide end-state architecture		
		Promote technological standardization to reduce organizational cost of ownership		
Add here more software architecture career goals.				

It is common for aspiring and experienced software architects to set multiple career goals in their career plan. Therefore, the goal-setting table can be expanded to include additional target occupations along with preferred duties, industries, and workplaces.

Setting Software Architecture Career Milestones

Unlike a career goal that signifies a decisive achievement in a professional journey, a milestone serves as a checkpoint to measure skill improvement and occupational progress. In the context of a software architecture career, a milestone not only denotes the proper time to ponder one's technological achievements, it is also a good time to prepare for the next career step.

> **CONCEPT**   Remember, each career milestone provides a good opportunity to evaluate if an individual's software architecture capabilities are up to snuff.

When reaching a software architecture career milestone, it's time to ask these questions:

Career trajectory   Am I on the right trajectory to achieving my personal preferences and professional goals?

Satisfaction   Am I satisfied with my professional achievements so far?

Adequate solutions   Have I provided adequate software architecture solutions to meet critical business requirements?

Career improvement   Is there anything else I can do to improve my software architecture knowledge and performance to be able to provide superior technical solutions to business problems?

Career goal   Have I achieved my chief career goal?

Craft a list of milestones as shown in Table 3.4. In this example, there are two planned milestones to meet: 1) becoming an application software architect, and 2) serving an organization as a solution software architect. Preferred milestone duties, industries, and workplaces are indicated for each. Also specified is the timeframe for achieving each milestone: one year to fulfill the application software architect position and four years until the solution software architect job is realized.

Note that this example shows two milestones, each of which targets a different software architecture occupation. Multiple milestones, however, could be planned for a single occupation. It all depends on the career path that an individual chooses.

Table 3.4: Software Architecture Career Milestones Stetting

MILESTONE TO ACCOMPLISH	TARGET OCCUPATION MILESTONE	PREFERRED MILESTONE DUTIES	PREFERRED MILESTONE INDUSTRY	PREFERRED MILESTONE WORKPLACE
In 1 year	Application software architect	Promote programming frameworks that are embraced by enterprise architects and solution architects	Insurance	New Jersey
		Provide application-level design blueprints to the development teams		
		Facilitate, guide, and often participate in the software development process		
In 4 years	Solution software architect	Provide design blueprints	Insurance	Remote work
		Take part in integration efforts of business products in production		
		Provide technical management services to development teams		
Add here more software architecture career milestones.				

Decision-Making

Hasty career decisions never pay off. It's certainly not a good idea to pursue random employment opportunities without pondering the negative consequences.

Unvetted job propositions that may pay higher wages characteristically hinder career progress and only introduce disruptions to attaining professional objectives. Therefore, do not rush. Carve out a solid career plan that ultimately meets personal strategy goals.

So, what are the career decision-making steps that should be followed? What is unique about the software architecture decision-making process? And why is career decision-making so critical when planning future employment?

Decision-making activities must focus on career choices that individuals strive to accomplish. In other words, the decision-making process is about selecting the right career path after gathering enough information about various occupational options. This task in itself is not an easy one because there are endless opportunities to choose from, some of which are truly appealing.

CONCEPT   The rule of thumb suggests that the best career choice is also the most practical one. And the most feasible is the one that is aligned with an individual's software architecture capabilities.

Software architecture career decisions are driven by choices that are made because of professional preferences, technical capabilities, and software architecture talents. Only when all these traits are brought into consideration does the right decision become clear.

Finally, consider the decision-making activities of software architecture career planning:

Gather career path choices.   Compile a list of software architecture career path choices. The "Carving a Software Architecture Career Path" section in this chapter elaborates on various career path options.

Study the choices.   Carefully analyze all career path choices that are on the table.

Choose the best career path.   The best career path is the one that aligns with professional preferences, technical and social capabilities, and personal career goals.

Analyze the feasibility of the chosen career path.   Consider the alternatives. Analyze the practicality of the chosen career path. And answer the questions, "Is it practical? Does it comply with personal professional preferences?"

Action Planning

The execution of a software architecture career plan must be driven by a solid scheme that ultimately meets predefined *goals*. In addition, the action plan should be guided by a compelling *approach*—as outlined in the previous section. So why is such an execution plan needed? A professional career is typically prone to failure if an action plan is absent. The same outcome may apply to a plan that's not well thought out or meticulously outlined. In the case of a career failure, the stakes might be high and the results irreparable. Waste of valuable time, compensation reduction, and professional demotions may be some of the harsh consequences for disregarding the significance of a career strategy.

When mulling over the activities that should be incorporated in a software architecture career action plan, consider including rudimentary tasks that can promote the fulfillment of professional goals. Remember, though, that these tasks ought to be achievable and practical. The action plan must never comprise futile activities that result in negligible career outcomes. Tasks are beneficial if they bring about tangible results. Hiring a career coach, joining a software architecture social media group, acquiring a laptop, and even purchasing a business suit are examples that typically contribute to employment efforts.

The Impediments to Completing an Action Plan's Tasks

Be aware that an action plan is merely a plain list of tentative tasks, some of which may never be executed. They are specified, though, just in case time and circumstances allow. When the time arrives to execute the action plan, we may find out that some tasks cannot be accomplished. All in all, the obstacles to the action plan could be infinite. In most cases, the chief impediment to the plan is due to underestimating the duration of the tasks.

CONCEPT Generally, career action plans are always subject to change because of unexpected hindering events or even execution time constraints. Consequently, the planned tasks may never be implemented.

Create an Action Plan Table

With this prior knowledge, create an action plan as shown in Table 3.5. Focus on the four columns: Target Occupation/Goal, Task, Task Specification, and Estimated Task Duration. In this case, the target occupation—security architect—is the eventual *professional goal*. Obviously, the tasks ought to be related to the occupation. It is also important to specify the estimated timeframe for completing each task. If the duration is unknown, then provide an execution time range.

Table 3.5: Software Architecture Career Action Plan

TARGET OCCUPATION/ GOAL	TASK	TASK SPECIFICATION	ESTIMATED TASK DURATION
Security architect	Certification	Acquire cybersecurity certification	10–25 weeks
	On-site conferences	Attend cybersecurity conferences	5–10 days
	Social networking	Pursue social networking to learn more about the cybersecurity industry	Constant effort
	Study	Study publications, such as books and journals about new cybersecurity penetration testing and risk assessment technologies	2–6 months
	Self-assessment	Use self-assessment tools to discover and verify cybersecurity skills	3 weeks
	Learning	Learn about cybersecurity frameworks	10–20 days
	Training	Take security awareness training	3 days
	Contacts	Update contact information for friends, co-workers, and recruiters	Constant effort
	Resume	Prepare a compelling resume that demonstrates cybersecurity experience and knowledge	2–5 weeks
	Employment searching tools	Discover employment search tools to find available cybersecurity jobs	Constant effort
	Employment opportunities	Search for potential employers who seek cybersecurity talents	Constant effort
	Interviews	Prepare for cybersecurity interviews	At least 2 weeks before an interview
Add here more action plans.			

Career Planning Step 4: Plan Career Execution

There is a substantial difference between *action planning* and *execution planning*. As elaborated in the previous section, there is no guarantee that an action plan will be fully executed. On that account, the rule of thumb suggests that there are no safe action plans—all are subject to change since myriad things may go awry during their execution.

The execution plan that's proposed here, therefore, should include alternative tasks just in case anything goes wrong. Moreover, the plan must consist of contingency activities to fall back on. It should include a backup strategy. It should include "what if" conditional statements to deal with the unknown and to address unforeseen events that can easily derail a career path.

CONCEPT   Recall that the better we plan for random career impediments, the better we're prepared for dodging them. Therefore, an execution plan must be flexible enough to adjust to changes in the software architecture field, attuned to trends in business and technology, and in harmony with industry transformations.

To carve out an efficient and realistic execution plan to alleviate fulfillment and timetable risks, consider the proposition of the two use cases that follow:

- "Use Case I: A Software Architecture Career Execution Plan with Alternative Tasks"
- "Use Case II: Optimized Software Architecture Execution Plan"

Use Case I: A Software Architecture Career Execution Plan with Alternative Tasks

Since it's difficult to circumvent negative impacts on almost any career execution plan, let's examine options that can mitigate risks. Namely, never assume that all tasks assigned to a career action plan (as shown in Table 3.5) are going to be fulfilled. Therefore, come up with alternatives that can replace the original ones. Or devise a different task that may take a shorter time to accomplish. Or just avoid setting tasks that are impossible to carry out.

First, Create a Base for an Execution Plan

To create a realistic career execution plan, start with the career action plan example as described in the section "Action Planning." Simply copy Table 3.5. This will be the base for the career execution plan that is discussed here.

CONCEPT   Remember that every action plan must be driven by a predefined goal. This obviously must apply to the execution plan as well.

First understand the predefined goal. In our case, the target occupation is security architect. Then understand the related tasks to be accomplished. Next, note that the Estimated Task Duration column specifies the projected time for completion. Now the time has come to refine the execution plan. Ask these rudimentary questions before fine-tuning the plan:

Realistic plan   Is the overall execution plan realistic when it comes to achieving the specified goal?

Understandable tasks   Do the tasks make sense? Are they understandable? Defined well? Clear?

Promoting goals   Do the all the tasks promote goal achievement?

Practical tasks   Are all tasks practical?

Pragmatic task durations   Are the estimated task durations pragmatic? Can the tasks be accomplished within the specified timeframe?

Second, Tweak the Base Execution Plan

Now, let's tweak the execution plan if any of the provided answers calls for modification. Table 3.6 shows the changes to the plan. The modifications to the tasks are displayed in gray.

First replacement   The On-Site Conferences task was deleted and replaced with the Virtual Conferences task.

Second replacement   The Self-Study task was deleted and replaced with the Cybersecurity boot camps task.

Table 3.6: Software Architecture Career Execution Plan with Alternative Tasks

TARGET OCCUPATION/ GOAL	TASK	TASK SPECIFICATION	ESTIMATED TASK DURATION
Security architect	Certification	Acquire cybersecurity certification	10–25 weeks
	~~On-Site Conferences~~	~~Attend cybersecurity conferences~~	~~5–10 days~~
	Complete this task instead:		
	Virtual Conferences	Participate in virtual cybersecurity conferences	2–5 days
	Social networking	Pursue social networking to learn more about the cybersecurity industry	Constant effort

TARGET OCCUPATION/ GOAL	TASK	TASK SPECIFICATION	ESTIMATED TASK DURATION
	~~Study~~	~~Study publications, such as books and journals, about new cybersecurity penetration testing and risk assessment technologies~~	~~2–6 months~~
	Complete this task instead:		
	Cybersecurity Boot camps	Take cybersecurity boot camps to focus on current penetration testing and risk assessment technologies	2–3 weeks
	Self-assessment	Use self-assessment tools to discover and verify cybersecurity skills	3 weeks
	Learning	Learn about cybersecurity frameworks	10–20 days
	Training	Take security awareness training	3 days
	Contacts	Update contact information for friends, co-workers, and recruiters	Constant effort
	Resume	Prepare a compelling resume that demonstrates cybersecurity experience and knowledge	2–5 weeks
	Employment Searching Tools	Discover employment searching tools to find available cybersecurity jobs	Constant effort
	Employment Opportunities	Search for potential employers who seek cybersecurity talents	Constant effort
	Interviews	Prepare for cybersecurity interviews	At least 2 weeks before each interview
	Add here more action plans		

To make the execution plan more realistic, the deleted tasks were replaced with their alternative tasks. To be more specific, the changes to the execution plan were made to shorten the estimated task durations for two chief reasons:

■ The estimated duration for the On-Site Conferences task would have taken longer than necessary (5–10 days) and required physical attendance at conference facilities. For these reasons it was replaced with the Virtual

Conferences task (2–5 days duration) that would be conducted on the Internet.

■ The estimated study task's duration is between 2–6 months. For practical reasons it was replaced with the Cybersecurity Boot Camp task, with only 2–3 weeks estimated duration.

Use Case II: Optimized Software Architecture Execution Plan

Unlike Use Case 1 (presented in the previous section), Use Case 2 is all about shortening the goal achievement time range. There are a few pragmatic reasons for doing this, especially when it comes to veteran software architects.

Experience   Experienced software architects who aspire to become security architects typically need shorter preparation time.

Prior studies   They may also be able to ace interviews with limited training and self-study.

Conferences   They may already have attended cybersecurity training and conferences.

Resume   The estimated time for honing their résumé and preparing for interviews may be shorter.

To reflect these reasons, Table 3.7 shows these eliminated tasks (shown in gray): On-Site Conferences, Study, Learning, and Training. In addition, for the same pragmatic reasons, the estimated task duration for the resume is not completely eliminated, but shortened from 2–5 weeks to 1 week.

Table 3.7: Optimized Software Architecture Career Execution Plan

TARGET OCCUPATION/ GOAL	TASK	TASK SPECIFICATION	ESTIMATED TASK DURATION
Security architect	Certification	Acquire cybersecurity certification	10–25 weeks
	On-Site Conferences	Attend cybersecurity conferences	5–10 days
	Social networking	Pursue social networking to learn more about the cybersecurity industry	Constant effort
	Study	Study publications, such as books and journals, about new cybersecurity penetration testing and risk assessment technologies	2–6 months
	Self-assessment	Use self-assessment tools to discover and verify cybersecurity skills	3 weeks

TARGET OCCUPATION/ GOAL	TASK	TASK SPECIFICATION	ESTIMATED TASK DURATION
	~~Learning~~	~~Learn about cybersecurity frameworks~~	~~10–20 days~~
	~~Training~~	~~Take security awareness training~~	~~3 days~~
	Contacts	Update contact information of friends, co-workers, and recruiters	Constant effort
	~~Resume~~	~~Prepare a compelling resume that demonstrates cybersecurity experience and knowledge~~	~~2–5 weeks~~
Estimated task duration is adjusted to 1 week:			
	Resume	Prepare a compelling resume that demonstrates cybersecurity experience and knowledge	1 week
	Employment Searching Tools	Discover employment searching tools to find available cybersecurity jobs	Constant effort
	Employment Opportunities	Search for potential employers who seek cybersecurity talents	Constant effort
	Interviews	Prepare for cybersecurity interviews	At least 2 weeks before an interview
Add here more action plans.			

Self-Discovery Process: The Six Ws

One of the most challenging efforts when planning a career is self-discovery. The term *self-discovery* is all about being able to look in the mirror and face the very fundamental, and at times daunting, questions that every professional should ask before embarking on or while pursuing a software architecture occupation. This discovery process may seem uncomfortable to those who attempt to be in touch with their feelings, desires, aspirations, and dreams. But there is nothing more satisfying than facing reality and then finding out that the self-discovery process was indeed worth pursuing.

Here are some queries that typically cross aspiring software architects' minds: "Are my technical and social capabilities suited for a software architecture career?" "Am I good enough?" "Will I be able to pull it off?" "What if I fail. . .?" "Who should I consult?" "What will I need to prepare?"

For those who have already been working in the field, these reflective questions are common: "Am I an effective software architect?" "Am I fulfilling the goals that I set for myself before embarking on current career?" "What is the contribution of my work to the organization?" "What would be my next step to progress in the field?"

The self-discovery process, however, should not preclude applicants from consulting friends, family, or co-workers about their future endeavors. Getting advice from veteran software architects is another way of discovering the hurdles that one may experience during a professional journey.

So which questions should candidates ask themselves to discover if a career in software architecture is suitable for them? Should these questions be about the skills that they must possess? Should these questions be about their communication competence? Should they be about the ability to provide effective solutions? Should the questions be about their decision-making capabilities?

Clearly, the number of questions to be asked is infinite. Software architecture candidates should therefore employ a personal guiding strategy called the *Six Ws*. As elaborated in the sections that follow, the strategy encompasses six categories of questions employed to discover personal aptitudes, character, behavior, and the ability to provide feasible solutions under the weight of growing business demands and technical challenges.

The "Why"

The "why" questions must be related to prior knowledge about the software architecture practice. There must be something about it that a candidate finds compelling, exciting, and fascinating. And the answer should not be "because it's cool." Nor should it be associated with the prospects of hefty earnings. True, experienced software architects are typically well paid. But the motivation ought to be more than income. It must be about the intangible rewards, the dedication, and the daily persistence needed to enact organizational positive change.

CONCEPT A candidate should be motivated by the opportunity to promote organizational software architecture best practices, standards, and policies. Candidates' decisions to pursue such a career should be driven by the opportunity to foster technological innovation, propel enterprise transformation, and drive business growth.

The "why" question is not easy to answer because it demands research, industry studies, and high motivation to uncover the reasons for becoming a software architect. But persistence pays off. Taking the time to understand the software architecture field and then being comfortable with personal strategic decisions may be a lengthy endeavor. Many applicants typically worry about making imprudent career decisions, asking themselves if software architecture is the right field for them. This self-discovery process can take a while.

If the answer to the "why" self-question is unsatisfying to some, that should not be a reason to give up. There is no excuse for throwing in the towel so early in the game. Surrendering to failure even before rationalizing the reasons to pursue the software architect career is not encouraged. The efforts to discover the chief motivations must go on.

Therefore, attempt to answer the queries that follow. And persist in the self-discovery process with utmost determination.

Career   *Why* is a software architect career what I really want?

Practice   *Why* is the software architecture practice so compelling to me?

Investing   *Why* should I be investing my time in improving my software architecture skills?

Quitting   *Why* do some of my co-workers quit their jobs as software architects?

Accomplishing   *Why* does the software architecture occupation prove so difficult for some to accomplish?

Politics   *Why* do software architects often engage in office politics rather than focusing on their own duties?

Software development   *Why* do software architects not develop software as often as they would like to?

Software architecture and software design   *Why* is software architecture analogous with software design?

The "Who"

Only a handful of professionals tend to flourish in the software architecture industry without the helping hands of others. We must be thankful to those generous individuals who are willing to help with career planning and development. They typically endow us with knowledge and experience that is immensely important to our self-discovery and decision-making process. They stand by us when we need to learn more about the software industry, when we hesitate to make bold career moves, when we are unsure about our software architecture career planning, and when we are uncertain about our ability to provide solutions to business problems.

CONCEPT The only way to accelerate our search for viable first-hand software architecture information is to network with others.

Networking means that we must reach out to people who possess undocumented knowledge about the industry, the policies, the best practices, and the standards. Networking also means that we maintain a respectful dialogue with professionals who can boost our confidence in ourselves. Networking is a part of what we need to do to advance our careers in this industry. Networking is a big part of what experienced software architects must do to achieve professional milestones and goals.

But we must also contribute to this dialogue despite our lack of knowledge or hesitation to pursue new career avenues. So how do we give back? How do we strengthen the dialogue with career enablers whose help we seek? The simplest answers to these questions must be driven by the belief that everyone brings talents to the table even if they are limited in scope.

Finally, when seeking to advance in the software architecture industry, find useful facilitators such as co-workers, mentors and trainers, or even IT recruiters. Without the benevolent gestures of these individuals, our career may stall.

Consider the number of the "who" self-discovery questions that aspiring, beginning, or even experienced software architects ought to ask when planning a career road map.

Self-identity   Who is best suited for a software architecture job? Can I do it? Do I have the right qualifications to become a software architect? To answer these questions, take the software architect self-assessment that is offered in Chapter 4, "Self-Assessment for Software Architects."

Career enablers   *Who* should I seek help from to promote my software architecture career?

Collaboration   *Who* are the people with whom I should collaborate to promote my career?

Architecture organization managers   *Who* is in charge on an architecture organization?

Interviewers   *Who* are the typical software architecture interviewers? Discover their backgrounds and technical strengths.

Duties   *Who* can shed light on software architecture duties?

The "What"

"What actually is a software architect?" and "What do architects do?" and "What is Software architecture practices and diciplines are discussed in chapter 1, "Software Architect Capability Model?" are general questions that applicants must ask to become familiar with the job they are applying for. These questions could also pertain to experienced software architects who are in the process of discovering new avenues for professional advancement. Growing business demands and technological challenges propel these veteran architects to rediscover the contribution of software architecture to the enterprise.

On a more personal level, the self-discovery aspect of the "what" questions are affiliated with the duties that one will be asked to perform. In other words, common queries are "What will I be required to deliver as a software architect?" and "What would then be my daily schedule?" For experienced architects the more applicable questions could be, "What would be my new software architecture duties in the face of business transformation?" and "What type of deliverables will I be required to submit for technological innovation projects?"

Self-Discovery Questions for Software Architecture Candidates

Consider the self-discovery questions that apply to software architecture applicants:

Software architecture   *What* is software architecture?

Industry standards   *What* are the typical responsibilities of software architects? Are there any industry standards for architecture roles and duties?

Occupation   *What* would be my duties as a beginning software architect?

Practices   *What* is a software architecture practice?

Disciplines   *What* is a software architecture discipline?

Architect type   *What* kind of a software architect would I like to be?

Pursuing   *What* do I need to do to become a software architect?

Required skills   *What* are the required skills for succeeding in the field of software architecture?

Skills   *What* are my qualifications to become a software architect?

Design capabilities   *What* are my software design capabilities? (Refer to Chapter 1, "Software Architect Capability Model," to learn how to assess personal skill competencies.)

Deliverables   *What* will I be required to deliver as a novice software architect?

Daily schedule   *What* will be my daily schedule as a beginning software architect?

Self-Discovery Queries for Software Architects

The next set of the self-discovery queries are provided for software architects who seek to advance their career and enhance professional performance.

Solution architect   *What* are the steps for becoming a solution architect after a few years of performing application architecture duties?

Enterprise architect skills   *What* technical skills must enterprise architects possess?

Enterprise architect duties   *What* do enterprise architects actually do?

Technological modernization   My organization has decided to embark on technological modernization efforts. *What* would be my responsibility as an enterprise architect to foster the enterprise's ongoing technological transformation?

Consumer-centric strategy   Our business strategy calls for constructing consumer-centric driven applications. *What* architecture styles should I recommend to foster my organizational strategy?

Cloud transition   *What* software architecture best practices, standards, and policies should I embrace to promote our organization's transition to the cloud?

Next career move   After a few years of practicing software architecture, *what* would be my next career move? Should I stay in the same field?

Software architecture managers   *What* do software architecture managers do?

The "Where"

The "where" self-discovery type of questions pertain to locations. In this context, the term *locations* does not necessarily refer to a geographical region or continent—although it could. Some of the questions refer to the virtual meaning of the term, which, for example, may reveal the candidate's industry preferences, technological environments, and perhaps lines of business. "Which line of business would benefit the most from my software architecture talents?" or "In which industry can my skills make a greater impact on technological decisions?" are some of the key questions that applicants ought to answer before making a career move.

> **CONCEPT**   Recall that the answers to the "where" self-discovery questions must be predicated on the specific business and technological skills of the software architecture applicants.

For example, the question, "Will my business knowledge be valuable to the organization's credit card line of business?" pertains to one's capability to provide solutions to a particular line of business. Furthermore, "Are my current skills suitable enough to be engaged effectively in a cloud migration initiative for the banking division?" is visibly a self-discovery query that is affiliated with cloud architecture technical abilities to contribute to a specific financial institution. The same principle applies to applicants who prefer to work for particular industries, such as automobile, wireless, and construction.

As indicated, geographic locations, such as cities, countries, and continents, should not be ruled out when attempting to answer the "where" self-discovery questions. It's well known that some cities or regions predominately support technological development environments and innovation centers. Other geographical locations are more affiliated with certain industries, such as agriculture, semiconductor, and tourism. These geographical locations may affect applicants' preferences when it comes to career planning and even work relocation.

Consider the examples of questions that pertain to the "where" self-discovery questions:

Line of business   *To which* line of business will my software architecture skills contribute the most?

Industry   *Which* industries are the most appealing to me?

Geographical location   *In which* city, region, or continent would I like to live and work from?

Work relocation   If I were offered a software architecture job, would I agree to relocate to my new workplace?

Technological environment   *To which* technological environment will my software architecture skills contribute the most? Cloud ecosystem? Integration environment in production? Data warehouse environment?

Office location   *Where* is my preferred work environment? Home office? Corporate offices? Client sites? Small office with a few co-workers, large work environment, or in an office with no co-workers?

The "When"

The "when" type of self-discovery questions refer to the right time during a career to resign from the current occupation and move on to a different one. Many applicants, and even veteran software architects, struggle with decisions about their career moves. They typically grapple with career changes and life-altering determinations.

CONCEPT   Those who lack the tenacity to make timely and bold career moves characteristically fail to obtain fulfilling employment opportunities.

Career moves are never easy. And nothing can make applicants, or already practicing software architects, comfortable enough about embarking on new professional endeavors. If there's any consolation, it's common to feel uneasy about changing workplaces, meeting new co-workers, or being assigned to new projects.

> **CONCEPT**   One of the most challenging tasks is to ensure that the new career move is about moving up the professional ladder.

But nothing is guaranteed in this fast-paced business world. In some cases, the next career move turns out to be disappointing—not as it was perceived or planned. Mustering the courage, though, to take career-changing risks despite a potential setback may pay off in the long run. Simply put, learning from mistakes and circumventing them in the future is the chief benefit of failed or lackluster career moves.

Do not rush, though. Before even contemplating a move, ask these pivotal questions: "Am I ready?" "Am I prepared?" "Have I considered the risks?" "Have I fulfilled my current milestone?" "Have I exhausted the prospects to advance in my current occupation?" These questions are all about the "when." And nothing is more important than timing.

To summarize this discussion, consider the chief "when" self-discovery type of questions that must be addressed before investing time and resources during a professional career journey:

Readiness   Am I ready to make a career move *now*?

Timing   If not now, *when* would be the right time?

Pre-training   Would it be wiser to take software architecture training that can prepare me better for moving to the next career milestone?

Preparations   *When* would be the best time to start preparing for a career move?

Resume updating   *When* should I start updating my resume?

Availability   *When* should I let recruiters know that I'm available for my next career move?

The "How"

The "how" self-discovery question pertains to the manner by which one achieves the desired career goals. Obviously, there is no prescribed method to meeting the software architecture professional objectives. The road to success is always challenging since the pace of business transformation and technological evolution is rapid and utterly demanding. But despite unforeseen hurdles, applicants and currently practicing software architects ought to adopt a road map for achieving success. In other words, there must a step-by-step program with milestones, tasks, and an accomplishment ladder to promote personal goals.

> **CONCEPT**   Simply put, the "how" self-discovery queries focus on *how* to become a software architect who is able to provide viable business solutions. And for those who are already practicing the art of software design, these types of questions center on *how* to grow and succeed in the field.

Furthermore, to carve out a software architecture road map for success, one must plan achievable milestones and goals. The purpose should be, therefore, to plan attainable and feasible steps that clearly answer the "how" questions (refer to the "Career Planning" section to learn about action planning and career execution).

"How" Self-Queries for Software Architecture Applicants

The "how" self-questions are never easy to answer. And there is no need to panic about the planning and undertaking efforts for becoming a prosperous software architect. It's all about dedicating the time and taking the appropriate measures that can change someone's course of life. Applicants, therefore, must recognize that an effective personal strategy with "chewable" goals can make a big difference between success and failure.

Moreover, there is no limit to what one can do to advance a personal career. These efforts may include engaging a personal software architecture career coach who will help usher in an exciting occupation that may last years or decades. In addition, finding a helpful community that can shed light on software architecture duties and responsibilities would contribute immensely to achieving professional goals.

On the quest for career opportunities, keep in mind these "how" questions. When the time comes, attempt to answer them as the career road map becomes clearer.

Acing a software architecture interview   *How* to ace a software architecture interview? Elaborate on an effective approach to beating the competition.

Successful software architect   *How* does a software architect meet business requirements? Provide a business problem and explain how to solve it by employing technological means.

Personal road map   *How* to plan a personal career road map for becoming a software architect?

Practical road map   *How* to structure a practical career road map with archival milestones and goals?

Software architecture career coach   *How* to find the right software architecture career coach?

Software architecture communities   *How* to find communities that share useful information about the software architecture industry?

"How" Self-Questions for Practicing Software Architects

The questions that follow are presented for those who are currently pursuing the art of software architecture and have already participated in providing technological solutions. These queries identify challenges that software architects meet while serving their duties as solution providers. The term *solution providers* in this context refers not only to technologists chartered to fully understand organizational problems but to those capable of satisfying business requirements. Moreover, only with fruitful collaboration with co-workers and executives are software architects able to accomplish their technological vision and mission.

Business requirements   *How* to analyze business requirements when asked to provide software architecture solutions?

Software architecture frameworks   *How* does an effective software architect facilitate technological solutions by promoting architecture frameworks?

Impact time-to-market   *How* do software architecture frameworks impact the acceleration of time-to-market and organizational expenditure reduction?

End-state architecture   *How* to devise an organizational end-state architecture road map that meets the demands of business transformation?

Obtaining architecture vision support   *How* to persuade executives, managers, and peers to buy into software architecture visions? Describe the approach for accomplishing it.

Communicating architecture solutions   *How* to effectively communicate a proposed software architecture solution?

Technological transformation   *How* to plan and execute an organizational technological transformation such a cloud migration? Provide a road map to facilitate such technological evolution.

Carving a Software Architecture Career Path

A software architecture career does not progress in a straight line. Career goals and professional success can never be smoothly achieved without encountering challenges such as business trends and technological transformations. Furthermore, there will always be changes on the horizon that will impact the way business is conducted and the manner in which technological solutions are offered. Consequently, these shifts impact hiring demands and employment opportunities.

When a career is launched, expect to be challenged by winding roads, constant hurdles, and endless speedbumps. And nothing seems to be straightforward when trying to survive in uncharted territories. But this experience should not deter anyone from conquering what appears to be the impossible. Professional career journeys are not easy. This is what makes them so interesting and exciting, though. Do not fret! Carve out a software architecture career path to achieve personal and professional goals. Be determined and take chances.

These challenges call for devising a professional career path, a map that visually presents individual moves from one milestone to another. It must have a beginning and should focus on goals. In essence, the road map should be followed to achieve professional and technological objectives. It's an itinerary that illustrates work experiences and occupations in a sequential order. It also depicts personal preferences and software architecture capabilities to provide practical solutions to organizational problems.

The 4D Software Architecture Career Perspectives

Every aspiring, beginning, or experienced software architect has different career objectives. Some lean toward supervisory positions in the software industry. Several envision a more technical role in IT. And a few would like to be involved in promoting organizational culture by fostering enterprise strategies. Consequently, before making the next employment move, be aware that career goals can be pursued in different ways and influenced by diverse agendas. When it comes to making career decisions, professional competencies and personal preferences drive most employment decisions.

As illustrated in Figure 3.2, we focus here on four different career perspectives: social-driven, technology-driven, management-driven, and strategy-driven. Each of these views represents a unique approach to achieving professional goals. Employ them to carve out a realistic career path. But before even determining which career perspective to embrace, make sure that the questions presented in the section "Self-Discovery Process: The Six Ws" have been answered. The answers to these queries can shed light on personal preferences and career objectives.

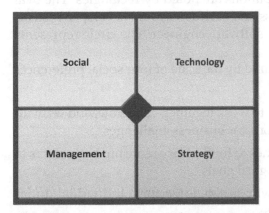

Figure 3.2: The 4-D Software Architecture Career Perspectives

The sections that follow elaborate on the four software architecture career perspectives, each with their respective career charts and paths. These views can be employed to carve out a career path that coincides with personal preferences, employment goals, and individual professional missions. Note that it's common to be drawn to more than one career perspective. And therefore, there is nothing wrong about carving out multiple career paths. For example, an individual may be interested in exploring the management and technical career development views. Both of these perspectives can add immense value to the career strategy since the view is not confined to only one perspective.

Social-Driven Career Perspective

This career view centers on the social skills and preferences of those who *seek to promote their professional objectives by forming robust partnerships* in their workplace. The term *social-driven career perspective* refers to personal traits and abilities that can foster collaboration with co-workers, managers, and organizational executives. But these alliances can even go beyond a company's boundaries. It also involves forming and strengthening relationships with members of technology communities and their influencers in the software industry.

CONCEPT   The benefits of pursuing a career driven by social incentives are vast. By and large this career strategy tends to foster workplace communication, accelerate productivity, and open the door for new employment opportunities.

Social-Driven Career Chart

Figure 3.3 shows an example of a social-driven career chart where various IT roles are located. The architect occupations are noted by rectangles. The oval shapes are dedicated to other IT professions, such as software developer, systems administrator, business analyst, and software engineer. The circle represents the college graduate.

Each position on the chart is measured by the scale of four social preferences and personal traits.

Collaborative   Depicts the ability to work together, cooperate, and team up to provide technological solutions for business challenges

Sociable   Refers to one who inclines to form companionship with others to promote business and technological goals

Self-sufficient   Pertains to one who is able to perform individual duties without the assistance of others

Introverted   Refers to an individual whose occupation does not benefit from social interaction with others

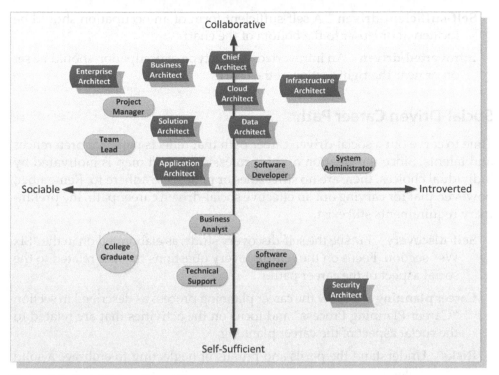

Figure 3.3: Social-Driven Career Chart

Note that on this social-driven career chart, for example, an enterprise architect role ought to be both highly collaborative and highly sociable. This is because the corresponding role is located on the top-left corner of the social-driven career chart. In contrast, a security architect, shown on the far-right corner of the chart, is known to be notably both self-sufficient and introverted.

Carve Out a Social-Driven Career Chart

When planning a career driven by social motivations, do not be confined to the example shown in Figure 3.3. And do not hesitate to place on the chart a variety of other occupations, even if some may not reflect personal objectives. Attend to these simple chart-carving principles.

Collaborative-driven   A collaborative-driven type of occupation should be located at or near the top of the career chart.

Social-driven   A social-driven occupation should be positioned on or near the left side of the chart.

Self-sufficient-driven   A self-sufficient form of an occupation should be located at or closer to the bottom of the chart.

Introverted-driven   An introverted-driven type of occupation should be set on or near the right section of the chart.

Social-Driven Career Path

Time to carve out a social-driven career path that reflects personal preferences and talents. Since the creation of this professional road map is motivated by individual choices, there are no strict rules or policies to adhere to. Remember, however, that for carving out an effective social-driven career path, the preliminary requirements still exist.

Self-discovery   Pursue the self-discovery study, as elaborated on in the "Six Ws" section. Focus on the self-discovery questions that are related to the social aspect of the career path.

Career planning   Follow the career planning process as described in section "Career Planning Process" and focus on the activities that are related to the social aspect of the career planning.

Risks   Understand the perils and pitfalls of neglecting to embrace a solid career plan.

Preferences and goals   Stick to the personal preferences and professional goals that can be promoted by social interaction and collaboration.

Obstacles   Avoid U-turns and hurdles that can slow career progress. And ponder how social competencies can alleviate the impact of obstacles.

Create a Social-Driven Career Path

Figure 3.4 illustrates an example of a social-driven career path. It's created to depict a road map that begins at a software developer level. As shown, an individual who sets this career path aspires to become an enterprise architect. Clearly, this definitive professional occupation is also the ultimate career goal. But there are no shortcuts when it comes to achieving the career objective. Unless it's an exception, the path to the goal typically must meet intermediate milestones.

As illustrated in Figure 3.4, there are two occupational milestones to be successfully fulfilled before becoming an enterprise architect: application architect and solution architect. Obviously, the career path indicates that without achieving these milestones, the software developer would never be able to accomplish the goal of becoming an enterprise architect.

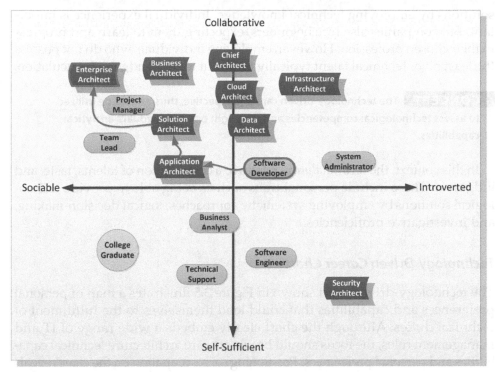

Figure 3.4: Software Development to Enterprise Architecture Career Path

When planning a professional road map akin to the example that's illustrated in Figure 3.4, it would be helpful to create a career path catalog, a simple list, or a table of milestones and goals to be achieved. Table 3.8 demonstrates this task. It was created to reflect the depicted social-driven career path in Figure 3.4. In addition, find the individual traits and professional preferences of the software developer in the table's "Driving Social Career Preference" column.

Table 3.8: Software Development to Enterprise Architecture Career Path

CAREER PATH	MILESTONE/STATE	DRIVING SOCIAL CAREER PREFERENCE
Current position	Software developer	Collaborative, introverted
Milestone	Application architect	Sociable, collaborative
Milestone	Solution architect	Sociable, collaborative
Goal	Enterprise architect	Sociable, collaborative

Technology-Driven Career Perspective

The technological perspective of every software architecture role is the essence of this profession. Software architects must understand and be capable of devising solutions by employing technical knowledge. Individual experience is important. But companies also hire beginners, expecting them to learn and progress in their chosen profession. However, employing individuals who do not possess the least bit of technical talent typically turns out to be a budget miscalculation.

> **CONCEPT**   The technology-driven career perspective, thus, should be utilized to assess technological competencies and shed light on an individual's analytical capabilities.

In this context, the term *analytical* relates to a combination of talents, taste, and judgment. These include personal traits such as being able to provide technological solutions by employing systematic approaches, logical decision-making, and investigative proficiencies.

Technology-Driven Career Chart

The technology-driven chart shown in Figure 3.5 illustrates a map of personal preferences and capabilities that could lend themselves to the fulfillment of technical duties. Although the chart clearly embeds a wide range of IT and management roles, the focus should be on software architecture technical capabilities and personal preferences. Positioning each occupation on the chart reveals the four technological scales affiliated with each career perspective.

Nontechnical   Measures the personal preference of an individual to carry out an IT position that does not necessarily require in-depth technical skills

Analytical   Pertains to an individual's analytical skills, thorough logical thinking, and science-driven problem-solving approaches that can promote potent technological solutions

Technical   Bears on the ability to offer business solutions and foster technological modernization by applying frameworks and industrial expertise

Nonanalytical   Reflects an individual's preference to take on an IT duty that does not necessarily require analytical skills

Note that in this technical-driven career chart, for example, the cloud architect, security architect, and software developer ought to be exceedingly analytical, and obviously technical, to effectively perform their duties. Conversely, the program manager, product manager, and chief architect do not need to possess deep technical skills or even superior analytical talents. In essence, they assume leadership, management, and executive duties. And their occupations call for different types of skills. Refer to the section "Leadership-Driven Career Perspective" that follows to learn more about the necessary leadership talents.

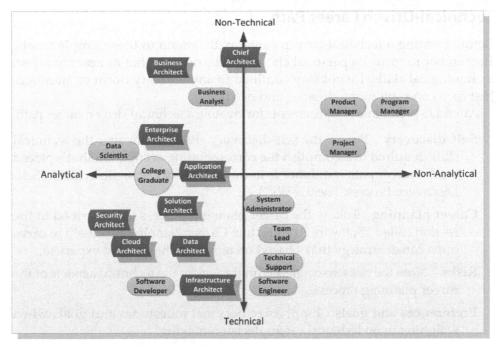

Figure 3.5: Technical-Driven Career Chart

Create a Technology-Driven Career Chart

As depicted in Figure 3.5, the technical-driven career chart example applies to capabilities and preferences that illustrate personal contributions to business solutions. Remember, when creating the career chart, focus chiefly on technical proficiencies. And do not be confined to the illustrated example. Additional occupations can be added to expand the technical-driven career view.

Consider this general guidance for locating the related occupations on the technical-driven career chart:

Non-technical-driven An occupation is positioned at or near the top of the career chart to indicate a professional preference.

Analytical-driven Position the corresponding job at or near the left side of the chart.

Technical-driven A technical-driven IT or business occupation should be placed at or near the bottom of the career chart.

Non-analytical driven This career preference should be sited on or close to the section of the chart on the right.

Technical-Driven Career Path

Before creating a technical-driven career path, attend to these simple tenets. Remember to focus on personal choices and priorities that noticeably reflect technological skills. Do not stay confined to any industry norm or standard. Just focus on aspirations, dreams, and needs.

Attend to preliminary requirements for creating a technical-driven career path.

Self-discovery   Pursue the self-discovery study to uncover the technical skills required to accomplish the corresponding occupation that's placed on the career path (guidance is in the self-discovery section called "Self-Discovery Process: The Six Ws").

Career planning   Follow the career planning process (as described in the section called "Software Architecture Career Planning Process") to carve out a career strategy that's based on technical choices and expertise.

Risks   Note the risks associated with the lack of the technical aspects of the career planning process.

Preferences and goals   Emphasize personal milestones and goals when weighing in on technical career decision-making.

Obstacles   Dodge potential hindrances to technical career achievements.

Develop a Technical-Driven Career Path

Take a moment to view Figure 3.6, which represents a technical-driven career path. It illustrates a professional journey that commences at the software engineering level. As is apparent, the chief architect role is the identified goal in this career path. As with all life aspirations, fulfilling a goal that is located on top of the "food chain" is not an easy endeavor. It's nothing short of an arduous and complex voyage. It's also an outstanding achievement that only the most talented and lucky ones happen to fulfill. But recall, nothing is unachievable!

Figure 3.6 also depicts the planned milestones on the way to achieving the ultimate goal. The agenda of this career path includes three milestones: solution architect, enterprise architect, and chief architect (which is also the goal). Furthermore, according to the plan, not only must these milestones be successfully pursued, the individual who started on this professional journey ought to be well on the road to conquering the top architecture position in the enterprise. Consequently, the milestones should serve as evaluation checkpoints to measure intermediate achievements. These intermediate career assessments call for taking time to measure the effectiveness and contribution of an individual to enterprise projects.

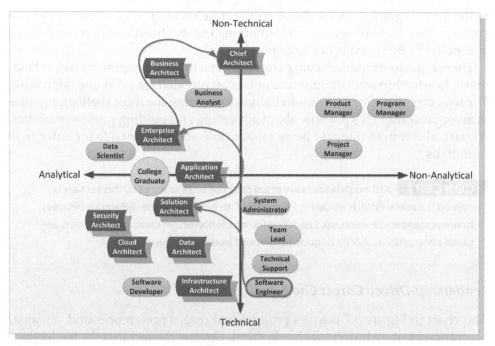

Figure 3.6: Software Engineering to Chief Architecture Career Path

A technical-driven career path, akin to the example that's illustrated in Figure 3.6, should also be accompanied by a table that summarizes the path to success. Create a career path similar to Table 3.9. Moreover, insert individual traits and professional preferences in the table's "Driving Social Career Preference" column.

Table 3.9: From Software Engineer to Chief Architect Career Path

CAREER PATH	MILESTONE/STATE	DRIVING SOCIAL CAREER PREFERENCE
Current position	Software engineer	Technical
Milestone	Solution architect	Technical, analytical
Milestone	Enterprise architect	analytically-focused
Goal	Chief architect	Nontechnical

Leadership-Driven Career Perspective

The leadership-driven career perspective is advised for those who plan to climb the professional management ladder within the organization. Moreover, this career view offers another window of opportunity for individuals who possess natural management skills. These special talents tend to promote enterprise culture, steer technological transformation, and establish company standards and policies. But is everyone fit to be a leader?

There is no doubt that achieving a management role is an impressive career landmark. Leadership roles, though, are not recommended for everyone. Managing IT projects or directing business initiatives are among the most challenging roles in an organization. It's not only about governing and guiding professional staff; it's also about planning and being responsible and accountable for enterprise initiatives.

> **CONCEPT** Although leaders are often referred to as managers, this section is named "Leadership-driven Career Perspective" to emphasize the difference between management and leadership. Leaders influence followers. In contrast, managers are given enterprise authority to govern, rule, and exercise power of control.

Leadership-Driven Career Chart

The chart in Figure 3.7 mirrors professional career preferences and personal aspirations that an individual has in mind. Despite the fact that the leadership-driven chart encompasses positions that may not entirely reflect one's ultimate goals, the rule of thumb calls for extending the range of employment opportunities. That is to say, there is nothing wrong about placing milestones on the career chart that may be considered worth pursuing in the long term. But in this regard, draw more attention to goals that are chiefly related to software architecture occupations.

Consider the four leadership-driven scales that are reflected in this career chart and attempt to relate to one or more of them:

Decision-maker　One who holds governing, administrative, and supervisory authority to promote the business and oversee technological initiatives

Leader　A socially respected figure who influences followers to impact vital decision-making and organizational problem-solving processes

Problem-solver　Provides effective solutions to business and technological challenges by applying professional expertise

Team player　One who collaborates with management and co-workers to promote successful business and IT initiatives

Bear in mind that according to the example in the career chart (Figure 3.7), most of people in the software architect roles are considered leaders and problem-solvers. These are the enterprise, solution, and application architects. They are classified as leaders because of their duties to provide technical solutions and spearhead vital enterprise initiatives. Conversely, those in the top management positions, such as the enterprise architect, IT director, and product manager, are mostly employed to make prudent decisions for promoting the business.

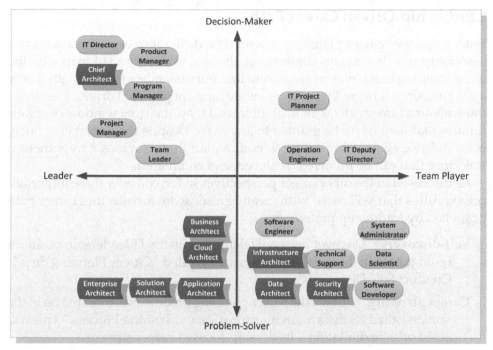

Figure 3.7: Leadership-Driven Career Chart

Create a Leadership-Driven Career Chart

Once again, just as with the other career perspectives discussed thus far, create a chart for the leadership-driven career that reflects the ambition and enthusiasm to lead. But the chart should center primarily on the talents to provide powerful solutions for business problems. Furthermore, a systematic approach to placing occupations on the chart is strongly encouraged. Avoid setting random milestones, dodge aiming at unachievable or unrealistic goals, and create a realistic leadership-driven career chart.

With the emphasis on the software architecture professional field, the list that follows provides guidance for placing IT and business positions on the leadership-driven career chart:

Decision-maker This position is located at or adjacent to the top of the career chart to show an occupational inclination.

Leader Place the related milestone at or near the left side of the chart.

Problem-solver A leadership-driven occupation should be set at or about the bottom of the chart.

Team player This career preference should be situated on or close to the right portion of the chart.

Leadership-Driven Career Path

Without proper career planning, it would be difficult to envision a path to a leadership role. It's always challenging, though, to draw a road map with the understanding that it may never materialize. But remember, a career path is only a proposition, a scheme that reflects a wide range of personal drives. Therefore, think about a career path as an intangible road map, a virtual window of opportunities that may never be granted to any of us. Despite the uncertainty, there is no defense against neglecting to craft a plan that provides a hypothetical trajectory that can be followed, achieved, and conquered.

As discussed in the other career perspectives so far, consider these important prerequisites that will assist with creating a software architecture career path propelled by leadership preferences:

Self-discovery   Discover personal talents that justify IT leadership positions (guidance is in the self-discovery section called "Career Planning Step 1: Conduct Self-Discovery").

Career planning   Pursue the career planning process as elaborated on in the section called "Software Architecture Career Planning Process." This will assist with formulating a leadership-focused career strategy.

Risks   Be aware of the pitfalls caused by the absence of a solid career path that could shed light on fulfilling leadership roles within the organization.

Preferences and goals   Highlight the various milestones to achieving software architecture goals.

Obstacles   Avoid career round-trips. Stay on course and focus on the planned leadership goals.

Develop a Leadership-Driven Career Path

Figure 3.8 depicts a leadership-driven career path that begins at the data architecture position, moving on to serve as an application architect, and then becoming a team leader. The next milestone is assuming the project manager role, just before ascending to the program management level—the ultimate goal.

It seems that assuming a team lead position after serving as an application architect would be a miscalculated career move. But the strategy to gain management experience by shifting the direction to a leadership role justifies this professional journey. This is a common occurrence with many IT professionals because the preference is to gain technical experience at the outset of the career path before reaching the executive levels. In fact, many executives claim that they started their careers as software developers and then progressed to fulfill IT director levels.

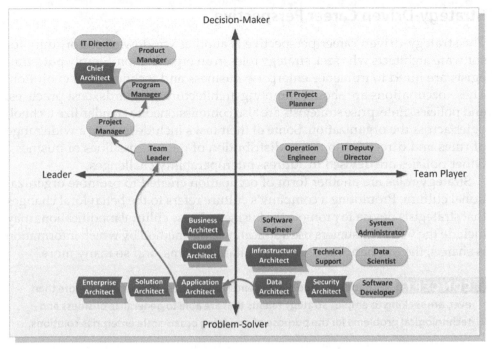

Figure 3.8: Data Architecture to Program Management Career Path

Table 3.10 outlines the chief milestones that the data architect ought to achieve. This is the same career path that is illustrated in Figure 3.8: application architect, team leader, project manager, and program manager. The latter is also the eventual goal. Keep in mind that leadership-driven career paths of this kind typically tend to be long because of the vast experience needed for management positions. Unforeseen impediments to a career path never fail to arise, and a complex and lengthy career path is typically doomed to fail. For that reason, avoid planning a career path with stacks of milestones. Plan a concise career strategy. Stay practical. Stay focused!

Table 3.10: From Data Architecture to Program Management Career Path

CAREER PATH	MILESTONE/STATE	DRIVING CAREER PREFERENCE
Current position	Data architect	Problem-solver, team player
Milestone	Application architect	Problem-solver, leader
Milestone	Team leader	Decision-maker, leader
Milestone	Project manager	Decision-maker, leader
Goal	Program manager	Decision-maker, leader

Strategy-Driven Career Perspective

The strategy-driven career perspective is another window of opportunity for software architects who seek strategy roles in an organization. Simply put, strategists are hired to influence enterprise business and technological evolution. These occupations are about promoting architecture standards, best practices, and policies. Enterprise strategists are also commissioned to standardize technologies across the organization. Some of their tasks include issuing a wide range of rules and directives to tackle distribution of data across lines of business. Other policies are devised to address interoperability challenges.

Strategy roles are another form of occupation created to promote organizational culture. Promoting a company's culture refers to the behavioral changes that strategists devise to promote the business. These cultural modifications may include the ways consumers use applications, the method by which information is shared, the mechanisms used to maintain systems, and so many more.

CONCEPT   With today's large scale of enterprise issues, organizations, more than ever, are seeking to employ strategy talents that are able to generalize business and technological problems for the purpose of providing broad-scale enterprise solutions.

Strategy-Driven Career Chart

The strategy-driven career chart represented in Figure 3.9 includes two types of occupations, strategists and improvisers. Both collaborate on devising remedies for a wide range of business and technological challenges. On one hand, the strategists in this career chart are chartered to seek long-term, overarching, and holistic solutions for organizational imperatives. On the other hand, the improvisers are inclined to address a narrow scope of issues. When they work together, strategists and improvisers are capable of ensuring business continuity and technological stability.

In many circumstances, software architects demonstrate the capability to devise long-term solutions for recurring organizational problems. They accomplish this by employing architecture frameworks that offer best practices, standards, and policies. Moreover, software architects are idea-thinkers who are able to abstract and generalize private instances with the aim of formulating wide-scale solutions. The design blueprints they provide typically include patterns of solutions that can be applied to meet a large variety of business requirements and technical specifications.

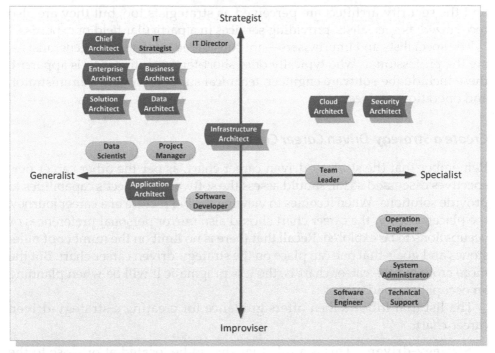

Figure 3.9: Strategy-Driven Career Chart

The personal and professional skills and preferences of the roles that are presented in the strategy-driven career chart are measured by applying these four unique scales:

Strategist A leader whose sole responsibility is to devise long-term and over-arching plans to achieve feasible firm-wide goals by employing methodical approaches

Generalist One whose broad expertise is leveraged to offer remedies for business and technological problems by conceptualizing holistic solutions

Improviser A professional who is able to offer immediate solutions, typically short term, for business and technological for burning business and technological problems

Specialist An expert in a particular field who offers a narrow scope of solutions to a small scale of problems

From a strategic point of view, note that the software architecture occupations located on the career chart (in Figure 3.9) are mostly considered strategists and generalists. These roles include the chief architect, enterprise architect, business architect, solution architect, and data architect. Moreover, the cloud architect and the security architect are perceived as strategists too, but they are also recognized as specialists, providing services in a particular field of expertise.

The specialists and improvisers—not considered strategists or generalists—are the professionals who typically offer short-term solutions. As is apparent, these include the software engineer, technical support, system administrator, and operation engineer.

Create a Strategy-Driven Career Chart

Remember that the strategy-driven career chart, as per the other career perspectives discussed so far, should assess the software architect's capabilities to provide solutions. When it comes to viewing the big picture of a career journey, the placements on the career chart should also mirror personal preferences or occupations to be explored. Recall that there is no limit on the number of milestones and goals that one can place on the strategy-driven career chart. But the more crowded the career chart is, the less pragmatic it will be when planning an occupation road map.

The list that follows then offers guidance for creating a strategy-driven career chart:

Strategy-driven This is a role that should be located at or close to the top of the career chart to show an occupational preference and reflect a particular talent.

Generalist Site this expert's job at or in close proximity to the left side of the chart.

Improvisation-driven The roles of solution providers who offer quick and typically short-term solutions should be positioned at or near the bottom of the chart.

Specialist The occupations of domain experts with particular areas of expertise should be placed on or adjacent to the right side of the chart.

Strategy-Driven Career Path

A strategy-driven career path, like any other type of road map, cannot be planned without prior study and exploration. In other words, research is required to discover character traits and capabilities to effectively fulfill strategy duties for the enterprise. Moreover, no matter what type of strategy role one is aiming at, self-discovery (see section titled "Career Planning Step 1: Conduct Self-Discovery") and self-assessment (Chapter 4) can contribute immensely to career decision-making.

If the career priority is to progressively grow in the field of software architecture and the emphasis is on attaining strategy jobs, then each millstone on the road to achieving the ultimate goal must be thoroughly planned. For example, no one should expect that the path from a software developer position to an IT strategy role can materialize overnight. The road to the definitive goal is typically long. And the better we plan, the greater is the chance to succeed in the software industry.

Before taking on the task of developing a strategy-driven career path, consider this vital checklist. This summarizes a number of items to be aware of:

Self-discovery   Answer the six "W" questions from earlier in this chapter before embarking on a software architecture career journey. Find out if the self-discovery unveils traits proper for the pursuit of strategy occupations.

Career planning   Take the time to study the career planning process (in the section called "Software Architecture Career Planning Process") to develop a software architecture strategy career road map.

Risks   Consider the consequences when failing to embrace a career plan driven by personal and professional preferences. A strategy role in the enterprise first requires a career strategy.

Preferences and goals   Goal-oriented professionals tend to fulfill occupation aspirations. They are also motivated by personal preferences. Never compromise on professional goals. Stay on course. Focus on organizational strategy roles only if personal traits seem to suit the corresponding occupation's duties.

Obstacles   There is nothing to prevent any talented professional from being offered a strategy job. However, ensure that the career path is indeed optimized to smoothly carry out professional goals without being bogged down by trivial employment opportunities.

Develop a Strategy-Driven Career Path

Figure 3.10 represents an example of a strategy-driven career path. It commences at the operation engineering level and aims to attain an IT strategist role. Although the goal seems farfetched, remember that there is nothing that's impossible to achieve if an adequate career plan is available. True, plans are always subject to change, but without them, the road to career success would be muddled and utterly confusing.

There is something intriguing about the career path example in Figure 3.10. The individual who plans this employment strategy has in mind to climb the leadership ladder—favoring strategic occupations and moving away from a job that focuses on a narrower expertise level. Indeed, this is a steep road to climb, but the career strategy is clear and sound. Moreover, the strategy-driven career path shown in Figure 3.10 includes midway milestone roles that do not seem to fall in this individual's comfort zone. These are the infrastructure architect, the enterprise architect, and the goal itself—IT strategist.

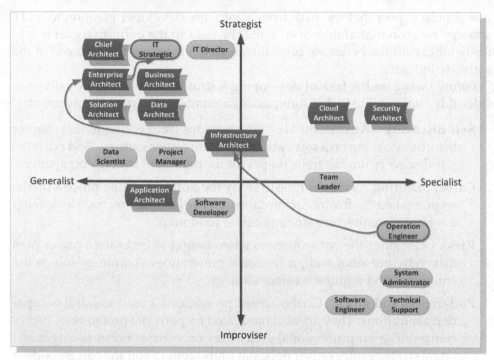

Figure 3.10: From Operation Engineering to IT Strategy Career Path

Review Table 3.11, which echoes Figure 3.10. Create a similar one that reflects personal choices and professional milestones and goals. There is nothing to fret about: the steps to achieving the ultimate objectives are not carved in stone. These can always be revised to reflect career challenges. There is no overnight success, especially when the goal is to become an influential strategist for the enterprise. No matter what kind of strategy role is in mind, plan a feasible career path, a pragmatic strategy that facilitates professional growth.

Table 3.11: From Operation Engineering to IT Strategy Career Path

CAREER PATH	MILESTONE/STATE	DRIVING CAREER PREFERENCE
Current position	Operation engineer	Specialist, improviser
Milestone	Infrastructure architect	Strategist, generalist
Milestone	Enterprise architect	Strategist, generalist
Goal	IT strategist	Strategist, generalist

CONCEPT   And once again, there is nothing wrong about being naïve, silly, and inexperienced at the outset of or during a career journey. Always meet success by using imagination. The sky is not even the limit.

CHAPTER

4

Self-Assessment for Software Architects

The software architecture self-assessment introduces rudimentary questions that can unveil the level of competencies an individual possesses to fulfill a software architecture role. By no means, however, are they intended to resemble interview questions. Nor will the earned scores for the selected answers necessarily reflect the overall knowledge of an individual who seeks a software architect position. Instead, these questions are designed to illuminate the chief areas of focus, interest, and fundamental concepts that software architects ought to understand; standards and best practices that should be ingrained in every software architect's mind; and areas to enhance should the scores be disappointing.

The self-assessment scoring system consists of four categories, each of which focuses on an assortment of different software architecture skills.

Social intelligence   This includes the communication, collaboration, and partnership formation skills needed to promote software architecture strategies and lead technological transformation and innovation.

Software architecture practice   This category includes best practices, standards, concepts, and general understanding of the software architecture practice.

Leadership This category includes talents required to lead technological change, promote software architecture vision, foster organizational culture, and facilitate the software development life cycle.

Strategy This group of queries can uncover an individual's capability to offer long-term technological plans, foster overarching solutions to business challenges, and introduce a potent end-state software architecture.

Social Intelligence

Social intelligence is a valuable skill employed for promoting software architecture agendas and visions. This talent encompasses communication and presentation capabilities that software architects ought to master. Without the abilities to connect, partner, and collaborate with business and information technology (IT) stakeholders, business initiatives are more likely to be doomed. Furthermore, constructive and tactful communication with decision-makers can galvanize support for business transformation and technological modernization.

Social networking, self-awareness, self-motivation, empathy, negotiation, communication, collaboration, and soft skills are only a few aspects that propel the questions presented in the sections that follow. Select only one answer in each of the 13 social intelligence categories. To complete the assessment, tally the scores as indicated in the section "Social Intelligence Skill Assessment."

Teamwork

The term *teamwork* refers to a group of professionals who collaboratively tackle business problems by employing their individual talents to fulfill software architecture goals and offer effective organizational solutions.

Question: What is the value that you see in software architecture teamwork?

A. Not important at all. Developers and architects do not need to collaborate on anything because software architects are running the show.

B. Somewhat important. Software architects are natural leaders, and they do not always need to collaborate on application and/or systems design with anyone else.

C. Software architecture is a practice that calls for teamwork. This collaboration should include a wide range of stakeholders, such as developers, team leaders, managers, production operation engineers, and executives.

D. It depends on what type of software architecture deliverables are required. If the mission is to deliver an enterprise technological solution, then collaboration is needed. For a small-scale project, there is no need for teamwork.

Partnership

Partnership pertains to relationships formed between two or more professionals or organizations who work together to achieve common goals. In the context of software architecture, these alliances are typically established to foster technological change and collaborate on construction of business products to meet business imperatives. Moreover, partners not only share joint responsibilities, but they're also liable for the negative consequences of their collective decision-making.

Question: Is it necessary to form partnerships with business and IT professionals when providing a software architecture solution to a business problem?

A. Partnerships only impede technological decision-making and the implementation of architectural solutions.

B. To a certain extent, partnerships can add value to a business solution, but they are not always necessary.

C. Partnerships should be established only with consumers of applications and systems. The software architecture life cycle does not require forming internal partnerships in the company to promote technological solutions.

D. There is no question that establishing partnerships with business and IT personnel, consumers, and even with software industry community members adds great value to software architecture solutions.

Self-consciousness

In social terms, self-consciousness is defined as self-awareness. It's a conscious knowledge of one's character, attributes, capabilities, motives, and ambitions. It's also about understanding the environment in which an individual operates and communicates with others.

Question: How does your self-awareness affect relationships with team members?

A. The more I understand myself, the better I'm attuned to the concerns and needs of my coworkers, managers, and customers.

B. Self-awareness does not have much effect on the rapport with my coworkers.

C. Self-awareness is just a term in psychology and should not be applied to relationships in my workplace.

D. High self-awareness is a mandatory trait that software architects must possess to be able to promote their designs and solutions.

Communication

In the IT world, the capability to use proper vocabulary for imparting concepts, ideas, and information is the crux of effective communication. Communication is not only about verbal competencies. It also relates to effective writing, presentations, or behaviors to facilitate the transmission of technological strategies, vision, and mission.

Question: What methods would you employ to effectively communicate technological solutions to business stakeholders, the software development community, IT managers, and enterprise executives?

A. I always describe the problem and then the solution even if no one understands my vision.

B. When I describe a remedy for a business challenge, I strive to simplify complex software architecture solutions. I always give visual examples and urge people to ask questions and challenge my solutions.

C. There is no need to embrace any communication method because no one in the organization understands what software architecture is.

D. My communication method calls for developing questionnaires, given to a wide range of professionals, for the purpose of collecting software architecture solutions and implementation ideas.

Networking

For numerous reasons, networking refers to the efforts of interacting with subject-matter experts to establish professional contacts and develop social relationships. Effective networking can be achieved by a variety of means, such as using computer applications or attending trainings, conferences, and conventions.

Question: Do you prefer in-person over online networking to achieve personal career goals?

A. Both are equally important to my professional career.

B. I prefer online networking because I do not have time to meet people face to face.

C. I prefer in-person networking because personal acquaintances and interactions are more reliable.

D. I do not understand why networking of any kind can promote my professional ambitions.

Soft Skills

Soft skills are personal attributes that enable an individual to interact harmoniously with professionals. Character traits and interpersonal talents typically influence how well one can communicate and collaborate with coworkers and management.

Question: What are your interpersonal skills that contribute the most to harmonious interaction with business and IT personnel?

A. Listening, empathy, conflict avoidance and resolution, flexibility, adaptability, and work ethic.

B. Listening to others is my greatest soft skill.

C. Soft skills are hard to learn, and it's questionable if they really help with interoffice communication.

D. Interpersonal skills typically do not resolve work conflicts.

Trust Building

Trust building is a process of establishing relationships that are based on the social principles of mutual respect, confidence, and reliance.

Question: Do trust building and transparency promote the quality of technological solutions?

A. The quality of software solutions has nothing to do with trust building skills. Applications and systems quality is always driven by smart software design and a dedicated workforce.

B. Trust building and interpersonal transparency skills can promote productive partnerships within an organization. Cooperation with subject-matter experts typically results in high-quality software architecture solutions.

C. The quality of technological solutions partially depends on developing relationships and trust-building traits. Successful software implementations are mostly the outcome of astute management and superb software architecture skills.

D. Trust building and transparency in a workplace foster good relationships with coworkers and managers. It's impossible, however, to assess how this bond affects the quality of the software.

Learning from Others

This social intelligence category demonstrates one's ability to gain knowledge from business and IT associates by listening, corresponding, and exchanging information.

Question: Is learning from peers and managers a valuable trait that can promote effective software architecture solutions?

A. Learning from others only adds to personal knowledge that can enhance technological solutions.

B. It depends on whom the knowledge is obtained from. Not everyone can contribute valuable wisdom and industry insights.

C. Learning should be pursued only by reading and attending training.

D. Learning from others is a long venture, a continuous effort to obtain knowledge that is not always useful.

Negotiation

Negotiation is a strategic effort to seek compromise and reach agreements by conducting dialogue and employing persuasion tactics to resolve conflicts and misunderstandings.

Question: How would you use your negotiation skills to advance a software architecture vision?

A. Nothing is negotiable about my software architecture vision because not everyone understands technology as well as I do.

B. During the negotiation phase, I typically do not give up completely on my software architecture vision. Some technological solutions are not negotiable.

C. To advance my software architecture vision, I'd adhere to these principles: 1) Use persuasion tactics—explain the advantages of the architecture solution; 2) Compromise on technological solutions; 3) Understand opposing positions and concerns; 4) Be a good listener and consider others' concerns and feelings; 5) Exercise patience and control emotions; 6) Establish fruitful relationships with the other side; 7) Strive for a win-win outcome; 8) Plan a negotiation exit strategy if compromise has not been achieved.

D. During negotiations I typically give more than what I take to please the other side. Usually, this negotiation approach saves time and improves relationships with others.

Self-presentation

Self-presentation or self-branding is affiliated with actions or behavior of an individual aimed at exhibiting a favorable image to be perceived by others.

Question: How can one's effective self-presentation influence business and technical decision-making?

A. Personal branding of software architecture leaders never contributes to business and technological solutions.

B. The self-presentation of technology leaders always affects decision-making in an organization.

C. Self-presentation has limited influence on partnerships and relationships in an organization.

D. Self-presentation is only one component of personal behavior that can affect organizational decision-making.

Teleworking

Teleworking, also known as *remote work*, refers to a flexible work arrangement that enables employees to perform their duties from an approved work site, such as a home office.

Question: Is remote work your preferred work arrangement?

A. Unlike work in an office, remote work never gets done, communication between team members is often poor, and managers are unable to control their employees.

B. I support employees who prefer to work from home.

C. I do not see any value in working in a corporate office.

D. Teleworking is necessary for employees who can provide proper justification.

Fellowship

Affiliation and belonging to business and technological communities and professional associations whose members share common interests is called *fellowship*.

Question: Can fellowship with technology communities contribute to the success of business products and software development?

A. Not always. It depends on the type of technical information these communities share.

B. I support joining online communities to learn more about advanced software architecture technologies as a means of enhancing applications and systems performance, integration, and operations.

C. Technology communities never contribute to the success of application and system implementations.

D. Technology communities that are sponsored by vendors are typically about marketing and promotion of their products.

Self-sufficiency

Professionals who perform their work duties without the aid of others are recognized as being self-sufficient.

Question: Would you apply for a position that calls for independent work and self-sufficiency?

A. I never feel the need to ask coworkers and managers for help on any professional matters.

B. Companies promote employee self-sufficiency to save time on interaction and communication with others.

C. Self-sufficiency demonstrates a high level of maturity. This especially applies to the capability of being responsible and accountable for assigned tasks and projects.

D. The term *self-sufficiency* does not contradict collaboration, partnership, communication, and information sharing.

Handling Customer Relationships

Relationships with coworkers, managers, and executives are typically different from affiliation with customers. This social intelligence category calls for special talents and communication capabilities to meet clients' requirements and satisfy their business imperatives.

Question: How important are relationships with customers to the successful implementation and integration of applications and systems?

A. It's important to create working partnerships with customers, understand their requirements, and consider their suggestions. But their contribution to development of business products is very limited in scope.

B. Customers typically do not understand technology, and there is no need to involve them in software design decisions and implementations.

C. Customers are a vital part of the software architecture life cycle, and their relationships with the software development community always shape business products.

D. Software architects should collaborate with customers only when their requirements are unclear.

Social Intelligence Skill Assessment

Each of the presented social intelligence skill assessment category questions calls for selecting only one answer that resonates most with an individual. It's advisable to print out Table 4.1 and then record the earned score in the "My Score" column.

Based on the earned point tally, the three competency ranges defined in the following list should indicate if an individual possesses adequate social intelligence skills to handle software architecture roles:

55–81 points   Above average score that shows an individual's capability to employ social intelligence to promote software architecture strategies, vision, and mission.

28–54 points   An average social intelligence score that calls for self-improvement, training, and studies.

1–27 points   Below average score that requires major improvement to social intelligence skills. It's recommended to take training classes and even hire a personal coach to strengthen social and communication skills.

Table 4.1: Social Intelligence Skill Assessment Table

CATEGORY	ANSWER	POINTS EARNED	MY SCORE
Teamwork	C	4	
Partnership	B	1	
	D	4	
Self-consciousness	A	4	
	D	4	
Communication	B	4	
	D	2	
Networking	A	4	
	B	1	
	C	2	
Soft Skills	A	4	
	B	1	
Trust Building	B	4	
	C	1	
	D	2	
Learning from Others	A	4	
Negotiation	C	4	
Self-presentation	B	3	
	D	4	

Continues

Table 4.1 (*continued*)

CATEGORY	ANSWER	POINTS EARNED	MY SCORE
Teleworking	B	2	
	D	4	
Fellowship	A	2	
	B	4	
	D	1	
Self-sufficiency	C	4	
	D	3	
Handling Customer Relationships	C	4	
Maximum Points to Earn		81	
My Score Point			0

Software Architecture Practice

The questions in this section are provided to assess the general capabilities to fulfill the role of software architect. They are designed to test the understanding and familiarity with software architecture best practices and standards. Moreover, the queries include topics such as software architecture strategy, vision, roles, system integration, interoperability, reuse, and distributed and federated architecture models. These are fundamental questions that every software architect ought to understand before embarking on a software design career.

Select only one answer in each of the 13 software architecture practice categories. Then tally the scores for the answers as guided in the section "Software Architecture Practice Skill Assessment."

Software Architecture Strategy

A software architecture strategy is driven by business imperatives. The strategy ought to be aligned with a business strategy and meet business requirements. Its chief components are the roadmap for technological implementations, architecture frameworks, and an execution plan for fulfilling business objectives.

Question: How useful is a firm-wide software architecture strategy?

A. It's imperative to carve out a software architecture strategy only because every institution must have one.

B. An enterprise-level software architecture strategy is not needed. Instead, every line of business should have a proprietary strategy that satisfies its own business needs.

C. A firm-wide software architecture strategy only increases a company's overhead. As an alternative, an organization should promote software architecture best practices, standards, and policies.

D. An enterprise-wide software architecture strategy is useful as long as its vision and mission are embraced by executives, managers, development teams, and operations personnel.

Software Architecture Vision

A software architecture vision delineates technological capabilities designed to address business imperatives and fulfill organizational goals. The vision also identifies approaches for achieving these objectives and proposes an overarching end-state architecture.

Question: Why should an organization carve out a software architecture vision?

A. To define technological *goals* that will satisfy business imperatives.

B. To identify technological capabilities and propose software implementations to meet business requirements.

C. To map out technological objectives to meet business goals.

D. There is no need for an organizational software architecture vision.

Software Architecture Role

Software architects are solution providers and decision-makers who are commissioned to align technological strategies with business imperatives. Their solutions are devised to ensure business continuity and facilitate technological transformation and modernization.

Question: Why do organizations hire software architects?

A. Software architects promote corporate civility and encourage teamwork to tackle social problems within the organization.

B. Software architects are employed to promote organizational culture and encourage adherence to architecture frameworks.

C. There are no particularly good reasons to employ software architects. Most organizations hire software architects to technically manage development teams.

D. Software architects are employed to lead technological initiatives by demonstrating leadership, creativity, and expertise in the field of computer science.

System Integration

Linking software implementations, such as services, applications, and systems is the process of system integration. This effort enables coordinated message exchange and data sharing in a distributed environment to boost computing resources, avoid operational redundancy, and promote functionality reuse.

Question: How do software architects achieve efficient system integration?

A. By merging a number of business applications into a single monolithic implementation to reduce network traffic and save servers.

B. The integration of organizational assets is more successful in cloud computing environments because of native cloud services.

C. Efficient system integration can be achieved by employing a variety of technologies, network devices, platforms, and infrastructure. These may include middleware products, gateways, application programming interfaces (APIs), connectors, and remote procedure calls.

D. Most system integration efforts are inefficient, and therefore businesses never benefit from bringing together distributed systems.

Interoperability

Interoperability refers to an architecture attribute that enables heterogeneous computer systems and production environments to communicate with each other and share information.

Question: How do software architects promote business and technological interoperability?

A. Promoting interoperability is not the role of software architects. Instead, they must master the art of software design and deliver useful architecture blueprints.

B. There is no need to promote business and technological interoperability because it's merely a concept that never materializes.

C. Software architects typically enable business and technological interoperability by devising proper system integration patterns, adopting powerful middleware platforms, and using robust infrastructure.

D. Interoperability is promoted by embracing software architecture frameworks.

Software Reuse

Software reuse is an architecture best practice that calls for utilizing existing software rather than developing new implementations.

Question: Why do software architects foster software reuse?

A. Reduces redundancy of business and technical functionality.

B. Increases productivity and minimizes software development cost.

C. Increases maintenance and operation efficiency of software implementations in production.

D. Accelerates time to market.

Distributed Architecture Model

The distributed architecture model is all about the *disbursement* of autonomous software implementations *deployed* to different environments and maintaining communication over networks to offer business and/or technological solutions.

Question: Why do enterprise architects often embrace the distributed architecture model?

A. Architects shy away from the distributed architecture model because it raises concerns about data synchronization.

B. The distributed architecture model offers technological stability because it promotes high cohesion.

C. The model eliminates the need for a centralized architecture scheme.

D. The implementation of the distributed architecture model increases scalability, enhances security, alleviates single point of failure risks, elevates data and process redundancy, and ensures business continuity.

Federated Architecture Model

Federated architecture is a pattern in enterprise architecture that strengthens *interoperability* capabilities to enable information sharing between large ecosystems and institutions, such as production environments, lines of business, and organizations.

Question: What is the benefit of devising a federated architecture model?

A. There is no justification for devising a federated architecture environment because it typically increases message exchange volume.

B. Federated architecture promotes the development of loosely coupled applications and systems.

C. Architects embrace the federated architecture model to enable business and technical interoperability between computer systems.

D. To establish a decentralized computing environment, alleviate application dependencies, and increase the performance of business functionality.

Architecture Styles

An architecture style describes a structural implementation and integration of an environment and the systems that encompass architecture patterns and design patterns.

Question: Provide an example of an architecture style.

A. Layered architecture.

B. Monolithic architecture.

C. Service-oriented architecture.

D. API gateway.

Architecture and Design Patterns

Architecture patterns and design patterns are employed to devise reusable solutions to business and technological problems. Both are employed to address repeatable challenges, standardize organizational technologies, increase productivity, and accelerate the software development life cycle.

Question: What is the difference between architecture patterns and design patterns?

A. An architecture pattern is devised to address a broader business problem than a design pattern is.

B. There is not much difference between these types of patterns.

C. Design patterns are subsets of architecture patterns.

D. Architecture patterns represent solutions for enterprise-level challenges, and design patterns provide solutions on smaller scales.

Componentization

Componentization is a design process that calls for breaking down a software implementation, such as an application, into smaller parts, namely, components. Each of these components consists of related functions that provide partial solutions to business or technical problems.

Question: Why is one of the most critical duties of a software architect to devise componentization of software implementations?

A. To achieve high cohesion of software implementation.

B. To increase software reuse, performance, maintainability, and reduce implementation complexity.

C. To shorten the software development life cycle.

D. Componentization of software implementation is not necessary because it renders tightly coupled applications.

Software Architecture Frameworks

A software architecture framework offers guidance and governance for the software development life cycle. The framework typically includes standards, best practices, and policies for software implementations, deployment, configuration, integration, and maintenance.

Question: What is the difference between architecture standards, best practices, and policies?

A. They are all the same.

B. Unlike policies, best practices are standards that are the same.

C. Standards represent technical consensus for building applications and systems. Best practices are about the "how" to build business products. And policies are not a part of an architecture framework.

D. Standards are accepted industry norms. Best practices are recommended procedures. And policies are rules for implementation.

Software Development

Software development is the process of constructing software implementations such as applications and systems.

Question: Should software architects develop source code?

A. Software architects should focus on application and system design, deployment, integration, configuration, and maintenance in production. Therefore, the rule of thumb suggests that they should not engage in programming.

B. In addition to their design duties, software architects must be part of development teams because of their superb programming talents.

C. In essence, all members of any software development team are architects.

D. Software architects are not required to possess software development skills.

Software Architecture Practice Skill Assessment

Table 4.2 consists of four columns: Category, Answer, Points Earned, and My Score. The corresponding answers to each question in a category carry points. Add up the earned points and place them in the corresponding My Score column.

Based on the earned point tally, the three competency ranges defined in the following list should indicate if an individual possesses satisfactory software architecture practice skills:

67–99 points This score range indicates that an individual possesses adequate skills to provide software architecture services.

34–66 points This score range calls for training and self-study to improve the software architecture practice skills.

1–33 points This score range necessitates major improvement to software architecture practice talents. Pursue professional networking to learn more about software architecture disciplines and take architecture training to broaden professional knowledge.

Table 4.2: Software Architecture Practice Skill Assessment Table

CATEGORY	ANSWER	POINTS EARNED	MY SCORE
Software Architecture Strategy	D	4	
Software Architecture Vision	A	4	
	B	4	
	C	4	
Software Architect Role	B	1	
	D	4	
System Integration	B	1	
	C	4	
Interoperability	C	4	
	D	1	
Software Reuse	A	4	
	B	4	
	C	4	
	D	4	
Distributed Architecture Model	B	1	
	C	2	
	D	4	

CATEGORY	ANSWER	POINTS EARNED	MY SCORE
Federated Architecture Model	B	2	
	C	3	
	D	4	
Architecture Styles	A	4	
	B	4	
	C	4	
Architecture and Design Patterns	A	4	
	C	2	
	D	1	
Componentization	A	2	
	B	4	
	C	1	
Software Architecture Frameworks	D	4	
Software Development	A	4	
	D	2	
Maximum Points to Earn		99	
My Score Point			**0**

Leadership

The answers to the questions in this section can shed light on an individual's capabilities to demonstrate technological leadership in the software architecture field. Leadership competencies are necessary for promoting software architecture strategies and contribute to decision-making that eventually impacts the foundation of enterprise performance. Leadership also comes into play during project management and technical facilitation.

The various question categories provided in the sections that follow are driven by important leadership skills, such as time management, decision-making, problem-solving, creative thinking, team building, and conflict resolution.

To self-assess leadership capabilities, only one answer should be selected in each of the 14 leadership categories. The total score for the selected answers can be revealed after following the instructions in the section "Assessment of Leadership Competencies."

Managing Time

One of the most important leadership skills that can boost workplace productivity is proper time management. Administrating time effectively is the result of setting software architecture priorities, identifying milestones, and rigorously executing plans to fulfill goals.

Question: What are the chief technological benefits of effective time management?

A. Improves the quality of applications and systems.

B. Increases teamwork's efficiency and productivity to fulfill software architecture goals.

C. Delivers business products on time.

D. Controls software architecture and development budgets.

Decision-Making

Astute leaders make decisions only after they analyze and understand the choices they individually learned about or that were presented to them by subject-matter experts. Therefore, the act of decision-making is merely about *selecting* the most effective option to resolve a complex organizational problem.

Question: What is your decision-making approach?

A. The best approach is to delegate this task to someone whose duty it is to make decisions.

B. 1) Understand the problem; 2) Devise a number of solutions to address the challenge; 3) Select the most practical remedy from the collection of possible solutions; 4) Introduce the solution for further vetting by stakeholders.

C. I have not adopted any decision-making method.

D. My decision-making approach is to offer solutions that on one hand minimize organizational expenditure and on the other increase work productivity. I typically make decisions that are practical and garner support from business and IT professionals. Without their support a decision could not be made.

Problem-solving

Problem-solving is a strategic venture that consists of a number of critical tasks that ultimately render a solution to a problem or a number of challenges. Problem identification, problem analysis, root-cause analysis, proposition of solutions, and final decision-making are the chief tasks of the problem-solving process.

Question: What leadership skills do you possess that demonstrate problem-solving capabilities?

A. I use creativity, team building and collaboration, and analytical skills.

B. I'm a good listener and my communication skills are excellent.

C. I tend to solve problems effectively because of my outstanding technical skills and vast experience in technology.

D. Generally, leaders are not commissioned to solve problems. They are required to supervise projects.

Diversity, Equity, and Inclusion

Diversity stands for the structural composition of a workplace that recognizes individual preferences and differences, such as ages, beliefs, ideologies, and ethnicities. The term *inclusion* promotes tolerance and civility toward staff with diverse backgrounds by involving them in vital business and technological initiatives. And equity pertains to justice and fairness in how they are regarded and treated.

Question: How do you encourage diversity and inclusion in your workplace?

A. I denounce any form of discrimination and inequality.

B. I promote an inclusive organizational culture that does not leave anyone behind despite their backgrounds and beliefs.

C. I strongly support interaction between individuals with different ideas, concepts, and education credentials.

D. It's not my job to encourage diversity, equity, and inclusion.

Responsibility and Accountability

A person who is assigned to a duty is responsible for its progress and satisfactory completion. An accountable party, however, refers to an individual who owns the duty's outcome and the impact of its deliverables.

Question: Can leaders be responsible without being accountable for their own work?

A. Leaders must always be responsible and accountable for their work.

B. Leaders are always responsible for their work. Their superiors, however, should be the ones who are accountable for the work.

C. No one should be accountable for others' work.

D. In essence, there is not a big difference between responsibility and accountability. Responsible people must be accountable for any work that they do.

Hiring Preferences

The screening of candidate software architects is driven by the preferences of the hiring companies and managers. This vetting process calls for assessing applicants' skills, breadth of knowledge, experience, character, and motivation.

Question: What are the most important traits that an aspiring or practicing software architect must possess?

A. Must be highly experienced, astute, nonconfrontational, a team player, and adhere to organizational software architecture best practices, standards, and policies.

B. Strategist, solution provider, creative, out-of-the-box thinker, self-sufficient, individualist.

C. Very technical, does not have to be a team player or sociable.

D. Beginner who understands the fundamental software architecture disciplines and is willing to learn on the job.

Creative Thinking

Creative thinkers typically offer imaginative and innovative solutions to address business and technological challenges. One of their main responsibilities is to foster solutions that simplify the complexity of business processes, data, and architecture.

Question: What creative thinking attributes do you possess?

A. Problem-solving, ability to think out of the box.

B. Open-minded, analytical thinker, risk-taker.

C. Good listener, innovative thinker, imaginative.

D. Willing to learn from others, consider others' ideas and solutions, non-judgmental, communicative.

Critical Thinking

Critical thinkers are in the business of analyzing, assessing, and scrutinizing design concepts, software development project ideas, and implementations to provide strategic and technical solutions.

Question: How can critical thinking be utilized to enhance leadership's decision-making?

A. Critical thinkers are objective realists who utilize their logical judgment and reasoning skills to devise effective software architecture solutions.

B. Good decision-making has nothing to do with critical thinking.

C. Critical thinkers tend to test technical concepts and hypotheses to understand enterprise problems and make better solution decisions.

D. Critical thinkers use their analytical skills to provide best-of-class solutions.

Being Proactive

In the context of the software architecture practice, being proactive means to avoid procrastination, assess operational risks, and take initiatives to avert business loss or technological mishap.

Question: Give an example of a leader who's being proactive by employing technologies.

A. Launching a data disaster recovery project to prevent future loss of information.

B. Training staff to protect private information and prevent cybersecurity threats.

C. I have no idea because our top-level executives do not like it when people are proactive. They always expect you to promptly respond to recurring challenges rather than take initiatives to prevent them.

D. Devising a proactive health management plan to help staff improve their lifestyle.

Establishment of Trust

The establishment of trustful relationships between coworkers and management is achieved if leaders can foster mutual respect, encourage civil communication, and increase the sense of personal reliability.

Question: How important is trust building to the success of your leadership role?

A. I focus merely on the technical aspects of my software architecture role. Therefore, trust building is not the most important part of my job.

B. For software architects trust building is a waste of time.

C. Since software architects are considered technical leaders, trust building is a critical trait that can facilitate the promotion of architecture vision and mission.

D. Not everyone must be engaged in trust building; it all depends on the leadership level. Only high-level executives must build trust with their subordinates.

Administrative Duties

Administrative work characteristically includes tasks that are not directly or necessarily affiliated with software architecture or technical leadership. These activities may pertain to budgeting, assessment of employee performance, and signing timesheets.

Question: What percentage of administrative work is acceptable to you?

A. 90 percent

B. 60 percent

C. 40 percent

D. 10 percent

Coaching and Training

Coaching is the act of assisting staff to achieve their personal and professional objectives, not only by illuminating the opportunities in the workplace but by teaching them how to focus on individual strategies and meticulously fulfill predefined goals.

Training bears a different structure of gaining personal knowledge. This form of study can be accomplished by attending training classes, taking online courses, and pursuing certification studies.

Question: Do you consider staff coaching or training an important part of a leadership role?

A. Coaching and training should be a part of every software architect's duty.

B. Not everyone possesses coaching and training skills. Therefore, these tasks should be given to professional instructors.

C. Coaching is definitely a part of a leadership role. Training should be conducted by professionals whose job is to instruct and mentor.

D. Effective coaching can help professionals achieve their career goals and ultimately promotes effective organizational solutions.

Team Building

Leaders employ their team building talents to promote collaboration on projects, encourage exchange of ideas, and support mutual efforts that result in fulfillment of objectives.

Question: Why is team building vital for the delivery of high-quality software products?

A. The encouragement of team bonding and positive communication typically renders the best breed of software applications because of positive and productive collaboration.

B. Software design is a collaborative discipline that requires the participation of highly qualified professionals. Building a team that can work together as a whole is the top responsibility of a leader who understands that the quality of applications and systems is driven by a team's professional capabilities.

C. Team building is not a task that leaders must take on.

D. Team building is not vital for producing high-quality software implementations. One person alone can deliver superb business products without the need of a collaborative team.

Resolving Conflicts

Conflict resolution is a leadership talent that brings people together even if they possess different opinions. No matter how radical the disputes over business, technical, or social issues are, conflicts can be resolved by seeking a compromise that is acceptable to all parties.

Question: What would be the method that you recommend to resolve conflicts about a technology solution?

A. There are always two sides to a conflict, especially when there are heated debates about technology solutions. My approach is to identify the source of the conflict and then formulate an agreement that's acceptable to every party.

B. I support a written agreement that specifies what everyone is willing to compromise on. Then I keep my eyes open to check if the agreement is executed correctly.

C. There is no need for leaders to resolve conflicts because of two reasons: 1) There are many of them; 2) Professional staff typically do not have any disagreements.

D. There are not so many conflicts between staff who work for strong leaders.

Assessment of Leadership Competencies

Table 4.3 includes four columns to use for answer scoring: Category, Answer, Points Earned, and My Score. Every answer found in the Answer column carries the corresponding score in the Points Earned column. The My Score column then should indicate the points that are related to the chosen answer. Based on the tally of the earned points, consider these competency ranges:

72–107 points   The leadership competencies assessment denotes that an individual earned enough points demonstrating the proper capabilities to fill an organizational leadership role in the space of software architecture.

37–71 points   This average points range calls for further studies and continuing education to enhance the individual's leadership skills.

1–36 points   Based on this assessment, it is suggested that an individual should broaden related leadership skills by pursuing training and self-studies.

Table 4.3: Leadership Competencies Assessment Table

CATEGORY	ANSWER	POINTS EARNED	MY SCORE
Managing Time	B	4	
	C	3	
	D	3	
Decision-Making	B	4	
	D	1	
Problem-Solving	A	4	
	C	1	
Diversity, Equity, and Inclusion	A	3	
	B	4	
	C	2	
Accountability and Responsibility	A	4	
Hiring Preferences	A	4	
	B	4	
	D	4	
Creative Thinking	A	4	
	B	4	
	C	4	
	D	4	

CATEGORY	ANSWER	POINTS EARNED	MY SCORE
Critical Thinking	A	4	
	C	4	
	D	2	
Being Proactive	A	4	
	B	4	
Establishment of Trust	C	4	
Administrative Duties	D	4	
Coaching and Training	A	1	
	B	1	
	C	2	
	D	4	
Team Building	A	3	
	B	4	
Resolving Conflicts	A	4	
	B	2	
Maximum Points to Earn		107	
My Score Points			0

Strategy

Software architects who are chartered to draw up long-term technological strategies, offer design solutions, provide architecture blueprints, and facilitate the software development life cycle must demonstrate strategic thinking aptitude. The answers to the queries in this section, therefore, are designed to assess the level of the strategic skills an individual possesses. The questions that follow in this category thus focus on talents required to lead technological initiatives, such as architecture strategy, strategic thinking, generalization, problem-solving, and software design approaches.

An individual's strategic skills can be evaluated by selecting a single answer in each of the 13 strategic competencies categories. The score tally can be revealed after following the guidance in the section "Assessment of Strategic Competencies."

Software Architecture Strategy

Driven by business imperatives, a software architecture strategy offers a long-term plan for advancing technological transformation and innovation. This mission underscores the necessity to enhance business capabilities and reenforce organizational competitive edge.

Question: What are the components of a software architecture strategy?

A. A strategy execution roadmap, software architecture execution plan, and software architecture frameworks.

B. A software architecture framework that devises best practices, standards, and policies.

C. A human resources department's list of employees.

D. An organizational chart.

Strategic Thinking

Strategic thinking is all about the capability to employ analytic skills to reveal enterprise vulnerabilities and develop long-term plans for shielding the business from internal and external threats.

Question: What traits make a good strategy thinker?

A. Resistance to change and technological conservativism.

B. The capability to define long-term goals, plan technological transitioning roadmaps, and provide enterprise technological strategies.

C. Carving out a career path and setting career goals.

D. Forward-thinking and conducting risk assessments to prevent the negative impact of technological disasters.

Problem Identification

Problem identification is pursued for discovering and understanding in depth a business or technical problem that needs to be rectified. This effort also requires a root-cause analysis of the problem to grasp the severity of the challenge.

Question: For what purpose must business problems be identified?

A. An effective software architecture solution cannot be devised if a business problem has not been identified or is unclear.

B. Business problems are the impetus for employing technological remedies. Therefore, they must be identified at the outset of every product development life cycle.

C. Every software development initiative must be driven by business requirements. And requirements cannot be delivered if business problems have
not been identified.

D. It's not the strategist's duty to identify business problems. Analysts are
the ones responsible for identifying the challenges.

Problem-solving

Problem-solving is a strategic venture that consists of a number of critical tasks
that ultimately render a solution to a problem or a number of challenges. Problem
identification, problem analysis, root-cause analysis, proposition of solutions,
and final decision-making are the chief tasks of the problem-solving process.

Question: Should strategists be commissioned to solve enterprise business
and technological challenges?

A. Organizations should not employ strategists to solve business or technological problems since they are not technical enough to lead software
development.

B. Only developers can solve business problems because their job is to construct applications and systems.

C. Strategists should take part in solving corporate challenges because they
possess unique talents to identify problems and offer overarching solutions.

D. Enterprise and business challenges can never be rectified by anyone.

Abstraction

The abstraction process is employed to blend particular problem characteristics and facts for rendering *universal ideas and concepts*. The chief use of this
practice contributes to the construction of business products and the software
development life cycle.

Question: Why do strategists tend to employ the abstraction process?

A. To break down concepts into more granular ideas.

B. Abstraction is actually the same as specification.

C. Strategists abstract specific problem instances to understand why businesses fail to perform and identify the reasons for organizational revenue
decline.

D. To identify the properties of particular problems to recommend standard
technologies.

Generalization

In the business world, generalization practices are used to encourage utilization and reuse of existing organizational assets. The term *assets* refers to any property that the enterprise owns, such as servers, applications, systems, network devices, and infrastructure components.

Question: Which of these answers specify the most compelling reasons for employing the principles of generalization?

A. Generalization is employed by strategists to discover reusable business and technical functions, accelerate software development efforts, reduce cost of ownership, and optimize application and system maintenance expenditure.

B. Strategists employ generalization to abstract small-scale problems for offering overarching organizational solutions.

C. Strategists never employ generalization. They are chartered to deliver technical specifications and focus on providing limited-scale solutions.

D. Strategists use the principles of generalization to foster technological standardization, optimizing the cost of the software development life cycle, and minimizing redundancy of business functionality.

Visualization

One of the most potent methods that strategists use to promote their goals is visualizing their visions. This is achieved by conveying ideas and solutions not only by using descriptive language but also by creating mental images that draw clear pictures in other people's minds.

Question: How do technological strategists use the power of visualization to promote software architecture visions?

A. Strategists use the power of visualization to vividly present their vision with analogies, anecdotes, and use cases to depict palpable and practical business and technological solutions.

B. Strategists use graphic presentations, such as diagrams, storyboards, charts, and illustrations to depict a coherent vision for end-state architectures.

C. Technological strategists hire graphic designers to produce slideshows that demonstrate a clear vision for software implementations.

D. It's impossible to visualize a solution before understanding business and technical requirements.

Software Design Approaches

Organizations typically adopt software design methods that drive development of services, applications, and systems. These approaches ultimately affect the manner in which software is implemented. In today's market there are a number of prevailing strategies that focus on different design styles, such as structural, functional, object-oriented, bottom-up, and top-down.

Question: What is the difference between the bottom-up and the top-down software design strategy?

A. They are actually the same but named differently.

B. The bottom-up design strategy starts from business requirements. The top-down begins with technical specifications.

C. The bottom-up strategy calls for building the software from the smallest components and then deriving the larger components. The top-down starts with the larger components and renders the smaller ones.

D. They are different: the bottom-up is managed by developers, while the top-down is governed by managers.

Simplification

The simplification process that strategists are often engaged in refers to deciphering intricate business requirements and transforming them into tangible technological solutions. Simply put, they ought to present a coherent and easy-to-understand long-term vision in the most digestible manner possible.

Question: Give an example of what strategists typically simplify to provide potent solutions.

A. Design blueprints and technical specifications.

B. Source code.

C. Concepts and ideas that drive tangible software implementations.

D. Business problems.

Analytical Capabilities

The capability to efficiently analyze business problems, understand the root causes of organizational challenges, and employ critical and creative thinking to draw up comprehensive business and technological solutions is a vital trait that strategists must possess.

Question: Give an example of how business risks can be averted by using strong analytical capabilities.

A. Assess risks to business continuity and offer remedies to avoid production environment failures.

B. Evaluate, select, and adopt off-the-shelf middleware products.

C. It's not mandatory for strategists to have strong analytical traits.

D. Devise artificial intelligence solutions to provide medical prognoses.

Influencing

Strategists rely on their capability to influence business and IT stakeholders to obtain their support and foster advocacy for long-term technological plans and projects.

Question: How can the power of strategic influence be employed to impact organizational decision-making when it comes to technological solutions?

A. Influential strategists can contribute to enterprise architecture directions and strategies by motivating and incentivizing their followers to embrace business and technological visions.

B. Strategists never influence organizational decision-making.

C. Influencing is all about affecting the decisions to develop business products and transform enterprise technologies.

D. It's not the strategist's job to influence anything.

Promoting Culture

Organizational culture affects human behavior and code of conduct, moral values, product development methodologies, business processes, and practices that are critical to advancing business missions.

Question: How does a strategist promote organizational culture?

A. Cultures cannot be promoted. They evolve with time. No one has control over how people behave, respect each other, use software, or communicate.

B. Enterprise culture must be enforced—not promoted.

C. A strategist promotes enterprise culture by aligning business strategies with technological strategies.

D. Culture can be promoted by embracing best practices, standards, and policies to shape organizational strategies and business product development.

Strategy Execution Plan

A strategy execution plan answers the critical question, "How can a carved-out strategy can be implemented?"

Question: What does a strategy execution plan consist of?

A. A strategy implementation roadmap with milestones and goals.

B. Policies and best practices for software development.

C. There is no effective way to execute a strategy because strategies never propel any implementation of business products.

D. Providing a strategy execution plan is counterproductive because no one adheres to enterprise strategies anyway.

Assessment of Strategic Competencies

Table 4.4 lays out four columns: Category, Answer, Points Earned, and My Score. The points for each answer are shown in the Points Earned column.

Based on the earned point tally, the three competency ranges defined in the following list should indicate if an individual possesses satisfactory software architecture strategic skills.

49–72 points   This point range shows that one possesses passable software architecture strategic talents.

25–48 points   This point range indicates that there is a need for further training to enhance the software architecture strategic capabilities.

1–24 points   If the earned points are anywhere within this range, significant improvements to software architecture strategic skills are required. Individuals are encouraged to pursue self-studies and take related training to improve the strategic capabilities affiliated with the software architecture practice.

Table 4.4: Strategic Competencies Assessment Table

CATEGORY	ANSWER	POINTS EARNED	MY SCORE
Software Architecture Strategy	A	4	
	B	2	
Strategic Thinking	B	4	
	D	1	

Continues

Table 4.4 (*continued*)

CATEGORY	ANSWER	POINTS EARNED	MY SCORE
Problem Identification	A	4	
	B	4	
Problem-Solving	C	4	
Abstraction	A	4	
	B	4	
	D	4	
Generalization	A	4	
	B	2	
	D	2	
Visualization	B	4	
Software Design Strategy	C	4	
Simplification	A	2	
	C	4	
Analytical Capabilities	A		
Influencing	A	3	
	C	4	
Promoting Culture	D	4	
Strategy Execution Plan	A	4	
Maximum Points to Earn		72	
My Score Point Total			0

Software Architecture Toolbox

In This Part

Part

3

Software Architecture Toolbox

In This Part

Employing Innate Talents to Provide Potent Organizational Solutions

Humans have employed the power of life study and experience to promote culture and advance social communication. This compound knowledge has enhanced our lifestyle and introduced novel technologies that have broken educational barriers.

But the notion that humans' social, economic, and technological achievements have been merely propelled by experience and incessant study is implausible. There is substantial evidence that we carry innate talents since birth—skills not necessarily learned through experience. Some of these natural abilities are affiliated with primal instincts, such as survival, endurance, security, and social bonding.

Clearly, the ongoing participation in life activities characteristically renders accumulation of information and accelerates the learning of skills. But life experience is not the only factor that contributes to the survival of human beings. Humanity has also withstood hardships and overcome calamities by applying innate skills. It has become evident, though, that the combination of the two—life experiences and inherent innate capabilities—is frequently utilized to enhance decision-making and to provide potent strategies to avoid threats to existence.

There is no indication suggesting that innate gifts cannot be learned during a lifetime. Adaptability, enthusiasm, curiosity, creativity, and self-discipline are known to be genetic traits that can also be developed and enhanced through life experiences because of survival necessities.

CONCEPT   Bottom line: everything can be learned, every talent can be honed, and every competency can be subject to improvement.

Innate Skills Promote Software Architecture Effectiveness

Because of the harsh survival game in the corporate world, software architects must bring not only professional expertise to the table. This would not be enough to excel in the software architecture field; nor would it substantially contribute to organizational technological superiority. Therefore, to boost software architecture capabilities, innate competencies should be recruited to render effective and potent business and technological solutions. The most prominent innate skills that can promote software architecture effectiveness are good judgment, communication, social involvement, design taste, logical inference, creativity, intuition, imagination, and curiosity.

CONCEPT   Although innate skills are deemed as genetically imprinted knowledge, there is no limit to the traits a software architect can improve, study, develop, and acquire. Don't despair. Never lose hope.

Remember: Survival, Survival, Survival

Surviving in the turbulent corporate world is one of the greatest challenges that a software architect must grapple with. The struggle to maintain technological leadership, to galvanize support for architecture vision, to tolerate ignorance, and to advance software architecture agendas are only a few survival difficulties that software architects typically face.

Moreover, there are limitless occasions to fail when it comes to corporate survival: there are no limits to corporate subsistence problems that eventually put a strain on technological progress; there are no limits to social and communication issues that hamper collaboration, partnerships, and teamwork; and there are no limits to the slew of leadership problems that can only diminish support for software development projects.

Therefore, these technological, social, communication, and leadership hardships only emphasize the need for innate talents that must be employed to address business and technological risks.

CONCEPT Software architects must recognize that the impediment to technological progress originates from unfitting individual agendas, priorities, and preferences. To tackle these problems, they must unleash the innate power of creativity to provide viable solutions. They must take proactive measures to dodge business calamities. And to be able to survive in the corporate world, they ought to adapt a situational awareness strategy that reduces the chance of failure.

Consequences of Failing to Invoke Innate Talents

It takes only one adverse incident to put strain on a network, an infrastructure, or an entire production environment. The list of business and technological impediments is long. These obstacles may be caused by a broad range of issues, such as software glitches, inadequate system scalability, or even failing software architecture strategy. Slow system-response time or accelerated consumption of computing resources (such as memory, disk, and network bandwidth) are only a few signs of a malfunctioning production ecosystem.

A devastating epidemic, war, terrorist attack, decapitating cybersecurity strike, and civil unrest are also a few examples of causes that can disrupt system operations and halt business transactions.

A well-architected production environment can successfully respond to these obstacles and avoid substantial disruptions to critical business operations. Moreover, the inability of architecture leadership to effectively address any of these challenges exposes critical *software architecture capability weaknesses* that typically prolong technological disarray, which is hard to reverse.

Therefore, software architects ought to invoke their innate traits, such as curiosity, analytical skills, problem-solving capabilities, or decision-making talents to prevent *self-induced blindness*. The term *blindness* refers to incapacity to understand business imperatives, assess business and technological risks, or analyze the feasibility of applications and systems in production environments.

Self-induced social blindness is another symptom of ignoring innate skills. This ignorance typically relates to software architects who neglect to communicate effectively with business stakeholders and refuse to collaborate with IT partners.

Software architects who focus on trivial problems, promote unimportant agendas, and underutilize their innate talents fail to fulfill strategic organizational goals. Consequently, organizations tend to abolish their positions because they fail to demonstrate business or technological value. Similarly, architecture organizations cease to exist if they fail to provide effective remedies to business problems. And management is displaced if it does not show strong leadership.

CONCEPT Unutilized innate talents can result in ineffective leadership, failure of imagination, and procrastination that delays preventive measures to promptly address looming risks. These deficiencies only introduce grave consequences to business and technical operations.

Employ Chief Innate Talents to Become an Effective Software Architect

The innate talents discussed in the sections that follow are possible to learn and develop throughout a professional career. Bottom line: there is nothing that can't be honed, studied, and practiced. Be aware that there are umpteen training aids, classes, and literature that can improve the innate skills that are desperately needed to provide potent organizational solutions.

Inadequate imagination, for example, could hinder the capabilities to provide effective design blueprints to solve business challenges. In the same fashion, creativity is another talent that is extremely valuable for accomplishing software architecture missions. Underutilized similar innate traits typically yield ineffective, mediocre, and in many cases impractical organizational solutions.

The four sections that follow introduce the most necessary innate talents that a software architect must possess. Again, these skills can be developed and improved during a career life span.

- The power of creativity
- The potency of imagination
- Software design aesthetic
- Curiosity attributes

The Power of Creativity

It's hard to imagine a successful technological environment chartered to offer solutions to remediate business challenges that does not promote creative thinking. A technological culture must then promote innovation by galvanizing staff to devise new ideas, propose alternatives to existing solutions, and open a dialogue for generating new possibilities.

An organization's culture that is bogged down by conservative ideas and that expects the "right" approach to solve enterprise problems typically shows signs of technological stagnation. And technological stagnation is a byproduct of cultural conformity that in many cases promotes fear that suppresses creativity. On the contrary, successful businesses acknowledge that there are no "right" answers to organizational problems, that multicultural and diverse dialogue only propel technological innovation, and that the best solutions to business risks do not stem from ideologies that censor or curb the appetite and enthusiasm for change.

The Benefits of Unleashing Software Architecture Creativity

Software architects ought to be working in a work environment that is willing to bear the costs and risks of technological experiments, accepts the consequences of implementation errors, and agrees to shoulder the consequences of deploying ill-designed applications to production. Obviously, these risks should be addressed in a timely manner to carry on business operations.

In essence, software architects typically thrive under leadership that recognizes the benefits of creativity and keenly acknowledges that instant success is improbable. Executives who are tolerant of software architecture failure in the interest of promoting design innovation characteristically benefit from effective technological modernization.

Software architects who stifle creativity because of the fear of failure typically promote technological development inertia. Fear of failure endangers creative thinking. Fear of failure provokes procrastination that gives rise to technological modernization paralysis. Fear of failure strengthens conformity to old ideas that never contribute to business innovation.

Unleash the Power of Software Architecture Creativity

Table 5.1 offers methods to enhance creativity when providing solutions to organizational challenges. It's the software architects' responsibility not only to diversify solutions to facilitate business growth but also to continuously develop creativity traits during their career.

Table 5.1: Guidance to Boost Software Architecture Creativity

CREATIVITY ENHANCERS	EXPLANATION
Consider a diversity of software architecture solution alternatives	Devise a number of solutions to solve a business or technological challenge. These choices enable the selection of the best design approach and increase the rate of software development success.
Experiment to increase the chance of software architecture success	Obviously, experiments can be pursued in preproduction environments. But there is no guarantee that these solutions would work in production. Despite the risk of ill-designed implementations, experiments typically increase the odds of software architecture success and enhance the learning experience.
Demonstrate social flexibility when providing software architecture solutions	Communicate with stakeholders, get advice from co-workers, and listen to others' concerns to learn more about their particular business and technological challenges and imperatives.

Continues

Table 5.1 (*continued*)

CREATIVITY ENHANCERS	EXPLANATION
Never say "no" before analyzing new ideas	Do not reject offhand any concept or idea proposed to resolve business or technical issues. Stay open even to the most improbable and unfeasible ideas. Employ analytical talents to explore opportunities rather than filter them.
Explore business growth opportunities and possibilities	Business growth should be one of the leading drivers when proposing software design solutions. Keep in mind that creative and effective technological solutions tend to increase business opportunities and exceed consumers' expectations.
Do not reemploy failed or outmoded technological solutions	Be attentive to environment evolution and technological trends. Shy away from proposing software architecture solutions that have failed or were popular for legacy implementations. Be attuned to industry developments and never stop learning about advanced solutions.
Always ask the "why," "what," "when," and "where" questions to promote creative solutions and generate more ideas	Ask a variety of questions to explore creative opportunities. For example: Why is this solution needed? What is its business contribution? What is the problem domain that the solution intends to solve? Why now? When will the solution be deployed to production?
Apply many usages to a single software implementation	There is not much sense in designing a software solution that cannot be used for multiple purposes. For example, an enterprise middleware solution can provide a myriad of functions, such as business orchestration, message routing, security enforcement, and more.
Combine ideas and concepts to create powerful software architecture solutions	Synthesizing multiple ideas and concepts typically renders multifaceted software architecture solutions that provide potent remedies to organizational problems.
Break conservative barriers: Instigate change	Promote business and technological change: devise new software design and development approaches, methodologies, technologies, applications, systems, and services.
Diversify architecture investments to reduce business risks	Support organizational investments in a wide range of software architecture projects, products, platforms, infrastructure, and production environments to enhance business capabilities.
Combine sources to facilitate a creative software architecture solution	Any design solution should combine multiple sources of data, protocols, interfaces, design and development tools, deployment platforms, and more.
Repurpose software implementations	Design software that can be used to offer different solutions for different problems.

CREATIVITY ENHANCERS	EXPLANATION
Reuse implementations	Avoid functionality redundancy by utilizing existing software rather than building or acquiring new products.
Invent software that has never existed before	There is no limit to software invention and innovation. Keep the ideas emerging to enhance production environments. Software is not just source code. It should be perceived as the embodiment of creativity, as a vehicle for growing the business.
Use convergent and divergent thinking to boost software architecture creativity	In the context of software architecture, convergent thinking is about centering on an accurately defined solution to a problem. In contrast, divergent thinking is a creative approach to solve a problem by devising multiple solutions to a single business or technological challenge. Use both convergent and divergent thinking to increase software architecture creativity.
Come up with alternative solutions to legacy implementations	Technological trends call for replacing legacy implementations with advanced software architecture solutions.
Unleash the power of imagination	Imagination boosts creativity. Software architects who can harness the power of their imagination possess the capability to visualize and/or conceptualize innovative software implementations and environments (the next section outlines the benefits of imagination).
Expand technological knowledge to increase software architecture creativity	Enhanced technical, business, and social knowledge always improve software architecture solutions.

The Potency of Imagination

One of the most powerful traits that propels technological innovation and business development is imagination. The faculty of envisioning a different world, or an alternate reality; the ability to visualize images that do not exist; and the capability to form new ideas or concepts that are not perceived by the senses can play pivotal roles in organizational transformation.

Moreover, in its purest form, imagination renders mental constructs (intangible ideas and concepts) that over time can be transformed into concrete software implementations. Consequently, software architects who are able to effectively mobilize the power of imagination are characteristically capable of devising groundbreaking design of applications, systems, and environments that immensely promote the business.

But what does imagination entail? What type of capabilities or personal characteristics do imaginative software architects possess? They are typically motivated, curious, and out-of-the-box thinkers; they are able to create new realities and promote business and technological change; and they are disposed to originating different worlds. Otherwise stated, imaginative software architects are capable of providing unique software solutions that can make a big impact on organizational culture, consumer behavior, and the way the enterprise does business.

Imagination must render software design that embodies the principles of aesthetics, such as beauty, completeness, balance, and good taste. Namely, software architecture is not only driven by science—it's also a branch of art that must be expansive enough to drive consumer satisfaction and promote business. Aesthetics innate skills are discussed in the section, "Design Aesthetic."

The Benefits of Harnessing Imagination

To provide creative software design solutions, an imaginative software architect is commonly engaged in an experimental and to some extent risk-taking process that ultimately may contribute to technological innovation. In other words, the power of imagination facilitates original design solutions that result in cutting-edge applications and systems.

But imagination not only facilitates superior design solutions; it can also benefit astute software architecture decision-making when it comes to development, deployment, and integration of products in production. This may entail the establishment of innovative software delivery and deployment approaches; employment of creative software integration and federation patterns; or adoption of advanced infrastructure and security platforms.

In addition, imagination can be employed to foster fruitful professional partnerships with business and IT stakeholders despite disagreements between the collaborating parties. It's all about unleashing the imagination to better negotiate and compromise on disputed strategies. Therefore, harnessing the power of imagination to embrace interorganizational social relationships is vital to promoting software architecture visions. Without such alliances, software architects are typically unable to establish meaningful policies, best practices, and standards vital to organizational culture.

Conservative concepts and habits always impede imagination. Software architects who resist change and are protective of archaic technologies may drag down organizational progress. The lack of software architecture imagination, therefore, yields mediocre business products that never fully satisfy clients. The absence of imagination is noticeable in malfunctioning production environments where services and applications are not integrated properly. And average business performance is typically due to the dearth of software design and technological ideas.

Unleash the Power of Imagination

One of the most intriguing processes that takes place during the product development life cycle is the origination of concepts and ideas that are largely driven by imagination. Obviously, this conceptual process leads to tangible software executables, such as services, applications, and systems that are deployed later to production. Simply put, imagination generates concepts and ideas that in time become reality. And without the thrust of imagination, business and technological solutions tend not to fully satisfy organizational imperatives.

This discussion emphasizes the need for unleashing the power of imagination to be able to propose state-of-the-art design blueprints. Without harnessing the might of imagination, for example, software integration may not entirely utilize advanced infrastructure capabilities. Moreover, the lack of imagination characteristically contributes to vulnerabilities of software products that are vulnerable to cybersecurity attacks.

Imagination is an innate talent that can be developed, honed, and enhanced during a career. And there is nothing that can stop a software architect from amplifying and stimulating the inner strength of imagination. Table 5.2 introduces drivers that unleash the power of imagination to effectively meet business and technological requirements.

Table 5.2: Chief Software Architecture Imagination Boosters

IMAGINATION DRIVER	EXPLANATION
Be playful but take things seriously	Playfulness is a mental state that brings joy and satisfaction to software architects while fulfilling their duties. This state also promotes the creation of ideas that can break down technological barriers. But being playful does not mean brushing aside software design milestones and goals.
Do not filter out bold ideas and concepts	Accept a diversity of software architecture ideas and innovative implementations. Embrace technological possibilities rather than attempting to narrow the array of audacious solutions.
Avoid stereotyping and prejudgment	Be open-minded. Do not fall prey to unconscious biases, preconceived notions, and unproved opinions about technologies and software architecture approaches. Assess first their feasibility and actual contribution to business imperatives.
Become a daydreamer	Daydreaming is a mental state that stimulates mind wandering and thoughts about personal hopes and wishes. These are aspirations and fantasies about fulfilling hypothetical goals that do not exist in reality. Software architects should recognize the power of daydreaming that contributes to the establishment of groundbreaking applications and systems.

Continues

Table 5.2 (*continued*)

IMAGINATION DRIVER	EXPLANATION
Trust intuition	Learn to trust your gut feelings when it comes to negotiating solutions and establishing partnerships with business stakeholders, vendors, and consumers.
Develop an appetite for experiences	Every software architecture project or initiative should be regarded as an exciting experience in pursuit of a business solution. Strive for technological experiences that can help hone software architecture capabilities.
Be rebellious and conservative in the face of change	Rebellion promotes business and technological change. Conversely, a conservative approach to managing change instills practicality and order during organizational transformation
Be flexible	To successfully promote software architecture agendas, be flexible. Compromise on software design goals. Negotiate wisely with stakeholders and IT partners on business and technical requirements. Fulfill your dreams by being flexible.
Claim personal space and time to work independently, but at the same time collaborate with others	Imaginative software design and integration solutions are typically created in isolation. In contrast, to be able to effectively rise to business and technological challenges, collaboration with partners is highly recommended. Therefore, there is nothing wrong with being extroverted and introverted at the very same time.
Take risks	Accept risk-taking as a part of every software design and architecture implementation.
Generalize solutions but be thorough	Address a wide range of organizational challenges by providing a broad scope of technological remedies. At the same time, adopt systematic approaches and do not overlook software design and implementation details.
Ambition, passion, and enthusiasm are imagination boosters	Ambition, passion, and enthusiasm boost imagination to extreme limits because they motivate software architects to provide creative and potent software solutions.
Ask challenging questions	Imagination flourishes when asking the hard questions about design solutions, such as practicality of applications and systems, business value, cost of ownership, and the price of implementation maintainability.
Shake up the status quo	Do not always accept traditional or archaic software architecture approaches and design solutions. Support technological transformation; employ innovative software architecture styles and design patterns; and devise advanced software development best practices.
Reject habits	Embrace new experiences by rejecting old habits. Be willing to rethink software architecture strategies and solutions.

IMAGINATION DRIVER	EXPLANATION
Focus on storytelling	Employ storytelling skills to promote ideas and projects: develop user and business stories to facilitate the development of software implementations; come up with use cases to assess feasibility of applications and systems.
Battle resistance to innovation and transformation	Pick the right organizational battles and fight resistance to business and technological change.
Use procrastination as a strategic device	Developing new ideas, concepts, vision, and strategies for software architecture should not be considered procrastination.
Learn how to connect the dots	Imaginative, astute, and advanced software designs tend to connect the dots of multiple sources of information and data. These may include multiple strategies, design approaches, visions, business processes, and best practices and standards.
Understand success patterns and models	Always copy success patterns and models to minimize expenditure and accelerate time to market. Utilize the power of creativity to borrow successful concepts and software design.
Naivete is only a plus	Frequently, courageous or audacious business solutions are driven by naivete.
Be spontaneous and also deliberate	Support spontaneous software architecture ideas that spur ingenious business products. But also stay on track with project milestones and goals.
Employ reasoning but do not abandon emotional involvement with projects	Software architecture duties call for analytical talents to provide solutions. But this process should not only include logical reasoning. Therefore, all software architecture offerings should involve emotional aspects that can balance the outcome of software development projects.
Be a nonconformist	Do not conform to old ideas, outdated concepts, and archaic software architecture dogmas if business and technical requirements call for innovative applications and systems.
Be courageous enough to fail	The fear to experiment with advanced software architecture ideas and implementations inhibits technological change.
Utilize imagination to devise applications, systems, and environments that do not exist	The introduction of software implementations that are not currently available to consumers is a sign of software architecture maturity.

Continues

Table 5.2 (*continued*)

IMAGINATION DRIVER	EXPLANATION
Unleash the imagination power that embodies all human senses	Software architecture duties call for the involvement of all human senses to promote exceptional software implementations.
Use the potency of the imagination to build aesthetic software applications and systems	Software architecture is not only about providing adequate technological solutions; it's also about involving artistic, tasteful, and aesthetic software design skills to meet users' visual satisfaction.

Software Design Aesthetic

Innate artistic skills encompass a large number of visual and nonvisual self-expressions that we use to convey feelings and depict humans' conditions. We rely on our senses to view the world in the way we choose; make aesthetic decisions to improve our lifestyle; and better communicate with friends, family, and coworkers. These unique talents help us to promote ideas, present ourselves to the outside world, and even advance our careers. The *artistic* means to illustrate our thoughts and feelings by creating new realities that are indeed limitless. And the flair for inventing things that do not exist is indeed ingenious.

Employing artistic talents, no matter in which field or occupation, is affiliated with the science of aesthetics. Architects characteristically use these innate expressive skills to generate ideas, develop concepts, and create software implementations that do not exist. Moreover, the development process of modern applications and systems calls for sensitivity to colors, shapes, structures, and space. But software construction is not only about the creation of visual formations. Building trailblazing business products must also involve the senses of sound, smell, taste, and touch to enrich the consumer experience.

Technical Proficiency and Aesthetic Talents Drive Software Design

To be able to offer practical design blueprints for developers, integrators, and operations personnel, software architects must demonstrate solid technical knowledge. Technical aptitude is then clearly a necessary skill employed to devise applications and systems, to promote technological innovation, and to foster software architecture strategies.

However, software architects who are driven only by their technical capabilities without employing aesthetic talents typically produce mediocre products. Merely satisfying business imperatives is not enough. The converse is also true: software architects who are primarily driven by their artistic talents are incapable of devising compelling and effective software architecture solutions.

The best business products on the market are those that have been architected by brilliant minds. These software implementations are not only innovative; they make sense, they are tasteful, they are easy to use, they perform well, they are intuitive, they please the eye, and they are simply beautiful. The rule of thumb then suggests that to achieve this ideal, the marriage of the two—aesthetic and technical proficiency—is essential for delivering potent business and technological solutions.

The Chief Contribution of Design Aesthetic Talents to Software Architecture

Throughout the history of computing, it has become clear that aesthetic talents contribute to software design solutions that exceed expectations and provide enormous business value. To understand why these aesthetic traits typically yield software products beyond the call of duty, it's necessary to recognize what they actually entail. Is it only about the ability to create impressive graphical user interfaces? Are these talents only about using striking color schemes and astounding images to embellish web pages? Are they only about embedding pretty buttons, drop-down boxes, and checkboxes?

Design aesthetic skills are not only about the visual presentation of applications or systems. They reach beyond the simplistic notion of what is perceived as beautiful or elegant. It's not always about what the naked eye observes. So, what are software design aesthetic talents all about?

In a general sense, these unique skills represent the personal wisdom of a software architect who understands software concepts, software structures and composition, software behavior, software relationship, information flow, and design patterns. But it's not only about understanding.

CONCEPT   It's about the ability to arrange software components in certain hierarchies, compositions, distributed formations, and patterns; the capability to position the software across production environments; the knack to orchestrate and schedule business transactions between software components; and the ability to establish communication between applications and systems.

When employing design aesthetic skills, an architect's job is then to strike the balance between the possible and the probable—the feasible and what cannot be accomplished—including all that pertains to design attributes such as timing, rhythm, synchronization, quantities, qualities, variety, dimension, and proportions.

Consider Table 5.3, which includes proposed areas of study and improvement to facilitate the delivery of effective business and technological solutions. Moreover, the items in this list accentuate the vital abilities that software architects ought to be aware of and possess.

It's never too late to develop such proficiencies. Persistence always pays off.

Table 5.3: Aesthetic Aspects of Software Design

DESIGN AESTHETIC ASPECTS	EXPLANATION
Aesthetic patterns	These patterns are predefined sets of aesthetic solutions that software architects can reapply when devising design solutions. The patterns promote architecture balance between software granularity levels, footprint, response time, taste, rhythm, appeal, composition, presentation, and more. In other words, the term *balance* refers to the state of software equilibrium between the too fast and too slow, the too big and too small, the too complex and too simple, etc.
Transaction progress and timing	During the design process, the software architect's ability to assess the performance of information exchange between software assets is an aesthetic skill.
Design evolution	Akin to an artist who paints a picture, a software architect should be aware that software design is an ongoing process, during which layers, tiers, and processes are being added gradually over time.
Design agility	The capability to visualize and design a nimble application whose behavior, structure, and presentation are able to support business or technological change.
Balance of design good taste	Design good taste is about the aspects that drive the development of applications and systems. Good taste in this context refers to discerning judgment about software usage, feasibility, business value, performance, presentation, and quality of information. It's all about the balance between too much or too little, too slow or too fast, too colorful or too conservative.
Good eye for design decisions	The capability to recognize good software design qualities and understand the contribution of technologies to a solution is a design aesthetic trait that ought to be developed during a professional career.
Design intuition	The ability to picture software design solutions without reasoning or prior analysis and experience.

DESIGN AESTHETIC ASPECTS	EXPLANATION
Design appeal	Software architects ought to understand consumers' needs, habits, behaviors, and preferences when designing applications and systems. Therefore, design aesthetic talents typically drive software architecture decisions that refer to client interaction, application performance, intuitive user interfaces, presentation of multimedia, and satisfactory content.
Distance and geography	Distance and geography are terms used to depict the manner by which software implementations, such as applications, are being distributed in a production environment. Software can also be dispersed across regions, countries, and even continents. Software architects ought to envision these distributions by devising proper design patterns. They should then utilize their design aesthetic skills when they are required to strike the balance between practical and unreasonable software distribution.
Design proportions	Design proportions pertain to the association between two or more software implementations, such as services and applications. This relationship is about the aesthetic comparisons of software structures, patterns, shapes, granularity, size, footprint, qualities, and attributes.
Design aesthetic perspectives	The ability to picture software from different points of view is a powerful design aesthetic trait. These perspectives enable architects to conceive software products from different angles, such as presentation (shapes, colors, fonts, images, etc.), functionality, appeal, usage, software structures, and software components. The ability to provide design blueprints that depict how these perspectives work together is an art in itself.
Hierarchies	Architects utilize aesthetic skills to devise software hierarchical formations, such as layered structures, parent and child component dependencies, and data categories and subcategories. These formations are depicted along with their attributes, behavior, or functionality in design blueprints.
Relationships	Being able to visualize sensible relationships and interfaces between software assets without rendering a complex architecture ecosystem is a design aesthetic skill that addresses challenges such as redundancy of message exchange or duplicate functionality.

Continues

Table 5.3 (*continued*)

DESIGN AESTHETIC ASPECTS	EXPLANATION
Layers and tiers	Software design aesthetic skills enable architects to visualize and arrange software modules or components in layers. This talent is also employed to design architecture that supports tiers in which applications and systems are distributed in a production environment or dispersed over different geographical locations.
Innovative software structures and distributed formations	Layers and tiers are traditional software architecture structures and distributed formations. Nowadays, to meet demanding business requirements, it's common for software architects to be called upon to devise software design that depicts innovative structures and formations. Creativity, imagination, and design aesthetic talents are the chief drivers that promote state-of-the-art software implementations.
Abstractions	In essence, ideas and concepts are abstractions that must materialize into tangible solutions. Aesthetic talents then must drive this process from its inception by making design decisions about software structures, behavior, functionality, and presentation.
Architecture dimensions	Architecture dimensions visualize three fundamental views of software: height, depth, and length (refer to Chapter 7 Structural Construction of Software Implementations in Multidimensional Environments for the discussion about 3D software design).
Software behavior	Some of the most important aspects of software behavior are about interaction with consumers, data processing, presentation of information, and communication with other software implementations. The ability to visualize and orchestrate software behavior is an important aesthetic skill that can render potent solutions.
Data and information flow	Data flows on a network in many visual patterns, such as star, tree, bus, and ring. To design such traffic flows, software architects must not only possess technical talents, but also aesthetic skills to drive architecture simplicity, optimize performance, and increase efficiency of transactions.
Connect the design dots	Most of the design aesthetic skills must be driven by sources of organizational and industry information that can contribute to effective architecture solutions. This vital data typically comes from business requirements, business and software architecture strategies, consumers' needs, and technological capabilities.

DESIGN AESTHETIC ASPECTS	EXPLANATION
Design composition	Composition is one of the most important aspects that shape artistic work, such as paintings, drawings, and sculpture. Design composition is an aesthetic skill that enables software architects to visualize abstractions. Design and integration patterns, for example, are visualizations of software structures and dependencies that are visible in production.
Software elasticity	Architects should possess the ability to envision and design software formations and functionality that can be scaled, contracted, or expanded in response to fluctuations in consumer demand, market trends, business transformation, or technical evolution.

Curiosity Attributes

Curiosity is an innate quality, often driven by an inquisitive appetite for gathering information about unfamiliar events and facts. This study and observation process is naturally prompted to rationalize the unknown, out of the ordinary, or unconventional. Moreover, curiosity is not always triggered because of survival concerns or affiliated anxieties. It's also set off to restore lucid reasoning and logical thinking to avoid confusion, uncertainty, and chaos.

Curiosity increases the motivation to study, examine, explore, and question the environment, conditions, and evolution of obscure subjects or unclear circumstances. Furthermore, curiosity qualities drive the necessity for knowledge acquisition. Curiosity also fosters cultural, social, and technological development. Without such an innate attribute, individual and social progression would not make significant headway. Without curiosity drivers, business and technological goals would be difficult to fulfill and stagnation would be the current state of affairs without the craving for exploration, adventure, and change.

Curiosity is a multifaceted innate attribute that not only drives the need for examination of occurring events or facts. Curiosity is also about the desire to understand individual, social, cultural, and technological behaviors. This may include comprehending evolution and the growth of entities, such as communities, businesses, living environments, and social landscapes. The ability to trace progression and understand behavioral trends is attributed to humans' curiosity.

The Contribution of Curiosity to Software Architecture

Curiosity drives the situational awareness of business and technological trends. Simply put, studying and monitoring the evolution of business and technological transformation are attributed to the drive of professional curiosity. Moreover, the capability to mitigate business and technological risks, protect organizations from business threats, save production environments from applications and system failure, and offer effective software architecture strategies are all the outcomes of meticulous studies and incessant observation.

Curiosity drives the necessity for personal knowledge acquisition. Gaining information is indeed a potent power that contributes to operational balance of applications and systems in production. The term *operational balance* refers to smooth execution of business transactions. It pertains to software design that strengthens business continuity and is related to efficient integration of software services that satisfy consumers' imperatives.

> **CONCEPT**   Software architecture decision-making that is not based on systematic knowledge acquisition characteristically contributes to an unbalanced production environment.

The arsenal of vehicles employed by organizational leaders to promote culture that ultimately influences behavioral change of staff and consumers is vast. Software architects, too, have the clout to foster change by devising frameworks that focus on best practices, standards, and policies. These frameworks offer design principles, software development standards, and deployment and integration best practices of applications and systems in production.

> **CONCEPT**   Curiosity is the agent of organizational culture promotion and behavioral change. Curiosity drives business transformation and technological innovation. Curiosity contributes to the software architecture industry, computer science, software development methodologies, and enterprise strategies.

The Influencing Facets of Curiosity on Software Architecture Practices

Without the influence of curiosity on software architecture, technological stagnation would more likely dominate the progress, evolution, and development of enterprise business. The curiosity inducing aspects, such as the urge to explore, examine, diagnose, and infer galvanize technologists to devise new ideas and concepts that lead to innovative software implementations. So, can humans' innate curiosity attributes be further developed to. . .

- Maximize creativity and imagination?
- Accelerate studies?
- Modernize software design approaches?
- Improve the ways newly acquired knowledge is applied to provide potent business and technological solutions?

The answer to these questions is a resounding "yes." There is nothing that cannot be learned, honed, or practiced. The primary challenge, however, is to increase the awareness that curiosity is a fundamental contributor to the duties of software architects. Therefore, they must be continuously informed. They must communicate with others to gain knowledge. They must be socially active to understand business challenges. They must keep track of new technologies. And they must understand how to employ their discoveries for the benefit of organizations.

Table 5.4 summarizes the chief aspects that software architects ought to be aware of when fulfilling their software design duties.

Table 5.4: Influencing Aspects of Curiosity

CURIOSITY ASPECT	EXPLANATION
Types of curiosity	These are intellectual, social, personal, and collective curiosity types that refer to organizational governance, business, and technological aspects. These types render discovery of enterprise conflicts, implementation errors, ill-designed applications and systems, and more.
Desire to know	Desire for information to accelerate business and technological progress.
Inquisitive interest and thinking	Exploring organizational challenges, people's concerns, technical problems, and business impediments.
Knowledge acquisition	Continuous appetite for gathering business and technical knowledge to be employed for software architecture problem-solving and decision-making.
Learning process	Embrace learning methods to increase exposure to information that can contribute to understanding of production environments and operations.
Learning by listening to others	Learning about concerns and ideas from consumers, business, IT stakeholders, and peers.
Types of knowledge	There is no limit to the types of knowledge software architects ought to gain. This may include information about business organizations, leveraged technology, industry trends, organizational governance problems and solutions, and business imperatives.
Source of knowledge	The sources of information gathering may include books, articles, white papers, press releases, social media, videos, news, conferences, magazines, and more.

Continues

Table 5.4 (*continued*)

CURIOSITY ASPECT	EXPLANATION
Application of knowledge	Acquiring knowledge just for the sake of hoarding information is not a practical practice. Software architects must adopt methods for applying knowledge to solve organizational problems. These approaches may include action plans and long-term or short-term objectives to apply the acquired knowledge.
Observation	Stay tuned to business problems and events, performance of applications and systems, technical incidents, business transformation, evolution of technologies, and more.
Exploratory behavior	Adopt a fact-finding and investigative behavior to understand the challenges that software design is facing when providing architecture solutions. For example, explore behavior of business and IT partners to understand how they operate. Examine applications and systems behaviors in production. Study how software architecture affects organizational change, culture, and behavior of consumers.
Personal development	Curiosity contributes not only to organizational development and progress; it can also enhance professional experiences and careers.
Investigatory responses to events	Business problems, technological challenges, consumer demands, and market trends typically trigger investigatory responses that lead to powerful business and technical solutions.
Questions driven by curiosity	Always ask challenging questions to learn about business problems, technical difficulties, malfunctioning software, ill-designed systems, and more.
Curiosity range	The range of curiosity is boundless. Never stop examining unfamiliar occurrences, facts, and behaviors of business and technical aspects. The exploratory effort should cover software architecture application levels up to the enterprise level.
Business and technological situational awareness	Keep track of events that will require software architecture response: development, evolution, and progression of events, ideas, implementations, and strategize how to respond to them.
Risk mitigation	The power of software architects' inquisitive behavior can help mitigate business and technological risks.

CURIOSITY ASPECT	EXPLANATION
Desire for change	Curiosity is the agent of change. Find opportunities to promote and advocate business and technological change and transformation based on individual experience and knowledge.
Elicit ideas and concepts	Curiosity elicits ideas and concepts that play vital roles in providing potent software architecture solutions.

CHAPTER

6

Software Architecture Environment Construction

Software architects ought to broaden the scope of their responsibilities beyond application-level design. Their duties must also tackle the challenges that software is facing in a *software architecture environment*[1] deployed to a production ecosystem. In addition, consider requiring architects to monitor and control the impact of software behavior on a production landscape at large.

To accomplish these duties, employ the presented software architecture environment construction discipline, a field of expertise devised to offer business and technological integration solutions to address enterprise challenges. This discipline provides design methods, guidance, best practices, and governing laws to promote a balanced software architecture environment.

CONCEPT   Recall that the software architecture environment construction is a discipline devised to foster effective integration of applications and systems in a software architecture environment hosted in production.

---

[1] Not including hardware, a software architecture environment consists of software implementations, such as applications, services, or systems that software architects are commissioned to design, test, integrate, and control in production.

Benefits of the Software Architecture Environment Construction Discipline

The chief objective of the environment construction discipline is to equip software architects with design capabilities that will promote a balanced software architecture environment in production. Ultimately, this equilibrium, a sought-after goal, will contribute to business stability and continuity. To achieve this, the environment construction discipline calls for design activities that focus on a software architecture perspective and yet remain cognizant of the operational constraints in a hosting production environment.

Moreover, the emphasis here is on the behaviors of software implementations and their influences on the runtime environment to fulfill its *state of equilibrium*. The state of balance of a software architecture environment in production refers to a variety of conditions that enable software implementations to operate efficiently and without major disruptions. For example, a lack of computing resources may fail applications and keep systems from accomplishing their tasks. Absence of architecture elasticity is another reason for performance degradation of software products.

The sections that follow answer the fundamental questions that refer to the environment construction discipline. Note that these queries pertain to the task of designing a software architecture environment that is hosted by a production ecosystem:

- How do you construct a software architecture environment in production, and what is the devised environment construction life cycle?

- What should software architects focus on when deploying and integrating software implementations in production?

- How do you establish a balanced software architecture environment that maintains business and technological continuity?

- What are the influences of software behaviors on a production ecosystem?

- What are the governing laws of software architecture environment construction?

- What are the best practices guiding the software architecture environment construction?

Must Haves: Problem Statements and Requirements

When it comes to software design practices, there is nothing more essential than requirements. Therefore, software architects should not pursue a design effort without clear requirements. Any attempt to provide software architecture blueprints predicated on arbitrary emails, verbal communications, or speculations about business or technical imperatives will, more likely, bring about financial and technological failure.

> **CONCEPT** There is no defense against launching a software development project without understanding business imperatives, problems, and requirements. There is no defense against adopting commercial off-the-shelf (COTS) software products without understanding associated business and technological problems. There is no defense against allocating human resources and budgets for constructing applications and systems without defining milestones and goals.

This assertion seems logical and agreeable to most technologists. Nonetheless, some software architects tend to launch design projects that are not driven by an institutional product development life cycle that calls for problem analysis and requirements. The consequences of such irresponsible undertakings are typically grave. Uncontrolled budgets, unanticipated expenditure, and loss of revenue are only a few of the risks that a business might be forced to bear.

Never Start a Software Design Project Without Understanding the Problems

There are typically two types of problems that software architects are called upon to provide solutions for: business and technological. There is no limit to the array of business problems that an organization can be challenged with. Some of these problems are affiliated with the loss of market share, harsh competition, lack of effective business products, and even the failure to execute business strategies.

Moreover, software architects are chartered to offer solutions due to technical challenges. Some of these problems are related to malfunctioning applications and systems, lack of computing resources, improper software integration, and the inability to comply with software architecture strategies.

Never devise software design solutions in the absence of business or technical problem descriptions. A corresponding problem narrative document characteristically answers the following questions:

Problem definitions   What are the problems?

Reasons   What are the reasons for the problems that occur?

Criticality   Do the challenges introduce substantial risk to the enterprise? How critical are the problems?

Prioritization   Which problems ought to be resolved first?

Never Start a Software Design Project Without Requirements

The same guidance should be applied to a *lack of business or technical requirements*. Embarking on a software design effort in the absence of requirements is a shot in the dark—a wild goose chase that accomplishes nothing. Consequently, design blueprints that are not based on requirements fail to demonstrate business value. Software implementations based on these blueprints do not meet business imperatives and are ultimately stripped away from production.

Furthermore, business requirements should provide the justification for designing, developing, or acquiring applications or systems. For example, if a banking firm cannot successfully compete in its industry because it lacks retirement accounts, then the requirements must drive the corresponding software architecture and development initiatives.

In the same manner, if an organization experiences technological challenges, technical requirements must be issued before any software design effort begins. For instance, lack of computing resources, performance degradation, and inadequate security policies would require technical specifications before software architecture solutions are provided.

Software Architecture Structures

There are two types of software architecture structures that represent differing levels of implementation: *micro level* and *macro level*. The former is associated with a building block, a skeleton that represents the underpinning formation of a software implementation. The latter can be visualized as the fabric of a software architecture environment, in which software products communicate with each other to provide broader business and technical solutions.

The sections that follow elaborate on these two different software architecture structure levels:

Micro level   Software implementation level structures

Macro level   Software architecture environment structures

Micro Level: Multidimensional Structures of Software Implementations

At the micro level, a structure denotes a supporting frame of a software implementation, such as an application, a service, middleware, or a data repository. In this context, the term *structure* is analogous to a house's framing, assembled to provide the construction with structure. This framing is typically made of steel, concrete, and wood.

In the software architecture world, a micro-level software structure is designed to *hold together* all the components of a software implementation. Generally, it supports programming logic that executes business or technical processes. These operations are referred to as *software behavior*. Message exchange, information sharing, business transactions, computing resource consumption, and data persistence are examples of software behavior that drive business or technical solutions. Again, such software behavior is always reinforced by a software structure.

Figure 6.1 illustrates the micro-level software structure concept. It depicts a structure, a building block that internally supports the construction of an application. This structure holds together programming logic that executes business processes, user interface procedures, data persistence operations, and message exchange routines.

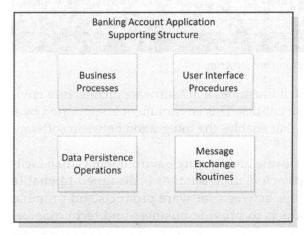

Figure 6.1: Micro-Level Supporting Software Structure Example

Note that Chapter 7 depicts the micro-level software structures as multidimensional formations: zero dimension, one dimension, two dimensions, and three dimensions. These geometrical building blocks can be used to support any programming logic, processes, services, or data.

Macro Level: 3D Software Architecture Environment Structure

A software architecture environment structure is a *3D geometrical and topological fabric* that hosts all deployed software implementations, such as applications, services, and systems. Moreover, this software architecture environment structure must be able to support the integration, interaction, and collaboration between its supported software implementations. To learn more about its topological and artificial intelligence (AI) capabilities, refer to the section "Software Architecture Environment: An Intelligent Topological Space."

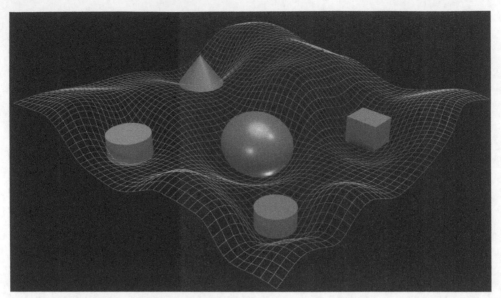

Figure 6.2: Software Architecture Environment Structure

Figure 6.2 depicts this notion. It illustrates a 3D software architecture environment with deployed software entities. This environment is supported by a geometrical structure—a fabric that enables the integration between software implementations.

Again, the integration of a software architecture environment is then facilitated by a *geometrical and topological structure* that is designed to enable communication and relationships between software products and promote collaboration of software products to provide business and technological solutions.

> **CONCEPT**   Recall that a software architecture environment structure is the 3D fabric that maintains a web of relationships between software implementations to foster collaborative solutions. The role of a software architect is then to construct balanced software architecture environments in production by leveraging the geometrical and topological attributes of their supporting structures.

Software Architecture Environment: Driven by an Uncontrolled Quantum Landscape Behavior

One of the most volatile technological landscapes is a software architecture environment that is hosted in a production ecosystem, in which stability and business continuity is never guaranteed. Not only are the behaviors of applications and systems unpredictable[2], but also the root cause of failure is often undetectable.

Moreover, the erratic nature of a software architecture environment is typically due to a growing number of evolutionary factors. Possibilities include technological modernization, continuous deployments, continuous integration, and even reoccurring modifications to software architecture.

In addition, malfunctioning or underperforming software implementations do not occur only by virtue of technological transformation. Gaps in architecture strategies, absence of effective methodologies to handle accelerating deployment pace, operational neglect, and management oversight are only a few of the reasons for deteriorating software architecture environments.

At the current time, there are, unfortunately, no effective approaches to remediating these shortcomings. Trial-and-error attempts to address business growth only add fuel to the fire. Speculative software architecture only exacerbates the already strained state of applications and systems. And a lack of professional and trained human resources further imperils the delivery of high-quality services to consumers.

Obviously, the expansion of software architecture environments is a sign of business and technological maturity. But as time goes by, the amassed technological stacks only add to architecture complexity, making it increasingly harder to maintain. Therefore, there is a vital imperative for addressing the growing deficiencies and limitations of a deployment site.

CONCEPT   There is also an essential need for minimizing unpredictable *quantum software behavior* in a software architecture environment.

Software Architecture Environment: An Intelligent Topological Space

The most intriguing aspects of a software architecture environment are the underpinning drivers that make software implementations work. That is, this environment that is supported by its geometrical structure enables applications and systems to exchange messages, disseminate information to consumers, distribute data across geographical boundaries, and more. These chief capabilities have been developed since the inception of computer science. To better understand the governing laws that propel such business and technical operations in a software architecture environment, it is important to study its driving qualities and attributes.

---

[2] System unpredicability draws an analogy between Heisenberg's uncertainty principle and production system behavior uncertainty: David Lindley, Uncertainty: Einstein, Heisenberg, Bohr, and the Struggle for the Soul of Science, Anchor Publishing, February 12, 2008.

One of the most powerful properties of a software architecture environment is the ability to treat software products as intelligent entities that can learn consumers' behaviors and work together to provide meaningful business or technical solutions. In other words, the software architecture environment regards software implementations as artificially intelligent decision-makers without the intervention of humans. This is certainly a unique and powerful *topological property* that a software architecture environment in production possesses.

Moreover, the ability to form social relationships that render integrated communities of software implementations is another topological property that drives operations in a software architecture environment. In other words, the ability to enable such social communication and AI behavior of software products is regarded as the ingenious topological property of a software architecture environment.

So, what are the factors that contribute to these software architecture environment topological properties?

- Traditional physical infrastructure that the hosting production landscape offers, such as servers and networking hardware
- Recent scientific research and developments that promote the utilization of AI hardware–based systems[3]
- Software architecture environment attributes granted at design-time by software architects

Software architects ought to leverage the power of design to boost the operational intelligence of a software architecture environment; employ the topological properties of the run-time environment to promote business growth; enable smart and efficient business transactions; and facilitate potent integration of software assets to enhance interactions between applications, services, and systems.

Refer to section "Software Architecture Environment Forces Drive Software Behavior" to learn how environmental forces can affect the operations of software implementations. In addition, the section "Software Architecture Environment Construction Life Cycle" offers design tools and methods to employ these environmental forces to balance a software architecture landscape.

Again, it's the software architects' duty to leverage these topological attributes when devising software integration design schemes. It's their responsibility to efficiently use the software architecture environment forces to promote a balanced architecture.

CONCEPT   A *topological space* is an integrated software architecture multidimensional environment driven by its topological attributes.

---

[3] AI hardware–based systems examples: https://research.ibm.com/blog/why-we-need-analog-AI-hardware or https://ieeexplore.ieee.org/stamp/stamp.jsp?tp=&arnumber=9057570

Deformation Aspects of a Multidimensional Software Architecture Environment

A software architecture environment continuously changes because of myriad reasons. Some of these reasons are related to business evolution and technological transformation and innovation. Others are related to ongoing maintenance and updates, such as continuous deployment (CD) and continuous integration (CI). Interactions between software implementations, consumption of computing resources, data growth, transaction volumes, and software behavior also impact a software architecture environment.

CONCEPT   The 3D software architecture environment constantly *deforms* when responding to these environmental changes or activities. When this deformation happens, the software architecture environment's dimensions and topology are modified as it reacts to business demands, technological imperatives, and software operations.

Improper integration, for example, that relies exceedingly on a centralized architecture style also impacts the dimensions of a software architecture environment. Furthermore, numerous other reasons cause a software architecture environment to buckle under the pressure of forces that operate in its space. Refer to the section "Software Architecture Environment Forces Drive Software Behavior" to learn more about software architecture attributes that impact a software architecture environment. Figure 6.3 illustrates a software architecture environment, depicted as a multidimensional geometrical formation that encompasses software products. The impact of these software implementations on the environment is noticeable by the dents they imprint on its foundations.

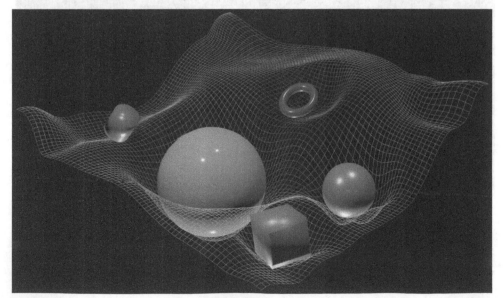

Figure 6.3: Software Architecture Environment Topological Space

Entanglement Effects in a Software Architecture Environment

Once applications, services, systems, or other software implementations are deployed to a software architecture environment, they begin to influence its topological space. As depicted in Figure 6.3, the dents that these software assets form in deployment go far beyond the influences of a confined and close vicinity. Not only does the deployed software consume the typically scarce supply of computing resources, but it can also put extreme strain on message exchange and information sharing with its peers. These runtime operation flaws are typically due to an unfit design of software integration and a correlation between autonomous software entities.

Message exchange, data distribution, and information sharing always affect interfacing software parties. It is critical to monitor these bidirectional influences carefully to understand integration consequences. Furthermore, no matter how far apart these software products are located from each other, they are *constantly entangled in a virtual or physical relationship that influence their behaviors*. Figure 6.4 represents a schematic depiction of the relationship between software entities in a software architecture environment.

Figure 6.4: Schematic Relationship of Software Entities in a Software Architecture Environment

However, the entanglement effect does not necessarily occur between software products that maintain tight (linked or physical) relationships. In other words, software entities that are not integrated or depend on each other can still be affected by the community of software products deployed to a software architecture environment.

Why does such an entanglement effect occur even when software entities do not associate directly? The reasons are affiliated chiefly with ill-designed software architecture computing space. Software integration and configuration failures, lack of intelligent deployment and monitoring utilities, improper architecture elasticity, and inadequate computing resources are only a few examples that negatively impact the equilibrium of software architecture environments. These environment design blunders only exacerbate the harsh competition of software implementaitons in the runtime landscape.

CONCEPT The inability to assess and mitigate the operational constraints in a software architecture environment as a whole is costly to organizations. Moreover, failure to evaluate the consequences of an ill-designed software architecture environment can introduce an irreversible business and technological calamity.

Software Architecture Environment Forces Drive Software Behavior

Software design principles and approaches typically *generate the forces* that can affect a runtime landscape of a software architecture environment. Arrangement of software formations, integration patterns, and information exchange schemes are only a few of the architecture aspects that produce these forces. So, what are these forces? How are they being generated? How do they impact software operations? What type of forces should a software architect be cognizant of? How should a software architect employ these forces to deliver solutions?

CONCEPT In simple terms, a software architecture force is an energy, power, pressure, wave, thrust, or drive generated by software runtime performance and behavior that can immensely affect operations in a software architecture environment.

Software architecture forces manifest themselves during message exchange, business transactions, consumption of computing resources, and other software runtime activities. These operations generate environmental pressures that can affect application performance, information sharing, data persistence, and more.

This section introduces four types of forces that dominate a software architecture environment. Software architects can leverage these forces to provide effective business and technological solutions.

Gravitational forces   A software architecture power granted to a centralized software implementation, such as a hub or middleware, to serve reusable services to consumers

Competing forces   A force that is employed by a software implementation to survive and compete against other products in a software architecture environment

Harmonizing forces   A force granted to software to control and coordinate operations in a software architecture environment

Disharmonizing forces   A force that does not promote environment harmonization in a software architecture environment

Finally, the strength of a software architecture force chiefly depends on organizational architecture best practices, standards, and policies. Architecture styles, architecture patterns, and design patterns also tend to influence the immensity of forces in a software architecture environment (refer to Chapter 9, "An Outline for Software Architecture Job Interview Questions," which discusses the differences between these styles and patterns). Moreover, the intensity of a software architecture force is measurable. For instance, data and message consumption can be calculable. Application and system response time can also be quantifiable. Network bandwidth utilization is another metric that can be assessed.

Probability Assessment of Software Operations and Behavior

As indicated, a software architecture force can be measured—just as application response time can be quantifiable. But this performance assessment can occur only after the software has been deployed to a software architecture environment. Any predictive models rendered by tools (currently being used by information technology [IT] organizations) merely illustrate *probable outcomes of software behavior*.

CONCEPT   These predictive modeling tools are driven by probability algorithms that cannot *precisely* foresee how a software implementation might operate and behave in a software architecture environment. And they are also unable to predict the quantum behavior of a computing space. Moreover, these modeling tools do not have the capacity to anticipate how a software architecture force will influence the topological space of a software architecture landscape.

Software Architecture Environment Positive and Negative Forces

Positive and negative forces may exist in the software architecture environment. The former is designed to balance a software architecture. The term *balanced architecture* depicts an environment in which applications, systems, and other software structures operate as designed. Namely, these software implementations do not cause severe outages, interrupt message exchange, or negatively impact the communication with their peers (refer to the section "Maintaining a Pragmatic Balance Between Competing Software Architecture Forces," which offers practical guidance for addressing the impact of negative software architecture forces).

Unfortunately, negative software architecture forces are in abundance. In fact, runtime environments are challenged constantly by negative energies that hamper the continuity of operations. For instance, the battle between applications to grab network bandwidth is a specific force generated because of improper employment of integration patterns. Similarly, a middleware platform may be under extreme pressure due to overwhelming transaction volumes.

CONCEPT   In this context, the ultimate objective of a software architect is to unleash positive environmental forces to promote business and technological solutions. In the absence of these unlocked energies, applications and systems would not be able to operate. And a software architecture environment would be incapable of promoting enterprise goals and strategies.

Software Architecture Environment Gravitational Forces

A software architecture gravitational force is a privileged power granted by design to a centralized software implementation, enabling it to integrate and connect distributed software products in a software architecture environment. The chief duty of this centralized implementation is to share information and exchange messages with its consuming applications, services, and systems. Therefore, an architecture style that relies on centralized software to exchange messages with its dependent consumers introduces gravitational forces in a runtime landscape.

A centralized software implementation, such as a message hub or middleware that serves consuming applications in a software architecture environment, possesses the properties of a software architecture gravitational force. Middleware is a message intercepting hub that features the quality of a gravitational force because it maintains a one-to-many type of association with its related consumers, such as applications and services. The well-known hub-and-spoke architecture pattern represents this concept. In this context, the hub is a message broker that resembles middleware functionality, designed to connect and integrate distributed software products.

But middleware alone does not embody the properties of a software architecture gravitational force. An enterprise-level application, such as employee benefits or customer contact information, also represents a gravitational force because of its close-fitting associations with related consumers, which depend on its exclusive services.

CONCEPT To sum up, centralized software implementations, such as message-oriented middleware (MOM), message hubs, message interceptors, message mediators, software intermediaries, gateways, central applications, and even load balancers possess the properties of a software architecture gravitational force. These implementations, typically employed by architects, integrate and connect distributed software products.

Figure 6.5 illustrates a schematic representation of two software hubs, presented by large spheres shown on opposite sides of the software architecture environment. They are surrounded by five linked dependent consumers (software implementations). This depiction shows how a topological space is affected by the gravitational forces of the central software hubs. As is apparent, the dent that the hubs imprint on the software architecture environment geometry deforms the entire runtime landscape. In other words, the illustration visualizes how central software entities may affect operations in a deployment environment.

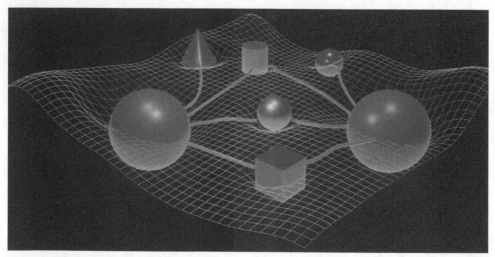

Figure 6.5: Impact Representation by Centralized Software Hubs on a Software Architecture Environment

The Impetus for Granting Software Architecture Gravitational Powers to Software Implementations

The centralization notion of software architecture grows out of design necessity, driven by best practices devised to promote software reuse, elimination of software redundancy, reduction of duplicate business processes, and more. For example, the term *design necessity* may also pertain to technical requirements that call for isolation or protection of organizational software assets, such as data or applications, from direct consumers' access. To address this design necessity, software architects typically employ centralized message interceptor hubs, such as message-oriented middleware (MOM) platforms, data access brokers, and gateways. In essence, by positioning any of these software intermediaries in central deployment locations they are granted gravitational powers.

Typically, management of a central software hub reduces runtime maintenance costs—but not without challenges. Consider these runtime difficulties: a hub may buckle under the pressure of overwhelming consumer demand for data. Moreover, inadequate supporting infrastructure to sustain hub operations may yield software performance degradation. These misfortunes are generally affiliated with a lack of computing capacity, ineffective software deployment and integration, and other software architecture deficiencies.

Software Architecture Gravitational Force Intensity

The strength of a software architecture gravitational force depends on the following key factors that software architects should be aware of:

- The more consuming applications and services utilize a centralized software hub's offering, the stronger its gravitational force.

- The strength of a software architecture's gravitational force is proportional to the size of data that its consumers demand. The higher the demand, the stronger the gravitational force of a centralized software hub.

The Cost of Unbalanced Software Architecture Environment Gravitational Forces

A centralized software hub, granted an excessive software architecture gravitational force, typically causes operation disruptions to business processes in a software architecture environment. Put differently, an extremely intense gravitational force is regarded as unbalanced. And it must be controlled and optimized to preserve the environment's equilibrium. In this context, the term *environment equilibrium* refers to a runtime landscape in which software architecture gravitational forces do not overwhelm the operating landscape. Namely, the community of software implementations is not being negatively affected by a centralized architecture style.

CONCEPT The dents imprinted by centralized software hubs on a software architecture environment's geometrical formation may impact many operational aspects, such as computing capacity consumption and performance.

The consequences of an unbalanced software architecture that unleashes extreme gravitational forces are grave and are discussed in more detail in the sections that follow in the coming pages.

- A centralized software entity that possesses an uncontrolled gravitational force tends to grab technological attention from issues with higher priority.

- The cost of maintaining software products with high-intensity gravitational forces outweigh its technological benefits.

- Software implementations with extreme gravitational forces contribute to software architecture complexity that is hard to manage.

Competing Software Architecture Environment Forces

To survive in a software architecture environment, applications and systems must be given satisfactory conditions to operate successfully. The term *satisfactory conditions* alludes to a myriad of technical requirements that enable software implementations to provide efficient solutions without being involuntarily interrupted, suppressed, impeded, or halted.

Computing resources is one of the leading environment conditions that must meet the operational requirements of a software product. For example, the lack of network bandwidth capacity or shortage of data storage introduces challenges to the execution of business and technical processes.

But the absence of adequate computing resources is only a single item in a long list of necessary conditions required by software implementations to operate at their fullest capacity. Suitable software scalability, efficient integration, architecture elasticity, disaster recovery, high availability, and adequate software configurations are also some of the most vital compulsory conditions that must be satisfied to optimize the operations of software products.

CONCEPT   As it becomes apparent, the community of software products must always survive in an environment in which the rising demands for computing resources and architecture excellence can strengthen their endurance capacity.

Software Architecture Environment: A Survival Game Space

There are concealed or noticeable survival contexts that take place between various software implementations in a software architecture environment. Evidently, not all software products possess the same capability to survive and thrive in a runtime landscape. Some are well-designed and given the technical conditions to expand their operations. They are nimble enough to withstand high transaction volumes. They are scaled properly to evade server outages. They are seldom interrupted. And the data that they aggregate is rarely lost. These software implementations are typically winning the environment survival game.

In contrast, software entities that are ill-designed tend to fail. They suffer performance degradation. They are slow to respond to consumers' requests. They are unable to recover after cybersecurity attacks. And they are highly susceptible to extreme fluctuation in data transmission volumes. These software entities are typically losing the environment survival game.

These two, the well-designed and the ill-designed software products, are not given an equal opportunity to survive in a software architecture environment. In other words, they are not assigned equal software architecture capabilities to compete in a runtime landscape. The software products with stronger competing powers can grab more computing resources to endure the competition, while the weaker ones typically succumb to resource starvation. Moreover, the stronger ones can leverage their superb design capabilities, while the losers do not possess adequate architecture powers.

CONCEPT   In an ill-designed software architecture environment, there is typically a finite quantity of computing resources. In this constrained runtime ecosystem, the harsh competition for survival is won only by superior software products that overcome the inferior ones because of the inequality in software architecture capabilities. From another perspective, applying here the game theory rule to a deficient design of a software architecture environment: the total gains are always equivalent to the overall losses in computing resources. So the net change in the sum of computing resources or architecture capabilities is always zero.

Maintaining a Pragmatic Balance Between Competing Software Architecture Forces

Among other design tasks, architects should impart *competing forces* to software products so they can endure the harsh survival competition in the software architecture environment. Consequently, the chief objective should be to maintain an optimal balance between the capabilities of software entities so they can attain the technical environment conditions for their proportional operational needs.

In other words, according to the operational requirements of each software product, it must be ensured that they possess adequate computing forces to safeguard their survival. This implies that not all software implementations call for the same level of architecture capabilities to withstand the challenging rivalry. For instance, some may necessitate more computing resources than their peers. Others may process higher volumes of data. And a few are designed to provide a smaller scale of solutions to business problems.

Architects must be cognizant of the disproportional service levels of software products. Therefore, a pragmatic design approach would be to carefully study the corresponding business requirements and technical specifications. Then correspondingly allocate to these software entities the architecture capabilities related to the criticality of their implementations and environment imperatives.

Mitigating the Competing Forces Challenge

To further secure the durability of software in a software architecture environment and mitigate the competing forces challenge, there are two critical aspects that must be addressed by software architects.

Business development   Responding to incremental business growth

Agile architecture   Enabling software architecture environment elasticity

The former must be given significant priority since business applications must be capable of broadening their solution scope for growing organizational problems. Strictly speaking, business products typically consume more of the software architecture environment's topological space and computing resources when business processes are added to them, when more programming modules are deployed, when additional services augment current business capabilities, and when more application layers amass on top of the old ones. Therefore, when enabling business growth, the intensity of competing forces is lessened, and as a result, software architecture balance is achieved.

Expanding software architecture capabilities is an additional aspect that architects must pay attention to when tackling the competing forces of software implementations. Boosting the technical abilities of a software implementation is affiliated with its ability to dynamically respond to the increase or decrease in business demands and satisfy related consumers. This trait is dubbed *architecture elasticity*.

The questions that follow are affiliated with decisions to enable architecture elasticity for software products:

- Are software implementations scaled enough to handle the upsurge in information sharing volumes?

- Are they adequately loosely coupled to improve software reuse?

- Do the employed integration patterns indeed promote a balanced architecture to reduce the competition for computing and environmental resources?

- Is the software architecture environment ready to accommodate the survival needs of software implementations?

Software Architecture Environment Harmonizing and Disharmonizing Forces

Deployed software products are designed to provide organizational solutions to problems by collaborating. This is one of the most vital goals of software architecture. Proper deployment and integration of software implementations are the decisive factors that promote harmonization in production. The term *harmonization* then refers to the relationship between software products that do not introduce conflicts of operations in a runtime ecosystem. By comparison, competing software forces, as described in the previous section, represent an example of conflicting powers that battle against each other to survive in a software architecture environment.

CONCEPT   A harmonized software architecture environment consists of implementations designed to promote synergetic solutions without canceling each other's powers. Therefore, the role of a software architect is to devise a solid and balanced ecosystem that ensures continuity of operations.

In contrast, disharmonizing software architecture forces are those that disturb the orderly execution of business transactions, powers that negatively impact the performance of applications, energies that do not promote software interoperability, and more. The list of software architecture forces that burden a runtime ecosystem is indeed limitless. Accordingly, software architects must assess the impact of the disharmonizing forces to reduce conflicts of powers in a software architecture environment.

Chief Properties of Harmonizing Forces in a Software Architecture Environment

Software architecture is not only about designing internal applications or systems. A substantial part of the design devises an environment in which software implementations coexist, work together, and share information to offer viable solutions. Every force in that environment must contribute its share, participate, and obey the general rules of proper integration. Once a software product breaks these rules and deviates from the collective responsibility to collaborate with its peers, the software architecture environment cannot offer effective solutions to business challenges.

Message exchange coordination, scheduling, and prioritization are chief properties of software implementations designed to promote harmonization in production. These software entities possess the forces to orchestrate, monitor, and control interactions between applications, services, and systems. For example, an enterprise service bus is typically employed not only to connect and integrate scattered applications in production, but also to coordinate, prioritize, and schedule the interchanges of a message. Without these software design characteristics, chaos typically dominates every aspect of a software architecture environment.

Table 6.1 identifies the leading attributes of software implementations designed to coordinate operations in a runtime environment. Some of the listed attributes are affiliated with software forces commissioned to aggregate and distribute data to consumers. The other design characteristics are all about the enablement of environment interoperability.

Table 6.1: Properties of Chief Harmonizing Software Architecture Environment Forces

DESIGN PROPERTY	FUNCTIONALITY
Prioritization	Prioritization of critical business and technical processes based on their criticality levels.
Orchestration	Coordination of message exchange between service producers and consumers.
Choreography	Messages follow predefined routes to exchange data without being controlled by central orchestration forces (such as message hubs).
Message synchronization[4]	Coordination of events or processes that must take place at the same time.
Message brokering	Message interception is a design property devised to isolate and protect data repositories and applications from consumers' direct access.
Collaboration enablement	Promotion of proper integration, interaction, and partnership between software products.
Application of security controls	Security controls are applied to lessen software vulnerabilities and interrupt environment harmonization by disrupting cybersecurity attacks.
Data aggregation	Aggregation and mining of data to serve applications.
Data accessibility	Permitting access to data by application programming interfaces (API), interfaces, and adapters.
Software reusability	Facilitating reuse and eliminating redundancy of software products, services, and processes.
Service centralization	Devising architecture styles that center on software hubs that intercept messages and exchange data with related consumers.
Integrating data source	Combining information from scattered data sources and repositories.
Integration of technologies	Compounding technologies to strengthen business and technical solutions.
Parallelism	Running asynchronous processes to enable simultaneous service operations.
Elasticity	Applying architecture capabilities to meet changing demands of business requirements and software implementations.
Contract-driven	Information sharing and data exchange to comply with service-level agreements.
Interoperability enablement	Enabling autonomous software implementations and heterogenous environments to communicate and exchange information with each other.

---

[4] Unlike message synchronization, environment synchronization (discussed in section "Use Case V: Software Architecture Environment Synchronization and Desynchronization Design Activities") refers to harmonization of a software architecture environment as a whole.

Chief Properties of Disharmonizing Forces in a Software Architecture Environment

Lack of software architecture strategies and failure to control orderly operations in a software architecture environment contribute to a *disharmonized runtime ecosystem*. This operational landscape characteristically contains negative software architecture forces manifested by the execution of software implementations that induce topological chaos.

When a production environment is thrown into such disarray, negative forces shoulder the blame for disruption to business processes and degradation in performance that result in failure to execute business transactions. Such ecosystem breakdown tends to limit software architecture elasticity and expansion of its capabilities. Furthermore, distressed environments like this typically do not respond effectively to trends in volumes of message exchange and information sharing.

Unbalanced architecture that is driven by tactical necessities tends to disharmonize a software architecture environment. The term *tactical necessities* means that the software design approaches are not based on strategic planning. And when an unplanned production landscape is unbridled, it tends to falter. Furthermore, as Table 6.2 shows, extreme design measures that drive software implementations are the chief culprits of a chaotic runtime environment. For example, radical software distribution or excessive software federation that span remote geographical territories generally disharmonizes the operations in a software architecture landscape.

Similarly, redundancy of applications and systems that tend to execute duplicated functions are major contributors to business ambiguity and instability of runtime environments. Lack of technical interoperability between heterogeneous systems is also a key factor that disharmonizes a software architecture environment.

Table 6.2: Properties of Disharmonizing Software Architecture Environment Forces

DESIGN PROPERTY	ENVIRONMENT IMPACT
Extreme isolation	Software products are isolated because they do not offer adequate interfaces or adapters to communicate with their consumers.
Radical software distribution	Software implementations distributed to extremely remote geographical locations with no control mechanisms to ensure data integrity and acceptable performance rates.
Excessive software federation	Excessive federation of software products that lack fitting technical or business interoperability capabilities.

Continues

Table 6.2 (*continued*)

DESIGN PROPERTY	ENVIRONMENT IMPACT
Redundancy and duplication	Redundancy of software implementations and duplication of business functionalities that compromise software reuse.
Decentralization	Decentralized software architecture with minimal control on coordinated information exchange.
Extreme data distribution	Distribution of information across large geographical locations with no emphasis on maintaining authoritative data sources.
Monolithic structure	Tight coupling of software products that limit architecture agility and reuse.
Asynchronous operations	Serial execution style of software operations that are performed one at a time and only when the running one completes its process.
Low availability	An environment that does not employ redundancy mechanisms to avoid outages of environment operations.
Technological incompatibility	A production environment that does not support standard technologies to enable effective integration and collaboration between software products.

Genetic Encoding of a Software Architecture Environment

It's hard to conceive that many organizations cannot reconstruct a software architecture environment once a disaster has struck. To put it differently, an organization must reassemble a runtime ecosystem when it's beyond repair because of a natural or technological calamity. Cybersecurity attacks, flooding, fire, and unrecoverable outages are types of catastrophes that can halt the operations of applications and systems for long durations.

True, most software architecture environments support disaster recovery (DR) facilities to provide operational redundancy in case of large-scale operational failures or breakdowns. But DR facilities typically do not provide full-scale recovery services to restore the original version of a runtime ecosystem. Nor do they replace business or technical operations for the long run.

Difficulties of Restructuring a Software Architecture Environment

The inability to precisely duplicate the original settings of an out-of-commission runtime environment introduces major challenges to an organization that cannot afford extended downtimes. The term *original setting* does not refer to reconstructing images of single servers or network configurations. It pertains to *reassembling a software architecture environment* driven by architecture strategies, design models, integration patterns, and architecture styles.

Although there are tools driven by programming and script languages to facilitate the restoration of a runtime environment, the difficulty of fully reconstructing it remains. Therefore, there is a need to encode a software architecture environment by capturing its holistic design attributes. And in due time, these properties can be restored. Otherwise stated, the reconstruction should include the fundamental software architecture characteristics that applications, systems, and data originally possessed.

Encoding a Software Architecture Environment

Nowadays, the motivation to encode a software architecture environment is more compelling than ever. This is because of the architecture complexity that dominates the runtime environment. To safeguard this intricate design, the environment topology space ought to be encoded and stored externally—not in the environment itself. Simply put, the genetic information of a runtime landscape should be deposited at a remote and safe location that can be retrieved later if reconstruction is needed.

The encoded information of a software architecture environment should resemble a three-dimensional image reproduced from its topology space. This information should render its encompassed components, such as software products, system configuration, integration patterns, architecture styles, application relationships, data, and more. In essence, the encoded information should resemble a hologram[5] that represents the genetic code of a software architecture environment ecosystem, in which processes and data are designed to provide business and technical solutions.

CONCEPT   This hologram should represent the authoritative genetic code of a software architecture environment. To reconstruct the original environment settings, the hologram should be decoded to reveal its topology dimensions.

Influences on Social, Behavioral, and Business Goals

The interminable transformation of a software architecture environment has immense implications on the social behavior of computer users. The alteration to this runtime ecosystem involves modifications to user interfaces, integration

---

[5] The hologram idea is modeled after Gerard 't Hooft's (arxiv.org/pdf/gr-qc/9310026 .pdf) and Leonard Susskind's (arxiv.org/pdf/hep-th/9409089.pdf) research.

patterns, the relationship between software products, infrastructure, data structures, security models, protocols, and more.

Such technological evolution influences how users handle communications with their co-workers, clients, and vendors. These changes even affect the way in which users handle information retrieval and data sharing. Software architecture is clearly the epicenter of every environment transformation that ultimately affects the behavior of applications, services, and systems. In light of these influences, user training and the adoption period of evolving technologies are required.

Moreover, business operations and goals can be hampered if the transformation of a software architecture environment is not gradual. This peril also applies to radical and instant software design changes. The rule of thumb then suggests that long-term planning, namely strategies, should mitigate the risks to business continuity.

Software Architecture Environment Construction Life Cycle

The environment construction process is effective if a software architect pursues multiple iterations to achieve an optimal software architecture construction. The term *optimal software architecture construction* delineates an architecture solution characterized by design attributes that are not radical.

For example, maintaining an equilibrium between a tightly coupled and loosely coupled software architecture manifests a *balanced software design*. Moreover, on the one hand, an excessively tightly coupled design produces software that is typically not nimble enough to enable rapid change and easy maintenance. On the other, an extremely loosely coupled design renders software that is hard to manage, monitor, and support in a software architecture environment. Therefore, an optimal software architecture requires applying the most advantageous composition between these two radical architecture decision choices.

CONCEPT   The environment construction life cycle calls for iterative design activities to attain an optimal software architecture composition. This design process is required to tackle challenging organizational problems in pursuit of effective software integration solutions.

To visualize the software architecture construction life-cycle idea, inspect Figure 6.6. It illustrates an example of circular life-cycle design activities that ultimately render a balance between two radical environment design attributes: excessively tightly coupled and extremely loosely coupled. Note that in this context, the design attributes *tightly coupled* and *loosely coupled* refer to a software architecture environment as a whole—not to a particular instance of an application or system.

Once this equilibrium and a middle ground design style have been achieved, the environment construction process concludes. The section that follows discusses various design activities used to achieve a balanced software architecture environment.

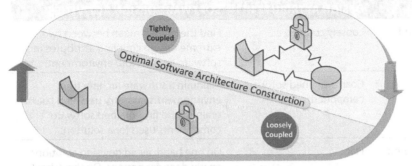

Figure 6.6: Software Architecture Environment Construction Life-Cycle Example

Software Architecture Environment Construction Process

As discussed in the previous section, the example in Figure 6.6 represents two radical solutions: excessively tightly coupled and extremely loosely coupled software design. This example highlights the need for a universal method to facilitate the formation of a balanced software architecture that would mitigate extreme design approaches. Therefore, any iterative environment construction process should be driven by gradual design to achieve a software architecture environment equilibrium.

> **CONCEPT**   Recall that software architecture environment construction must be driven by pragmatic design approaches to promote a software architecture balance. Such architecture symmetry should be maintained and safeguarded during the product design, development, deployment, and integration life cycle.

Creating a Software Architecture Environment Construction Balance Table

Before starting the software architecture environment construction process, it's highly advisable to create a list that identifies the properties that should be balanced and presented in a design blueprint. Consider the example depicted in Table 6.3. The information in the Design Attribute I and Design Attribute II columns represent two extreme design attributes that ought to be balanced. To populate these columns, study the project's technical specifications to gather the corresponding attributes and document them in a similar construction balance table. Moreover, the Software Design Activities column provides guides for achieving such equilibrium.

Table 6.3: Software Architecture Construction Balance Example

DESIGN ATTRIBUTE I	DESIGN ATTRIBUTE II	SOFTWARE DESIGN ACTIVITIES
Tightly coupled	Loosely coupled	Find the golden mean between two extreme design coupling attributes in a software architecture environment.
Fine-grained software components	Coarse-grained software components	Maintain a software architecture environment symmetry between coarse-grained and fine-grained software components used for a solution.
Extremely layered	Flat	On one hand, avoid devising solutions overly deep formations. On the other, shy away from flat structures if the design requires a layered software architecture environment.
Too federated	Isolated	Offer a middle ground software design that avoids unmanageable federated architecture but also does not support isolation of software implementations that hinder reuse and information sharing between production environments.
Tightly secured	Lightly secured	Circumvent software design that introduces tightly secured environments to avoid operation challenges. Yet, devise a reasonable amount of security controls to protect vulnerable implementations.
Tightly integrated environment	Loosely integrated environment	Shun software design that overemploys an excessive amount of integration facilities, such as interfaces, adapters, middleware, and gateways. Conversely, foster software reuse and information sharing by avoiding a loosely integrated software architecture environment.
Too many relationships	Too few relationships	Avoid unnecessary or redundant relationships between software products. But devise software architecture solutions that establish a reasonable amount of relationship between applications and systems to promote efficient data exchange.

Furthermore, design properties are not common in every blueprint that software architects deliver. Every deployment environment is different, every system necessitates distinct architecture styles, and every application is driven by unique design patterns. Therefore, balanced design solutions should be driven by a meticulous analysis of the environments and the software implementations that operate in the software architecture environment.

Software Architecture Environment Construction Design Activities

It'd be impossible to fulfill an *optimal software architecture environment construction* without a repetitive design process that satisfies the needs of an integrated business or technological solution. Simply put, a successful software architecture environment is a product of repetitive successions of design activities and architectural compromises. Furthermore, this iterative design process is employed to shape a software architecture environment. At the same time, however, software architects may also find it necessary to manipulate software structures, as is apparent in the list of design activities that follows and in the subsequent use cases. Refer to Chapter 7 to learn more about the structural construction of software implementations.

During this environment construction exercise, software architects can utilize 10 design activities to manipulate a software architecture landscape, as illustrated in Figure 6.7.

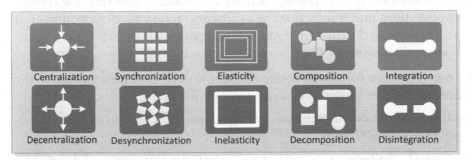

Figure 6.7: Design Activities

Composition   This activity is devised to consolidate, unify, augment, and aggregate software architectures to increase the solution scope of business and technological solutions.

Decomposition   This activity is utilized to break down a software architecture environment into subarchitectures to optimize business and technological architecture solution scope, functionalities, and capabilities.

Integration   This activity is employed to form a relationship between deployed software assets, foster software reuse, and distribute and federate software implementations in software architecture environments.

Disintegration   This activity is utilized to promote software architecture complexity reduction, consolidate software assets, reduce the distribution scope of software implementations, and unify software products.

Centralization   This design activity grants software architecture gravitational forces to software implementations. It also promotes reduction of software functionality redundancy, standardization of technologies, and consolidation of software intermediaries.

Decentralization   This is employed to reduce the intensity of architecture gravitational forces, promote architecture loose coupling, and foster optimal distribution and federation of software implementations.

Elasticity   This is leveraged to establish a nimble software design , provide adequate computing resources, improve software reuse and performance, and enhance software architecture agility to minimize the competing forces in a software architecture environment.

Inelasticity   This is used to fine-tune software architecture elasticity, optimize the consumption of computing resources, and reduce unnecessary clustering and scalability mechanisms.

Synchronization   This is utilized to enhance software architecture environment harmony and efficiently coordinate, choreograph, and orchestrate operations in a runtime landscape.

Desynchronization   This design activity is utilized to fine-tune the control of operations and transactions in a software architecture environment. It also can be used to loosen organizational policies that put strain on software and environment performance in production.

The use cases that follow elaborate on these design activities that drive the software architecture environment construction life cycle:

Use Case I   Software architecture environment composition and decomposition design activities

Use Case II   Software architecture environment integration and disintegration design activities

Use Case III   Software architecture environment centralization and decentralization design activities

Use Case IV   Software architecture environment elasticity and inelasticity design activities

Use Case V   Software architecture environment synchronization and desynchronization design activities

Use Case I: Software Architecture Environment Composition and Decomposition Design Activities

The most common environment construction tasks are the composition and decomposition design activities, during which software architects shape software architecture capabilities and business and technological solution scopes. Although this use case calls for the manipulation of software structures, the emphasis here is on the influence of software on its hosting software architecture environment. More specifically, the focus of this exercise is more on the distribution and federation of software architectures and less on modifications of internal software structures. The bottom line is that it's all about software architecture environment composition and decomposition.

To learn about the design activities that focus on manipulation of individual software structures, refer to Chapter 7.

The environment composition is about the arrangement and manipulation of software architectures in unique formations to broaden, optimize, or consolidate the scope of business or technological solutions for a wider array of problems. At its core, it's about combining software entities, augmenting and unifying architecture capabilities, and leveraging the environment hosting abilities to provide adequate computing power. This design activity employs four chief methods to achieve these software architecture goals: unification, augmentation, consolidation, and aggregation.

By comparison, the decomposition design approaches are employed to break down software architectures into subarchitectures. They are devised to trim down or completely remove software capabilities or architecture properties. These design activities ultimately render subsets of distributed architectures, business, or technical solutions across software architecture environments. The decomposition design activities offer four major methods of fulfilling these objectives: separation, detachment, decompiling, and insulation.

Both design activities are largely discussed in the section "Composition and Decomposition Design Methods."

Design-Time vs. Runtime Environment Composition and Decomposition Design Activities

Unfortunately, in many cases, the composition and decomposition of software architecture take place way after the software development process has been completed. In other words, organizations tend to remodel software formations and modify the architecture in a runtime environment—a post-design undertaking that may conflict with organizational architecture strategies.

Therefore, the appropriate time for performing composition and decomposition is during design time—not runtime. This is because the cost of design time is lower than applying changes to a live software architecture environment.

Moreover, composition and decomposition during design time merely render blueprints with no risks to a runtime ecosystem. In contrast, the efforts of modifying the software architecture environment and its implementations typically introduce risks to business continuity, integration, and data integrity.

Composition and Decomposition Design Methods

There are umpteen approaches for implementing composition and decomposition design activities. The rule of thumb advocates that the design activities for reshaping a software architecture environment and its implementations ought to be driven by methodological approaches. The methods for achieving practical modifications to software and its hosting environment depend on how architects choose to alter architecture attributes, such as reuse, coupling, decoupling, distribution, federation, and more.

For example, if the objective is to promote software reuse, architects typically apply architecture decomposition design activities that ultimately render sub-architectures that can provide solutions to a wider range of consumers. The same idea applies to technical requirements that call for breaking down monolithic software architecture styles. In this case, the decomposition design activity can be leveraged to reduce the inefficiency of tightly coupled architectures. Then again, if the goal is to eliminate software redundancy, the composition design activities can help to combine software architectures and unify their capabilities, functionalities, and attributes.

Table 6.4 introduces the chief approaches for carrying out the composition and decomposition design activities employed to manipulate software architecture that would ultimately impact the software architecture ecosystem. The changes to this environment should be accompanied by meticulous analysis and proof of concepts to justify such technical transformation.

Table 6.4: Methods for Software Architecture Environment Composition and Decomposition Design Activities

DESIGN ACTIVITY	METHOD	TASK
Composition	Unifying	Creating a unified software architecture by combining two or more software architectures, merging their attributes and functionalities, and increasing the overall architecture solution scope
	Augmenting	Gluing together two or more software architectures to leverage their mutual capabilities without changing or merging their attributes or functionalities
	Consolidating	Consolidating software architectures by removing redundant business or technical capabilities
	Aggregating	Broadening the business and technical solution scope of an existing software architecture by leveraging and aggregating the capabilities of other software architectures through interfaces only

DESIGN ACTIVITY	METHOD	TASK
Decomposition	Separating	Breaking down a software architecture into independent subarchitectures by establishing unique attributes and functionality for each separated sub-architecture
	Detaching	Unstitching two or more attached software architectures without changing any of their attributes
	Decoupling	Increasing the autonomous state of a software architecture by lessening their dependencies on each other by reducing interfaces and data exchange
	Insulating	Isolating of a software architecture by reducing its architecture capability and solution scope

Composition and Decomposition Process Outline

Figure 6.8 represents an example of three design states (A, B, and C) that are the outcomes of software environment composition and decomposition activities.

State A: Deficient design   Depicts monolithic architecture, a tightly coupled design formation that tackles a broad scope of business or technical problems. Note that monolithic architectures are typically subject to design decomposition to boost software reuse.

State B: Optimal design   Titled "Optimal Software Architecture Construction," state B is a result of a design decomposition activity that is performed on design state A or design composition activity on state C.

State C: Deficient design   An extremely decomposed software architecture environment that introduces only maintenance costs and operational challenges. State C is a result of two design decomposition activities on states A and B.

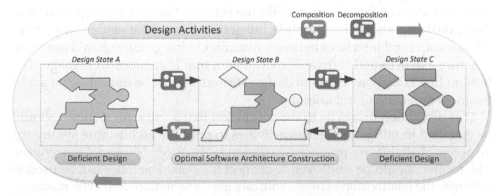

Figure 6.8: Composition and Decomposition Design Activities Example

As shown in Figure 6.8, two directions drive the architecture environment decomposition and composition activities. No matter from which direction these design activities begin, state B represents the optimal software architecture construction.

A, B, C direction   Illustrates a two-step software architecture environment decomposition

C, B, A direction   Depicts a two-step software architecture environment composition

Use Case II: Software Architecture Environment Integration and Disintegration Design Activities

The integration of software is always driven by business and technological imperatives that call for improving information sharing, reuse, performance, and efficiency of applications and systems. To achieve these goals, an organization ought to develop integration strategies, devising how the dots are connected in a runtime ecosystem. The phrase *connecting the dots* refers to software architecture practices that enable cost-effective dissemination and sharing of information across the enterprise. Also, it is about providing the best possible technical solutions to efficiently link and distribute software assets in a software architecture environment.

But integration is not only about connecting the dots or establishing a relationship between distributed business services. It is also about the reduction of software redundancy and scaling down technologies to address architecture environment complexity.

CONCEPT   Effective integration should institute a balanced deployment environment driven by symmetrical software architecture.

In achieving a symmetrical software architecture environment, design activities must focus on forming an equilibrium between "too much integration" and "too little integration." For example, integration should not render a myriad of relationships and interfaces between systems. Or, integration should not manufacture a distributed software environment that is arduous to manage. The bottom line is that any extreme design attributes must be optimized to avoid business or technological calamity.

This discussion brings us to the conclusion that a software architect should be engaged in mitigation design activities to promote architecture symmetry. To accomplish this, we propose two design tools: *integration* and *disintegration*. The former should be employed to connect the dots. The latter can be used to optimize the relationship between software implementations and even moderate the distribution and federation scheme of applications and systems.

When to Apply Integration and Disintegration Design Activities

Architects' hands are always full during the development life cycle of a software product. They are required to fulfill multiple activities to promote architecture strategies during that period. First, they must respond to business requirements by translating them into technical specifications. Next, they are commissioned to provide design blueprints and perfect them throughout the software development phase. Finally, they are charted to provide architecture guidance during the deployment, integration, and maintenance of software implementations in a runtime ecosystem. The bottom line is that software architects are employed to usher in all phases of the product development life cycle.

To effectively integrate software into runtime environments, the integration and disintegration design activities must begin at the inception phase of the business product development life cycle. In other words, the integration and disintegration design activities ought to be employed as early as possible to allow time for proof of concepts and validation of the design blueprints. The integration and disintegration design activities should not stop there. They must also persist through deployment, integration, and maintenance of software products in a software architecture environment—namely, during runtime. This would also be the time to validate architecture integration strategies against the real-time performance of deployed software assets.

Integration and Disintegration Design Methods

One of the most important aspects to ponder when working on the design of software integration is the objectives we aim to fulfill. Ask questions such as the following:

- What is the goal?
- Does the design solution satisfy the business or technical requirements?
- What are the proper integration and disintegration design methods to utilize?
- What integration patterns can promote the most effective solutions while meeting the software architecture environment constraints?

Table 6.5 includes tangible approaches to facilitate the fulfillment of software architecture integration goals. The four design approaches for software integration, shown in the Method column, foster fundamental best practices that software architects ought to be knowledgeable about: establishment of software relationships, reuse, distribution and federation, interoperability, and binding (founding contracts between software implementations). Moreover, the Task column identifies the design integration activities that ought to be performed.

In contrast, the methods for pursuing software disintegration design activities address different challenges that architects must tackle: optimization of software relationships, optimization of information workloads, distribution and federation scope reduction, and relaxation of software binding. These design approaches promote optimization of architecture environment complexity and the scaling back of software distribution and federation to strengthen the delivery of solutions.

Table 6.5: Integration and Disintegration Design Methods

DESIGN ACTIVITY	METHOD	TASK
Integration	Establishment of software relationships	Forming a one-to-one, many-to-many, one-to-many, or many-to-one relationship between software implementations
	Reuse	Enabling access to information and processes by providing connectivity mechanisms, such as APIs, adapters, and connectors
	Distribution and federation	Expending the scope of software architecture to include other organizational entities, such as lines of business and geographical locations
	Promotion of interoperability	Enabling heterogenous environments to communicate and exchange data
	Binding	Establishing exclusive contracts between software assets
Disintegration	Optimization of software relationships	Removing or consolidating unnecessary software relationships, interfaces, adapters, gateways, middleware, or other intermediaries
	Optimization of information workloads	Reducing data workloads and transaction volumes
	Distribution and federation scope reduction	Reducing the range of software distribution and federation across organizations and geographical locations
	Relaxation of software binding	Decreasing the number of contracts between software implementations across a software architecture environment

Integration and Disintegration Process Outline

Integration and disintegration design activities yield the best possible results when the process is bidirectional. In other words, to achieve an optimal software architecture environment construction, one ought to pursue repetitive integration and disintegration design activities. Consequently, the final design state is a manifestation of a symmetric software architecture landscape that grants production environment stability and strengthens business continuity.

Figure 6.9 represents such an iterative process, during which three design states are formed (A, B, and C) due to the employment of the integration and disintegration tools.

State A: Deficient design   This illustrates an excessively integrated mesh environment with point-to-point relationships between software structures. This configuration introduces architecture complexity that is hard to maintain and manage and poses risks to business operations.

State B: Optimal design   This optimal software architecture environment construction state is attained by the disintegration design activity on state A or integration on state C.

State C: Deficient design   This is an inferior design that illustrates weak integration between software structures in a software architecture environment. This style of configuration typically compromises software reuse and information sharing.

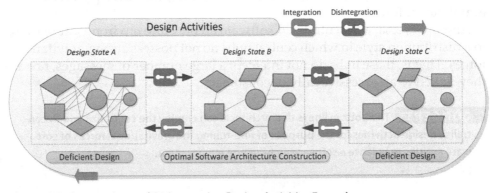

Figure 6.9: Integration and Disintegration Design Activities Example

Figure 6.9 depicts two design activities directions that can be repeated until an optimal software architecture environment construction is fulfilled. This design integration and disintegration life cycle is vital for achieving symmetry between two radical architecture options, which is reflected in state A and state C. Follow these two design directions that illustrate the transition between the three design states:

A, B, C direction   Depicts a two-step architecture disintegration activity

C, B, A direction   Shows a two-step architecture integration activity

Use Case III: Software Architecture Environment Centralization and Decentralization Design Activities

The centralization and decentralization design activities influence the arrangement of software assets in a software architecture ecosystem. Simply put, the term *arrangement* is all about the manner by which software implementations, such as applications, services, systems, and related infrastructure, are distributed in a multidimensional computing space. In the context of the centralization and decentralization design activities, the distribution style of software assets refers to how tight or loose the relationships are between consumers and their affiliated services.

In a centralized software architecture environment, consumers exchange messages with their service providers or applications through software hubs, such as middleware, gateways, data access points, or central service providers. The gravitational force of such hubs is determined by the number of their linked consumers (refer to discussion in the section "Software Architecture Gravitational Forces" about the influences of software architecture gravitational forces).

Software architects ought to be aware that the magnitude of consumers around a central hub determine the intensity of its gravitational force in a computing environment—the more consumers utilize a hub, the more powerful is its gravitational force.

And vice versa: a decentralized software architecture environment pertains to a distribution style in which central hubs do not possess strong gravitational forces. That is, these hubs do not intercept a large number of messages, nor are they linked to an excessive tally of consumers.

> **CONCEPT**   The bottom line is that architects can employ the centralize and decentralize design activities for the purpose of fine-tuning the gravitational forces of software entities to balance a software architecture environment.

When to Employ the Software Environment Centralization and Decentralization Design Activities

The centralization or decentralization of software is hardly ever the focus on the business departments or divisions, . Their attention is devoted to business strategies, business requirements, and business architecture. Thus, it's inconceivable that any business unit in an enterprise would attempt to dictate the employment of architectural styles, architectural patterns, or design patterns.

Also, business managers, analysts, or business architects wouldn't have much influence on software integration pattern decisions in runtime environments. These decisions are made mostly by the IT organizations that shoulder the responsibility for design, development, testing, deployment, and integration efforts.

When it comes to balancing a software architecture environment, the centralization and decentralization designing efforts should take place as early as possible during the development life cycle. Therefore, the planning and designing stages are the most productive and effective time frames in which devise a suitable balanced architecture.

Applying changes to existing software integration, however, is costly and may be disruptive to operations in a production environment. This is because architecture modifications to symbiotic software assets in a software architecture ecosystem would require extensive analysis and testing efforts to ensure business continuity. The perils to business are equally high when attempting to tilt the balance in favor of the centralized or decentralized architecture styles during the software development phase.

Centralization and Decentralization Design Methods

Consider Table 6.6, which elaborates on the chief design procedures employed to balance a software architecture environment. The Design Activity column includes the centralization and decentralization tools; the Method column lists four approaches for each design activity, and the Task column offers corresponding software design approaches.

As shown, the centralization tool introduces four methods of software environment design: consumer grouping, software reuse, consolidation of software intermediaries, and increasing software gravity forces. These environment construction approaches promote the centralization of software products by leveraging software intermediaries, such as hubs or middleware.

In contrast, the decentralization design tool includes four chief approaches: federation, increasing deployments of software intermediaries, decreasing software gravitational forces, and extending software distribution scope. These environment design methods are devised to promote the distribution and federation of software assets across an organization or geographical locations.

Table 6.6: Centralization and Decentralization Design Methods

DESIGN ACTIVITY	METHOD	TASK
Centralization	Consumer grouping	Grouping consumers by their service interests
	Software reuse	Promoting reuse of software by eliminating functionality redundancy and fostering consolidation of service providers
	Consolidation of software intermediaries	Reduction of software hubs in a software architecture environment
	Increasing software gravity forces	Increasing consumer access to software hubs

Continues

Table 6.6 (*continued*)

DESIGN ACTIVITY	METHOD	TASK
Decentralization	Federation	Transforming a centralized architecture to a federated distribution style
	Increasing deployments of software intermediaries	Extending the number of software intermediaries in a software architecture ecosystem
	Decreasing software gravitational forces	Reducing the number of consumers for existing software hubs
	Extending software distribution scope	Extending the reach of business services to remote geographical locations

Software Architecture Environment Centralization and Decentralization Process Outline

Figure 6.10 demonstrates the three design phases that employ the centralization and decentralization design activities. This design life cycle depicts three software architectures environment states: A, B, and C. No matter from which state a software architect chooses to use the design tools, the ultimate goal is to achieve a balanced software architecture for a particular environment. In this context, the term *ultimate* refers to a design symmetry that achieves balance between a centralized and decentralized distributed runtime landscape.

State A: Deficient design This design stage demonstrates a radical centralized software architecture environment with extreme gravitational force that can influence large sections of a production landscape. As apparent in the center, a software hub offers multiple interfaces to its potential consumers. In addition, this state results from the centralization design activities that are applied to state A and then state B. A highly centralized software architecture environment typically comes with perils to performance and response time. This is because of the potential high volume of transactions that the software hub must process.

State B: Optimal design Note that state B refers to an optimal software architecture environment construction. It demonstrates a design equilibrium that it's achieved between the two radical states: A and C. In other words, to obtain such architectural construction balance, a software architect ought to choose between states A and C. In contrast, state B represents a design compromise between these two extreme distribution styles that are modified by the centralization and decentralization design activities.

State C: Deficient design This is considered as another deficient design scheme that resulted from the repeating decentralization design activities, starting at stage A and continuing through stage B. State C, therefore, does not possess a strong gravitational force. It also depicts an impractical architecture construction since it does not promote reuse, nor does it foster consolidation of software functionality.

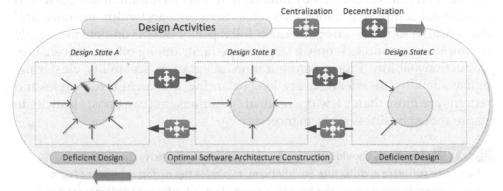

Figure 6.10: Centralization and Decentralization Life-Cycle Design Activities Example

Moreover, Figure 6.10 depicts examples of the centralization and decentralization design activities that a software architect may employ during the software design life cycle. This design process is illustrated in states A, B, and C. Consequently, dependencies between software assets may be altered, the intensity of gravitational forces may be modified, and the integration scheme of a software architecture environment may be changed.

Consider the two possible centralization and decentralization design directions as illustrated in Figure 6.10:

A, B, C direction   Depicts two software design decentralization steps

C, B, A direction   Illustrates a two-step software centralization design activities

Use Case IV: Software Architecture Environment Elasticity and Inelasticity Design Activities

As discussed in the section "Competing Software Architecture Environment Forces," *elasticity* is one of the most decisive attributes that impacts the survival of software in its deployed environment. This assertion implies that not only must a software implementation be nimble enough to withstand the competition game in production, but the environment itself must offer adequate conditions to accommodate the imperatives of applications, services, systems, and infrastructure.

NOTE   Software architects, be aware that it's not only design decisions and approaches that must empower software to thrive in the cutthroat endurance challenges of a production ecosystem. The hosting environment ought to be agile enough to promote business growth and technological transformation as well.

Furthermore, elasticity and inelasticity refer to vital architecture attributes that software architects must always be cognizant of. So, what are the conditions that foster software and its hosting environment agility? Nimbleness, in this context, can be achieved by allocating to the environment adequate and incremental computing resources (such as network bandwidth, memory, and disk space) so software can operate at its full capacity. But the on-demand supply of computing resources is only a single ingredient, among others, that ensures production stability. Proper configuration, integration, scalability, clustering, high availability, disaster recovery, load balancing, and architecture styles and patterns are more than a few operational conditions that can boost elasticity to ensure robust business performance.

NOTE   Architects should leverage the elasticity and inelasticity design tools to balance a software architecture environment, minimize the negative impact of *competing forces* in production, and boost the survival rate of software implementations in a challenging deployment ecosystem.

When to Employ Elasticity and Inelasticity Design Activities

Software and environment architecture elasticity is known to be achieved chiefly during product deployment, configuration, and integration in production. But nothing should stop software architects from also devising elasticity mechanisms during the planning, design, development, and testing stages. Therefore, the rule of thumb suggests that elasticity should be incrementally realized throughout the product development life cycle.

As mentioned in the previous section, elasticity is enabled by umpteen software and environment architecture features that typically contribute to a nimble software architecture landscape. Again, these traits include scalability, clustering, and even incremental and adequate supply of computing resources. Architecture agility concerns, therefore, should meet the specific requirements of every single stage of the life cycle.

For example, during the design phase, agility is characteristically affiliated with software clustering, instances, scalability, and architecture patterns. Then again, during the product deployment, configuration, and integration stages, message load balancing, failover, and high availability contribute to operation nimbleness and stability. In conclusion, during each software life-cycle stage architects should ensure that agility is the forefront of their concerns.

During all phases of a product life cycle, agility testing should be conducted to understand how durable a software implementation is. The hosting environment fitness should also be examined to ensure that it can sustain the data workload, transactions, and information exchange.

Elasticity and Inelasticity Design Methods

Note that Table 6.7 includes only a limited number of methods that refer to the elasticity and inelasticity software design activities. But with such an abbreviated set of design methods, software architects will still be easily able to deduce the usage of these design tools. As shown, the Design Activity column identifies the two activities. Next to each activity, find the related four listed design approaches under the Method column. The Task column introduces the task that is related to each design method.

As shown in Table 6.7, the elasticity design activity can be driven by each of the four software design methods: boosting scalability, increasing clustering capabilities, adding load balancing and failover technologies, and enhancing high-availability capabilities. These design approaches are devised to increase software and environment elasticity capabilities. In other words, by boosting the nimbleness characteristics of a software implementation and its hosting environment, software products will be able to withstand the harsh competition in a production landscape.

To limit the elasticity level of a software or its related environment, and to fine-tune an architecture balance, four design methods are proposed: limiting high-availability capabilities, reducing clusters, reducing load balancing and failover mechanisms, and reducing scalability. Note that these design approaches are devised merely to consolidate or eliminate unnecessary elasticity mechanisms to simplify architecture complexity. And they are not provided to reduce software or environment performance capabilities.

Table 6.7: Chief Elasticity and Inelasticity Design Methods

DESIGN ACTIVITY	METHOD	TASK
Elasticity	Boosting scalability	Increase software horizontal and vertical scaling instances
	Increasing clustering capabilities	Add more computers or nodes to run software's parallel tasks
	Adding load balancing and failover technologies	Raise the number of load balancer and failover devices
	Enhancing high-availability capabilities	Expand environment high-availability sites
Inelasticity	Limiting high-availability capabilities	Reduce environment high-availability sites
	Reducing clusters	Optimize the number of computers or nodes to decrease software's parallel tasks
	Reducing load balancing and failover mechanisms	Limit the number of load balancer and failover devices
	Reducing scalability	Decrease the number of software horizontal and vertical scaling instances

Software Architecture Elasticity and Inelasticity Design Process Outline

Figure 6.11 depicts the elasticity and inelasticity design activities and their related states: A, B, and C. There is no particular direction that a software architect pursues. Note that this schematic presentation of software design does not imply that there should be only three architecture states.

In the real world, the design process may be accompanied by analyses and architecture evaluation tasks. Then again, the upshot ought to be a balanced software architecture environment—an optimal scheme that ultimately stems from repeatable elasticity and inelasticity design activities. And in due course, the optimal software architecture must be an outcome of good judgment and sensible design decisions.

State A: Deficient design   There is no defense against a design scheme that calls for implementing excessive elasticity mechanisms as is apparent in state A. Avoid such radical elasticity solutions. In addition, software or environment elasticity should not be promoted by employing extreme scalability gears. Nor should a software implementation, for example, be deployed to a large cluster of servers or nodes to boost its nimbleness if there is no justification for pursuing such technical solution. Not limited to these elasticity facilitators, this train of thought should be adopted to promote a balanced software architecture environment.

State B: Optimal design   This optimal software architecture construction denotes that a software entity is nimble enough to effectively compete and survive in a computing environment. To achieve such architecture equilibrium, the elasticity design activity has been applied on state C. The inelasticity design tool is employed to reduce the elasticity level of state A. Obviously, state B represents a design compromise between two radical choices: A and C.

State C: Deficient design   This design state depicts a rigid and inflexible environment that most likely would introduce perils to business operations. The architecture seems unscaled, and the single software implementation instance would not be able to withstand production ecosystem message workload pressures. Such software and environment design is utterly impractical. Software architects, therefore, should employ the elasticity design tool to rectify the potential risks associated with the apparent lack of agility.

Figure 6.11 depicts examples of the elasticity and inelasticity design tools that should be employed to achieve an environment equilibrium. The process for obtaining such balance is illustrated in states A, B, and C. This schematic life-cycle depiction shows two design directions.

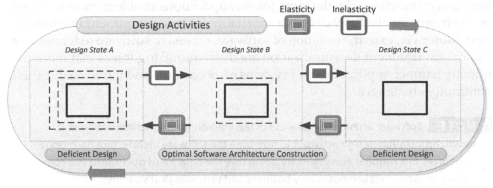

Figure 6.11: Elasticity and Inelasticity Life-Cycle Design Activities Example

A, B, C direction   Demonstrates the inelasticity design activity on states A and B that render state C

C, B, A direction   Depicts the employment of the elasticity design activity on states C and B that render state A

Use Case V: Software Architecture Environment Synchronization and Desynchronization Design Activities

As you may recall, the centralization and decentralization design activities, discussed in Use Case III, are chiefly about the distribution and arrangement of software assets in a software architecture environment. By contrast, the environment synchronization and desynchronization activities discussed here are leveraged to control the harmony level of operations in the same deployment landscape.

The term *harmony level of operations* then refers to the manner by which messages and data are being exchanged, controlled, managed, and disseminated on a computer network to promote a balanced software architecture. To learn more about this topic, refer to sections "Chief Properties of Harmonizing Forces in Production" and "Chief Properties of Disharmonizing Forces in Production."

To promote or demote the harmony of operations in a software architecture ecosystem, employ the environment *synchronization* and *desynchronization* design activities. By doing this, software architects can fine-tune the level of interactions, collaborations, partnerships, and information sharing in a runtime environment. The bottom line is that too much of a good thing is never good—namely, excessive harmony measures do not necessarily promote a balanced software architecture.

For instance, orchestration and choreography are architecture capabilities that promote harmony. However, excessive orchestration or choreography mechanisms that are employed to control messages may hinder performance of business transactions. By the same token, superfluous enablement of software or environment elasticity does not inevitably foster environment harmonization. Moreover, extreme isolation of software, excessive software federation, or radical environment decentralization are disharmonizing forces that more frequently hamper applications and systems response time and introduce business continuity challenges.

> **NOTE** Software architects: make use of the environment synchronization and desynchronization design activities to fine-tune the software architecture harmonization forces in a runtime ecosystem. By doing this, the balance of operations in a computing environment promotes only business and technological stability.

When to Employ Environment Synchronization and Desynchronization Design Activities

There are many design concerns that must be addressed in a software architecture environment, especially with message exchange and data sharing coordination and orchestration challenges. There are numerous consumers and service providers that trade critical information on a network. And there are a myriad of partnerships that are formed dynamically without human intervention. These umpteen interaction activities call for carving out communication strategies to foster stability in an error-prone runtime environment.

But communication strategies alone could not fully tackle architecture complexity levels. Therefore, to adequately prepare for the impact of a high volume of data transfer and the distribution of information in production, there is a need for devoting significant attention to behavior of software during each product development life-cycle stage. In this context, the term *behavior* is affiliated with how software responds to data requests, how it interacts with peer service providers, and how consumers trade information in a computing landscape.

Consequently, tackling environment harmonization ought to be one of the most overriding tasks during each product development life-cycle stage. Simply put, the synchronization and desynchronization design activities should be pursued during the planning, designing, development, testing, deployment, and integration phases. Although synchronization and desynchronization are typically invisible software architecture properties, testing time should be devoted to promote environment harmonization and operation stability.

Environment Synchronization and Desynchronization Design Methods

The environment synchronization and desynchronization design tools, listed in the Design Activity column of Table 6.8, can be used to control the harmonization level in a computing environment. In addition, these two activities are accompanied by corresponding design methods (listed in the Method column). The Task column elaborates on how to apply these methods to achieve the desired harmonization level in a software architecture landscape. Note that this table includes an abbreviated list of software environment design approaches for the environment synchronization and desynchronization design activities. Software architects, therefore, may consider augmenting this list with additional methods and tasks that are related to specific organizational concerns.

To enhance environment synchronization of operations, such as message exchange, information sharing, or distribution of data, consider these four methods: message harmonization, process parallelism, centralization, and contract-driven partnerships. This prevailing environment synchronization concept calls for enhancing the operational harmony level by setting message control mechanisms, coordinating interactions between software assets, and centralizing message orchestration and choreography capabilities.

By comparison, the environment desynchronization design activity in Table 6.8 lists four methods that can be used to reduce software dependencies and fine-tune an environment that overcontrols message exchange, coordination, and prioritization. To achieve these software architecture environment desynchronization effects, employ the listed design activity methods: decentralization, defederation, software isolation, and long-range software distribution.

Table 6.8: Chief Synchronization and Desynchronization Design Methods

DESIGN ACTIVITY	METHOD	TASK
Environment Synchronization	Message harmonization	Apply message coordination and control mechanisms, such as message orchestration, choreography, message synchronization, and prioritization.
	Process parallelism	Coordinate and prioritize the execution of parallel processes.
	Centralization	Recommend software architecture styles and patterns that promote reliance on central hubs.
	Contract-driven partnerships	Focus on contract-driven implementations that promote data exchange harmonization.
Environment Desynchronization	Decentralization	Reduce central software hubs and software intermediaries.
	Federation	Advocate federation of processes and data across organizational boundaries.
	Software isolation	Devise mechanisms to isolate and protect software.
	Long-range software distribution	Distribute software implementations to remote geographical locations without message control mechanisms.

Software Architecture Environment Synchronization and Desynchronization Design Process Outline

Figure 6.12 represents three design phases that take place during the software and environment architecture life cycle. This design process spans stages A, B, and C. Moreover, state B depicts an optimal software architecture construction—a compromised design solution favorable to states A and C. And it represents a balanced environment obtained after employing the synchronization and desynchronization design activities.

State A: Deficient design   This design state depicts a "highly harmonized" software architecture environment, formed by repeatedly employing the environment synchronization design tool on states C and then B. Recall that applying unnecessary and excessive environment synchronization mechanisms to promote environment harmonization would only introduce needless controls over messages, more likely raise software architecture complexity, and in many cases hamper software performance.

State B: Optimal design   This optimal software architecture construction is obtained by using the environment desynchronization and environment synchronization tools on states A and B, respectively. Remember that in the real world, there are no specific rules, guidance, or design sequences to achieve the ultimate software architecture environment equilibrium. In fact, the achievement of an optimal software architecture construction depends chiefly on good judgment and experience in the software design field.

State C: Deficient design   This state represents a deficient design because it lacks environment harmonization forces to balance a software architecture environment. It resulted from the repeating environment desynchronization activities that operated on states A and then B. And it's considered a radical software solution with no environment-balancing forces.

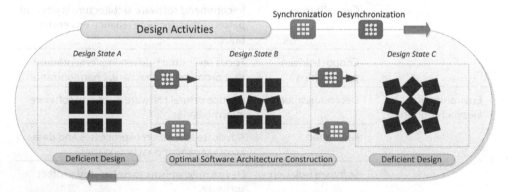

Figure 6.12: Environment Synchronization and Desynchronization Life Cycle Design Activities Example

As stated previously in this section, no particular design process order is required to perform the iterative sequence of environment synchronization and environment desynchronization activities. Note, however, that Figure 6.12 is merely a schematic software architecture construction life cycle that illustrates two possible directions.

A, B, C direction   The Desynchronization design activities start at stage A, which renders stage B, and the latter results in stage C.

C, B, A direction   Stage C is the starting point for the synchronization design activities, then B, and finally A.

Construction Laws of a Software Architecture Environment

It'd be impossible to ignore the interdependencies between a software architecture environment and production ecosystem. The governing laws of chance and probability are a constant battle for software architects who strive to stabilize a software architecture environment. That is, flawless operations in a runtime landscape are never guaranteed—not even by superb software architecture strategies—nor by employing superior technologies. Therefore, a potent approach to mitigating unpredictable environment performance is to employ balanced software design.

The chief laws of a software architecture environment construction reflect these assertions. Software architects ought to be aware that design blueprints never assure runtime stability, nor do they guarantee flawless business execution.

Production environment is an uncontrolled quantum ecosystem   Technological stability and business continuity are never guaranteed in a software architecture environment.

Inseparability   Software implementations are inseparable from any integrated software architecture environment.

Entanglement   Software implementations, whether integrated, separated, or isolated, always directly or indirectly affect each other.

Social behavior   Changes to software architecture environment typically impact users' social behaviors.

Information preservation   Nothing can guarantee data safety and integrity in a software architecture environment, even when software architecture redundancy mechanisms are employed to avert data persistence and transformation loss.

Software architecture gravitational forces   Architecture forces granted to software implementations tend to deform software architecture environment topology spaces and thus impact runtime operations in production ecosystems.

Competing software architecture forces   The stern competition for computing resources in a software architecture environment is won by software products that are driven by superior design.

The zero-sum game   In an ill-designed software architecture environment, the total computing resource gains are always equivalent to the total losses of software implementations. Therefore, the net change in the sum of computing resources or architecture capabilities is always zero in such an inefficient software architecture ecosystem.

Intense gravitational force   Extreme gravitational powers assigned to a software implementation manifest in an unbalanced software architecture environment.

Harmonized software architecture   Deployed software products that do not introduce conflicts of operations promote a balanced software architecture environment.

Best Practices for Software Architecture Environment Construction

The best practices laid out in Table 6.9 are devised to balance a software architecture environment. This guidance calls for leveraging the power of the gravitational, competing, harmonizing, and disharmonizing software architecture environment forces. To accomplish this, expand your institutional business and technological knowledge; understand the enterprise problems and imperatives; study meticulously the organizational production environments; and learn about the various architectures that make up the deployment landscapes.

Moreover, pay attention to design approaches that are offered in section "Software Architecture Environment Construction Life Cycle." Leverage these methods to achieve an environment equilibrium by applying integration and applications, services, and systems behavior balance in a software architecture ecosystem.

Table 6.9: Software Architecture Environment Construction Best Practices

BEST PRACTICE	SOFTWARE DESIGN TASK	EXAMPLES
Software behavior control in a software architecture environment	Grant balanced forces to software implementations to promote state of equilibrium in production.	The four chief software architecture forces discussed in section "Software Architecture Environment Forces Drive Software Behavior" are gravitational, competing, harmonizing, and disharmonizing.
Consolidation of software architecture gravitational forces	Reduce redundancy of gravitation forces to promote architecture balance and foster software reuse.	Consolidate hubs, brokers, gateways, data access layers, message interceptors, message orchestrators, and centralized applications.
Extreme intensity of software architecture gravitational forces	Assess and monitor the workload volumes of gravitational forces to preserve computing resources in production.	Reduction in data exchange workload and the number of consumers can level off the gravitational power of message hubs and introduce environment stability.
Starvation for computing resources	Mitigate competition for computing resources in a software architecture environment by devising effective capacity planning strategies.	Allocate sufficient computing resources, such as network bandwidth for software implementations, to reduce the impact of the survival game in a software architecture environment.
Information preservation	Utilize redundancy mechanisms to minimize breaches to data integrity and information loss.	Redundancy mechanisms may include high-availability environments, DR environments, backup facilities, data synchronization with clustering, server scalability, and automatic failover.
Software architecture environment elasticity	Devise nimble design to promote business growth and increase software architecture technological capabilities.	Automate the scalability of software products and the expansion of computing resource capacity to satisfy the growing demands of business requirements. This may include an increase of network bandwidth, data storage, and memory.
Software architecture environment harmonizing forces	Foster software architecture balance by employing harmonizing forces in a software architecture environment.	Harmonizing forces in a software architecture environment possess unique capabilities, such as orchestration, choreography, prioritization, and message synchronization.

Continues

Table 6.9 (*continued*)

BEST PRACTICE	SOFTWARE DESIGN TASK	EXAMPLES
Software architecture environment disharmonizing forces	Reduce disharmonizing forces to promote software architecture balance	Disharmonizing forces are propelled by extreme software distribution, excessive architecture federation, redundancy and duplication of functionality, and more.
Genetic encoding of software architecture environment	Develop approaches and organizational standards for encoding a holistic view of a software architecture ecosystem for reconstruction purposes.	Encoding mechanisms may include 3D holograms, metadata ontology, taxonomies, and preservation of environment integration properties, such as cataloging of interfaces and software products' relationships.
Impact on users' social behavior	Lessen extreme impact on users' social behaviors by planning and conducting gradual technological transformation.	Gradual technological transformation may be promoted by measured adoption of advanced middleware products, applications, and systems.

Structural Construction of Software Implementations in Multidimensional Environments

Throughout the past several decades of software development and architecture, software products do not seem to operate in a flatland.[1] Specifically, they do not survive in a predominately flat landscape without substantial elevation variations.

On the contrary, now more than ever, we understand that the prevailing properties of a production environment are affiliated with space, volume, shapes, and software implementation placement. Moreover, this geometrical and multidimensional run-time ecosystem is saturated with integrated, distributed, and federated software entities positioned in relative reference points. A superior navigation system is then needed to locate these software implementations in such multidimensional computing space.

Software products, too, possess multidimensional properties. Their spatial dimensions, such as width, length, and height, require an effective software construction process that considers their geometrical attributes. This design life cycle must also guarantee that software better adapts to its corresponding multidimensional architecture computing space. It also ought to ensure that applications, services, and systems can sustain the high pressure of transactions and effectively compete for computing resources.

---

[1] Published in 1884, the term *flatland* was first mentioned in the novella *Flatland: A Romance of Many Dimensions* by Edwin Abbott. The two-dimensional fictional world is depicted in the book as a square.

This chapter introduces a construction life cycle that centers on designing three-dimensional software implementations to tackle the challenges they face in a geometrical ecosystem. This architecture process is devised to ensure technological stability and business continuity.

The following topics are covered in this chapter:

- Software architecture solids: rudimentary geometrical design structures
- Software architecture dimensional model
- Software architecture computing space
- Distribution styles of software implementations in an architecture computing space
- Construction life cycle of software implementations
- Governing laws for software construction in a three-dimensional computing world
- Best practices for constructing software implementations

Software Architecture Solids: Rudimentary Geometrical Design Structures

The fundamental difference between *programming logic* and *software structures* is that the former is affiliated with business and technical functionality executed by computing processes; it simply lacks a supporting framework to hold together software implementations. The latter offers vital skeletons and rudimentary building blocks that hold together the operations of programming logic. Moreover, programming logic and software structures are interdependent. They cannot survive without each other, and it would be impossible to execute business or technical processes without the supporting attributes of software structures.

CONCEPT A software structure supports, reinforces, and contains programming logic and software processes.

This section introduces software architecture solids, which are elementary formations for software architect awareness. These basic software structures can be used to construct any software implementation or product, such as applications, services, or systems. The rule of thumb then suggests beginning the software building process with software architecture solids rather than employing complex structures that may be arduous to support.

CONCEPT With these software architecture geometric solids, begin the process slowly. Simplify and maintain technological cohesiveness to demonstrate clear strategy when providing software solutions.

As depicted in Figure 7.1, the following sections introduce six primary software structures:

Atomic Solid   A fine-grained, small footprint and unbreakable software structure

Composite Solid   A software structure that contains atomic and composite structures

Monolithic Solid   Nonmodular, coarse-grained, typically large-footprint software structure that is difficult to decompose

Interface Solid   A basic structural utility employed to facilitate the inbound and outbound exchange of information

Pipe Solid   A structure that enables the communication between software implementations

Data Solid   A structure that supports information persistence, processing, delivery, and exchange

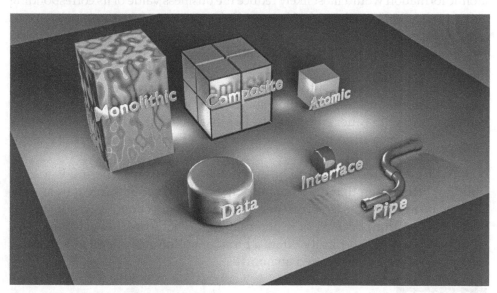

Figure 7.1: Software Architecture Solids

Atomic Solid

An atomic solid is the most fundamental software building block designed to offer a narrow solution scope. It is a fine-grained, unbreakable geometric structure that holds together programming logic designed to execute business or technical processes. These processes are execution units, such as routines, procedures, methods, or algorithms. Figure 7.2 illustrates this concept. It depicts an atomic structure that reinforces the existence of four different software processes.

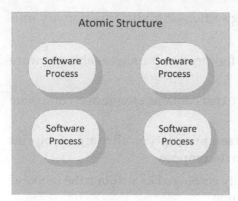

Figure 7.2: Atomic Software Structure

The atomic solid is unbreakable because it is impossible to break it down into smaller structures. It is impractical to chop up an already small formation designed to tackle a narrow range of problems. In addition, decomposing an atomic formation would most likely reduce the business value of its corresponding software implementations. A microservice's structure, for example, is atomic since it supports a limited number of processes. It is not only a microservice; any small software footprint, for that matter, is sustained by an atomic structure.

Furthermore, limited software capabilities supported by an atomic building block are not always self-sufficient. Specifically, the processes braced by such a tiny structure must augment their ability to provide satisfactory solutions by collaborating with other components. For instance, a microservice that offers login services may need to integrate with its peer services that identify users' credentials.

Software architects ought to be aware that an atomic structure is a solid building foundation that does not encompass substructures. In contrast, software reinforced by nested structures is categorized as composite (discussed in the next section) because of its internal hierarchal formations. Moreover, a composite structure typically offers a broader solution scope than an atomic structure because of its layered anatomy.

CONCEPT   At the onset of every software design endeavor, draw upon atomic structures to construct software implementations, such as services, applications, and systems. This practice involves employing atomic solids to circumvent or mitigate software architecture complexity. Again, start designing software with simple building blocks rather than introducing complex structures at the inception of the software development life cycle.

Composite Solid

A composite solid is a more complex software structure. It supports a wider range of processes to provide a larger scope of business and technical solutions. Furthermore, a composite structure is devised to aggregate atomic, composite, monolithic, and/or data software structures. Although it is not hard to comprehend this concept, such a hierarchical structure may introduce an intricated design formation that's difficult to implement, deploy, integrate, and maintain.

Figure 7.3 represents a schematic layout of a composite software structure that aggregates two atomic substructures and a single composite substructure.

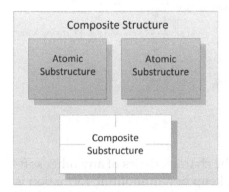

Figure 7.3: Simplified Composite Software Structure

Moreover, a composite structure maintains a hierarchical relationship with its corresponding child substructures. If this does not seem complicated enough, imagine a composite software structure that contains inner substructures, each of which encompasses its internal substructures. Furthermore, since there are no limits on substructure inclusion, a convoluted composite structure is not only hard to maintain in production but introduces collaboration challenges regarding software integration in a runtime environment as well.

Figure 7.4 illustrates a more complex composite software structure that incorporates two atomic substructures, two data substructures, and a composite software substructure. The latter encompasses its own two atomic software substructures, a monolithic substructure, and two data substructures.

CONCEPT   Composite structures do not offer compelling business value. Intricate compound structures like these are never easy to decompose because their internal substructures are interdependent. They are byproducts of unplanned technological evolution not promoted by solid software architecture strategies.

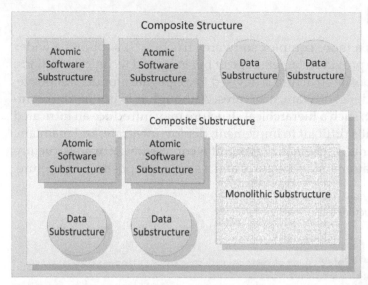

Figure 7.4: Complex Composite Software Structure

Monolithic Solid

A monolithic formation does not resemble the characteristics of any other software structure discussed thus far. Every makeup of a monolithic formation is unique. Their internal compositions are different because they are byproducts of organic technological developments that are not driven by design best practices and standards. In this context, *organic* refers to the unplanned evolution of software structures that keep morphing and growing without any software design strategy.

Although monolithic solids do not necessarily possess any distinguishable internal composition patterns, they are viewed as unbreakable software structures. These tightly coupled formations typically support symbiotic business processes, technical functionality, and data that are difficult or impossible to separate. They are not composed of software modules to boost source code reuse and ease programming maintenance. These design deficiencies indicate monolithic solids as legacy structures with limited integration and distribution capabilities.

However, monolithic structures are not outmoded just yet. Some organizations still support these formations with no end in sight. Their budgets are not allocated to lessen the business dependency on tightly coupled and bulky software implementations that devolve on monolithic structures. In some instances, such formations even survive generations of technological modernization efforts. Ironically, they keep growing and expanding as if there are no other innovative choices to consider.

CONCEPT   Architects should reduce design dependency on ubiquitous monolithic structures by fostering modular software construction and prioritizing budgets to mitigate performance risks that monolithic formation introduces to software architecture environments.

Interface Solid

The interface solid is an essential structural utility that facilitates outbound and inbound data exchange. This information trade is performed between software processes braced by their corresponding structures.

Figure 7.5 depicts this notion. Each of the two atomic structures, A and B, support corresponding software processes: the former comprises four and the latter two. Enabling information exchange involves each structure utilizing its own interface. Furthermore, a pipe solid must be positioned between these two interfaces to transmit data (refer to the following section "Pipe Solid").

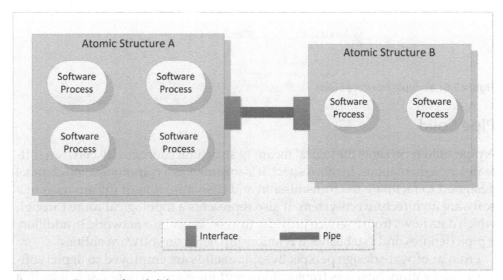

Figure 7.5: Two Interface Solids

CONCEPT   Each structure must utilize at least one interface to establish a relationship between software formations, and a pipe solid must be positioned between two interfaces to funnel data.

Few software products utilize a single interface when communicating with each other. Specifically, a software product may use multiple interfaces to exchange information with several software implementations. Figure 7.6 illustrates this idea. The composite software structure uses four interfaces for data exchange with three atomic structures: 1, 2, and 3. The latter is the only formation that utilizes two interfaces to communicate with the composite software structure.

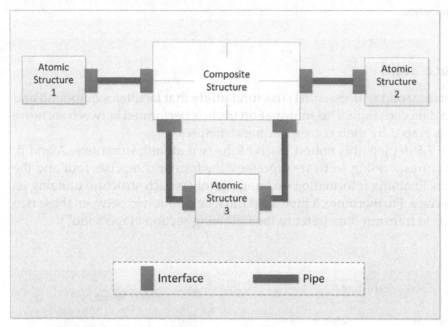

Figure 7.6: Multiple Interface Solids

Pipe Solid

A pipe solid represents the logical means of structural connectivity between software implementations. In this respect, it is regarded as a communication channel designed to facilitate the transmission and dissemination of information in a software architecture ecosystem. It also represents a topological route through which data flows from a service provider to a consumer on a network. In addition, a pipe denotes and establishes a relationship between software entities.

From a software design perspective, pipe solids are employed to depict software integration, business transactions, and message exchange schemes in a runtime environment. Without such correspondence and interaction capacity between deployed software, architects will not be able to offer design blueprints. Therefore, developers will be incapable of delivering executables. The bottom line is that business requirements and objectives will not be met.

The contribution of a pipe solid is evident when the discussion revolves around the logical integration of software products, services, and systems. The benefits of employing pipes to disseminate information are equally clear. However, what is the significance of connecting software structures with pipes? Why should one describe the relationship between software structures by linking them with pipes? The answers to these questions are discussed in the three sections that follow.

Inclusive Utilization of Pipe Solids

Refer to Figure 7.7, which illustrates the relationship between two software structures: composite structures A and B. The former contains three substructures: atomic substructure A.1, atomic substructure A.2, and composite substructure A.3. On the far right, the composite structure B encompasses two substructures: atomic substructure B.1 and atomic substructure B.2. The *inclusive association* between these composite structures (A and B) is established by two interfaces and a connecting pipe. This pipe is a funneling mechanism for distributing information and sharing between all substructures in the two composite formations, A and B.

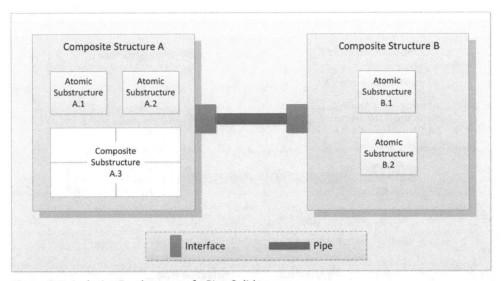

Figure 7.7: Inclusive Employment of a Pipe Solid

The scenario in Figure 7.7 demonstrates the utilization of a pipe solid to form an inclusive relationship between the two composite structures (A and B) with *disregard to the internal composition of either of them*. The design significance generalizes the relationship between the two composite structures (A and B) without delving too deep into their internal construction. Simply put, there is no clear indication of the specific relationships between the contained substructures in each of these composite formations.

CONCEPT   Employ pipe solids to depict an inclusive relationship between structures to describe an integration strategy in lieu of depicting details of software associations between their substructures.

Exclusive Utilization of Pipe Solids

Use the exclusive utilization of pipe solids to describe explicit interaction, relationship, links, and information exchange between software structures and/or substructures.

> **CONCEPT**   Software architects can use pipe solids to author technical specifications rather than general design solutions.

Figure 7.8 illustrates this idea by depicting the exclusive relationship between two software formations: composite structure A and composite structure B. The former encompasses composite substructure A.1, which contains three substructures: atomic substructure A.1.1, atomic substructure A.1.2, and atomic substructure A.1.3. Composite structure B, on the other hand, comprises two substructures: atomic substructure B.1 and atomic substructure B.2.

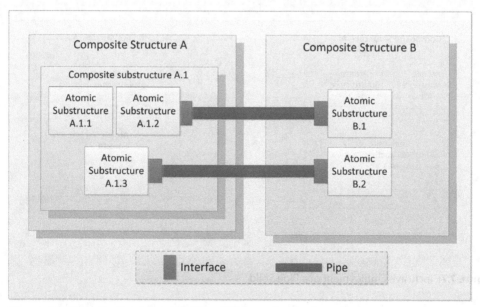

Figure 7.8: Exclusive Employment of Pipe Solids

As shown in Table 7.1, there are two established relationships: between atomic substructures A.1.2 and B.1, and between A.1.3 and B.2. These exclusive associations identify the integration and message routing between the internal substructures. This Table 7.1, the Exclusive Structure Relationship table, simplifies the view of these associations. It also specifies the message routing direction between the substructures: a relationship between atomic substructures A.1.2 and B.1 and information exchange between atomic substructures A.1.3 and B.2.

Table 7.1: Exclusive Structure Relationship

STRUCTURE	CONTAINMENT/ SUBSTRUCTURES	RELATIONSHIP
Composite A	Composite A.1	
Composite A.1	Atomic A.1.1	
	Atomic A.1.2	Atomic B.1
	Atomic A.1.3	Atomic B.2
Composite B	Atomic B.1	Atomic A.1.2
	Atomic B.2	Atomic A.1.3

Internal Utilization of Pipe Solids

Internal utilization of pipe solids depicts the inner communication between software substructures. To better understand this idea, refer to Figure 7.9, which illustrates the internal message exchange in composite structure A, which contains three substructures: composite A.1, atomic A.2, and atomic A.3. Furthermore, composite substructure A.1 encompasses its internal atomic substructures: A.1.1, A.1.2, A.1.3, and A.1.4.

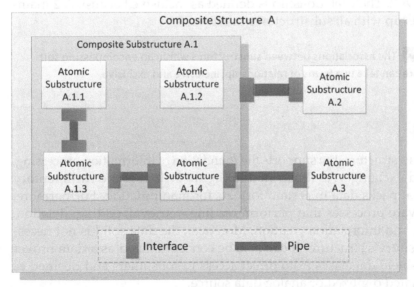

Figure 7.9: Internal Employment of Pipe Solids

Refer to Figure 7.9 to create a software structure association list similar to Table 7.2. It shows the structure relationships in the containment/substructure column. The relationship column identifies the association depicted by the pipe solid between two substructures, and the relationship type column denotes the type of association these substructures maintain.

Table 7.2: Internal Structure Relationship

STRUCTURE	CONTAINMENT/ SUBSTRUCTURE	RELATIONSHIP	RELATIONSHIP TYPE
Composite A	Composite A.1	Atomic A.2	Inclusive
	Atomic A.2	Composite A.1	Inclusive
	Atomic A.3	Atomic A.1.4	Exclusive
Composite A.1	Atomic A.1.1	Atomic A.1.3	Exclusive
	Atomic A.1.2	No relationship	
	Atomic A.1.3	Atomic A.1.4	Exclusive
	Atomic A.1.4	Atomic A.3	Exclusive
		Atomic A.1.3	Exclusive

For example, the table indicates composite substructure A.1, contained in composite structure A. The former also maintains a relationship with atomic substructure A.2. Their relationship is defined as inclusive because A.2 maintains relationship with all substructures in A1.

CONCEPT   The associations between substructures within an encompassing software structure can take two forms of relationship: inclusive and exclusive.

Data Solid

A data solid is a structure that supports the foundation of information processing, delivery, and exchange. As illustrated in Figure 7.10, it is the rudimentary formation that packs data in certain formats for manipulation. Furthermore, it hosts software processes that perform reading, retrieval, editing, deletion, replacement, and information creation. Moreover, the data solid is not necessarily a repository's structure. It can also be conceptualized as a data broker structure to shield databases from direct access to consumers and deemed as any encapsulated digitized or analog data source.

CONCEPT   To summarize, a data solid is a software structure designed to offer two chief functionalities. It containerizes arranged data in certain formats and braces software processes that offer data services to consumers.

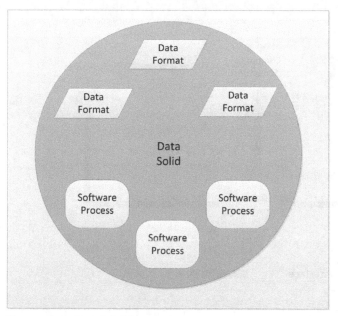

Figure 7.10: Data Solid Structure

Recall that a data solid is a structure, not the data itself. This formation is essentially an information organizer with various compartments for data formats available for specific consumers' needs. Data formats are the static or dynamic composition of information loaded in memory or saved to storage devices. For example, a data solid may accommodate formats such as arrays, stacks, linked lists, or queues.

Again, a data solid is merely the skeleton, the frame that holds all these information formats together and enables access to information through adapters and pipe solids. Just like with every other software structure discussed thus far, data solids can be integrated with their peer formations in the same fashion. Figure 7.11 illustrates a data solid utilization scenario in which three software structures, one composite and two atomic formations, make use of its structural capabilities.

In real life, data solids are found in abundance. They provide structural support for creating, reading, updating, and deleting (CRUD) operations across every software architecture environment. They grant access and information processing rights to tabular and/or nontabular data.[2] Furthermore, they constitute the building blocks of any data warehouse in production.

---

[2] *Tabular data format* refers to the structural arrangement of data in rows and columns. In contrast, nontabular data format pertains to unstructured composition of data that is stored in a repository.

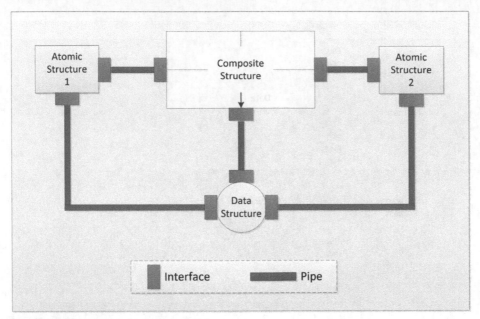

Figure 7.11: Integration of a Data Solid

CONCEPT   Most important, no information can be exchanged, served, manipulated, or distributed without the structural support of data solids.

Software Architecture Solids' Attribute Summary

Consider Table 7.3; it outlines the properties of the six design solids: atomic, composite, monolithic, interface, pipe, and data. Each column in the table specifies the affiliation of properties with a software solid.

Self-Sufficient   A structure that hosts software processes that do not wholly depend on other peer processes

Divisible   Refers to the feasibility aspect of decomposing a software structure

Distributable   A structure with the proper attributes for being distributed in a computing environment

Encompassing   A software structure that embeds substructures

Modular   A structure that supports reusable software processes or contains substructures that can be decomposed

Table 7.3: Software Architecture Solids Summary of Attributes

SOFTWARE SOLID	SELF-SUFFICIENT	DIVISIBLE	DISTRI-BUTABLE	ENCOMPASSING	MODULAR
Atomic	Not always	No	Yes	No	Not always
Composite	Not always	Not always	Yes	Yes	Yes
Monolithic	Yes	No	Not always	No	No
Interface	No	No	N/A	No	N/A
Data	N/A	Yes	Yes	Yes	Yes
Pipe	N/A	No	N/A	N/A	N/A

Software Architecture Dimensional Model

The fundamental necessity to illustrate space occupancy by each structure in a runtime ecosystem is the reason for depicting software dimensions. The software construction process calls for viewing a software implementation or a product from different dimensions. Architects, therefore, ought to provide blueprints that depict software structures in their single or multidimensional formations. The prevailing question that comes to mind now is what types of dimensions an architect can utilize to describe a software structure's geometry.

To answer this query, refer to Figure 7.12. It illustrates four types of software architecture dimensions that can be employed to depict structure sizes in a software architecture's space: zero dimensions, one dimension, two dimensions, and three dimensions. In addition, note the marking of the four coordinate lines, named *software architecture axes*:

L: Length

W: Width

H: Height

The sections that follow elaborate on these software architecture dimensions:

Zero Dimensions   A point, illustrated as a dot, possessing no geometrical length, width, or height properties.

One Dimension   The *length* of a software structure depicted by a straight or curved line that runs between two points. A series of connected lines (polyline) also illustrates one-dimensional software.

Two Dimensions   The *length* and *width* of a software structure (polygon) that illustrate a flat region in a software architecture environment.

Three Dimensions   Represents the *length*, *width*, and *height* of a software structure (polyhedron).

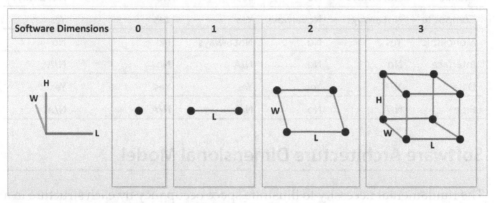

Figure 7.12: Software Architecture Dimensions

Software Architecture: Zero Dimension

The zero dimension of a software structure signifies a point in a software architecture space. In this environment, a point can be used to mark a position in a deployment landscape, specify a software implementation's geographical location, or denote a node on a network that a software product is affiliated with.

Although a point does not possess any geometrical properties related to structural software size (such as length, width, or height), it facilitates the mapping of software assets in production. Specifically, software implementations can be found at zero-dimensional points by leveraging a coordinate system. The section "Chief Features of Software Architecture Computing Space" discusses in detail coordinates in a software architecture environment space.

Furthermore, zero-dimensional points can be connected to illustrate relationships between software products and even depict message flows in a software architecture space. This topic is primarily discussed in the section "Software Architecture: Two Dimensions".

Figure 7.13 illustrates this concept. As shown, the white dots represent the zero-dimension points of software structures. Note that these points can be located anywhere in a software architecture computing space.

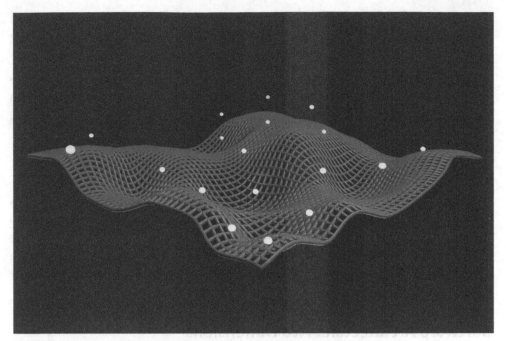

Figure 7.13: Zero-Dimensional Points in a Software Architecture Space

Software Architecture: One Dimension

Only the length between software structures is visible in the one-dimensional (1D) software world to illustrate their *relationships*. Simply put, this dimension illustrates the associations without depicting the software structures themselves. Accomplishing this requires straight or curved lines connecting the points (zero-dimension dots) in a software architecture space. For example, in Figure 7.14, point A and point B are linked by a line, and each point serves as a reference point for a software structure that is invisible in this illustration.

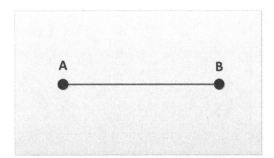

Figure 7.14: One Dimension in a Software Architecture Space

Furthermore, the 1D software architecture world not only illustrates business or technical relationships between software structures. It also identifies a variety of software capabilities and features, such as these:

Information Flow   Process flow, data flow, information sharing, message exchange, and workload direction between organizational software assets

Communication   Correspondence and collaboration between software implementations

Deployment Ranges   Regional and geographical distances between software deployments

Remember, in this 1D realm, the lines that connect points in a software architecture space also signify the distances between deployed software structures. The distances between these entities characteristically affect software performance and application response time. These operation influences are important aspects that should be considered when devising distribution, federation, and software integration.

Software Architecture: Two Dimensions

In the two-dimensional (2D) software architecture, a flatland world, software structures are depicted merely by their two dimensions: *length and width*. This view, depicted in Figure 7.15, represents only a single face of a software structure, disregarding its height. An illustration of a 2D structure does not divulge the entire space it would have occupied in a three-dimensional architecture ecosystem. However, in this flatland, the 2D software structure, measured by length and width values, provides helpful clues to the provincial real estate area that it requires for its operations.

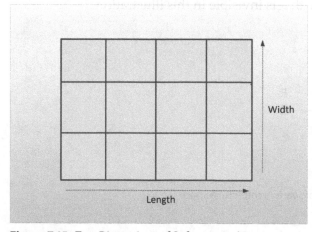

Figure 7.15: Two Dimensions of Software Architecture

CONCEPT   In a flatland software architecture world, the height of a hosted software structure is unspecified. Therefore, its hierarchical layers are invisible.

What Impacts the Length and Width Dimensions of a 2D Software Structure?

Table 7.4 depicts the aspects that impact the length and width of a software structure. As shown (in the "structure dimension" and the corresponding "influencing architecture factors" columns), scalability, consumers, interfaces, and computing resource consumption affect the length of a structure. However, granularity, modularity, and structural and source code complexity levels impact software structure widths. Finally, the metric column specifies how to compute a 2D software structure's length and width values.

Table 7.4: Examples of Influencing Factors on the Two Dimensions of Software Structures

STRUCTURE DIMENSION	INFLUENCING ARCHITECTURE FACTORS	METRIC
Length	Scalability	The number of instances of a software structure influences its length (i.e., horizontal scaling).
	Consumers	A software structure length is affected by the tally of the consumers that are served by its embedded software processes.
	Interfaces	The number of interfaces that a software structure supports affects its length's value.
	Computing resource consumption	The demand for computing resources by software implementation, such as memory, disk space, or network bandwidth, impacts the length of its supporting structure.
Width	Granularity	The number of processes, services, methods, and routines that a software structure supports defines its width.
	Modularity	The number of programming modules that a software structure braces impacts its width.
	Structural complexity level	The width value of a software structure is affected by the number of substructures that it encompasses.
	Source code complexity level[3]	Source code complexity level impacts the width of a software architecture structure.

---

[3] *IEEE Transactions on Software Engineering*, Volume: SE-2, Issue: 4, December 1976

The influencing architecture factors on software structure lengths and width may vary among organizations. For example, not all organizations would consider horizontal scaling as an influencing factor on the length of a software structure. Other factors, though, may be considered. Therefore, consider the table 7.4 an example that can be modified to reflect enterprise best practices and standards regarding specificity levels that should be illustrated in design models.

Software Architecture: Three Dimensions

As illustrated in Figure 7.16, the three dimensions of a software structure are length, width, and height. In this 3D software architecture world, a software structure appears like any other planet object. Namely, in addition to the length and width, we observe its height—commonly considered as the elevation of an object—that characteristically increases the level of software architecture specificity. Specifically, it enables architects to describe software attributes in design blueprints thoroughly. Moreover, schematically, the length is the longest side of a software structure, its width seems shorter, and its height emerges as a vertical dimension.

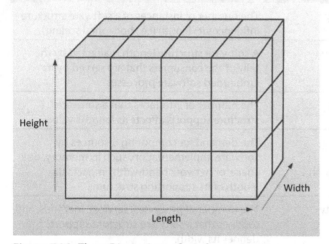

Figure 7.16: Three Dimensions of a Software Structure

Volumes of 3D Software Structures

In this three-dimensional (3D) world, software architects can specify the volume of a software structure. The term *volume* refers to the amount of space a software structure fills in a software architecture environment. In simple terms, every 3D software geometrical formation occupies the necessary space it needs to serve its affiliated consumers.

In the 3D computing world, volumes of software structures are calculated not only to visualize their size but also to be able to assess their operational needs for survival in a geometrical runtime environment. Operational needs pertain to various technical and architectural accommodations, such as elasticity, scalability, computing resources, high availability, and redundancy. Therefore, the volumes of software structures can provide metrics for these requirements.

Moreover, just like we would determine the volume of a simple formation, such as a living room, cube, brick, or shoe box, we would also be able to ascertain the volume of a software structure. For example, to determine the volume of a rectangular jewelry box, one would need to multiply its length by its width by its height.

CONCEPT   Keep volume calculations of software structures as simple as possible to avoid unnecessary composition complexity.

Increase in Software Architecture Level of Specificity in a 3D Computing World

The level of software architecture specificity is raised again with the 3D view of software. Here we are not only commissioned to identify the influencing architecture attributes on the length and width of a software structure (as discussed in the earlier section "Software Architecture: Two Dimensions"), we are also adding the height—a third dimension necessary to illustrate its altitude. The height of a software structure can be used to depict its elevation *above* any reference point, such as its base (length and width) or any point in a software architecture space. Moreover, the height of a software structure is a vital metric that can help to calculate its volume (magnitude), especially when comparing it to other structures.

As mentioned, in this multidimensional world, the length, width, and height depict the size of software structure in a software architecture space. These metrics identify the magnitude of a structure and its volume. Observe the influencing factor examples in Table 7.5 to understand this concept better. Note that the length and width dimensions have been established earlier in section "Software Architecture: Two Dimensions." Here we add the height—the third structure dimension—along with its influencing architecture factors and metrics.

Table 7.5: Examples of Influencing Factors on the Three Dimensions of Software Structures

STRUCTURE DIMENSION	INFLUENCING ARCHITECTURE FACTORS	METRIC
Length	Scalability	The number of instances of a software structure influences its length (i.e., horizontal scaling).
	Consumers	A software structure's length is affected by the tally of the consumers who are served by its embedded software processes.
	Interfaces	The number of interfaces that a software structure supports affects its length's value.
	Computing resource consumption	The demand for computing resources by software implementation, such as memory, disk space, or network bandwidth, impacts the length of its supporting structure.
Width	Granularity	The number of processes, services, methods, and routines that a software structure supports defines its width.
	Modularity	The number of programming modules that a software structure braces impacts its width.
	Structural complexity level	The width value of a software structure is affected by the number of substructures that it encompasses.
	Source code complexity level	Source code complexity level impacts the width of a software architecture structure.
Height	Software architecture layers	The number of layers affects the height dimension of a software structure (i.e., presentation, application, business, persistence, and database layers).
	Technology stack (solution stack)	The number of technologies developers use to construct software implementations affects the height of its supporting structure (i.e., programming languages, script languages, libraries, Web application frameworks, databases, data sources, web servers).
	Software architecture environments stack	The height of a software structure is influenced by the number of environments or infrastructures that its supported programming logic is compatible with (i.e., operating systems, clouds, data lakes, protocols, networks, virtualization, containers).
	Business or technical capability stack	Braced by its structure, the number of business and/or technical capabilities a software implementation offers (i.e., analytics, brokering, aggregation, interoperability, mobility, user interfaces).

As apparent in Table 7.5, the height dimension is influenced by four architecture characteristics or factors: software architecture layers, technology stack, software architecture environments stack, and business or technical capability stack. In essence, these layers depict hierarchical structure formations affiliated with the technologies, capabilities, and environments of the supported programing logic and processes. Furthermore, as discussed in the previous section, these influences on a software structure's dimensions are examples that can be used or replaced by other organizational architecture attributes or factors.

The height dimension of a software structure is one of the most useful metrics used to identify how compartmentalized a software implementation is. Specifically, the hierarchical layers of software technologies and capabilities would typically show to which extent software is componentized. This architecture attribute contributes to software reuse and the loose-coupling properties of software design. In addition, the height metric indicates how isolated its supported software components are.

Software Population Sustainability in an Architecture Environment Space: A Capacity Planning Challenge

Too often, organizations fail to assess the fitness of their production environments. The term *fitness* is related to companies' continuous capability to sustain the operational pressures of the hosted software products. And in this context operational pressures mean that every deployed software implementation typically burdens production uniquely.

For example, some software implementations strain the environment by pursuing a high volume of business transactions, while others necessitate extreme network bandwidth. Some serve an overwhelming crowd of consumers, while others demand advanced technologies to promote potent business continuity. So, with these collective operational challenges, the chief question that comes to mind is about the sustainability of a software population in a runtime ecosystem. Specifically, do organizations tend to control the population growth of deployed software?

What if these firms neglect to monitor and restrict the number of software implementations in an already strained deployment space? What if they do not employ control mechanisms to address extreme workloads of business processes? What if the overall geometrical volumes of the deployed software products overrun the computing space of a runtime environment? Finally, what is the sustainability level of a software architecture space?

Currently, there are no industry mechanisms to assess and understand the impact of the software population density on a production environment. Without proper monitoring mechanisms to mitigate the risks of a growing software population, the implications could be vast, and the consequences might even be dire. Furthermore, organically grown deployment environments that typically do not attend to software architecture strategies tend to disregard the impact of an expanding software community.

The uncontrolled increase in the software population only challenges the deployment, integration, and operations of software implementations. This state of affairs only introduces production chaos that's hard to manage. Furthermore, the architecture complexity level of the runtime environment only rises. Therefore, tackling the software population density issue in a software architecture environment should become a top priority when carving out a deployment and integration strategy. The chief mission would then be to formulate best practices to promote the software occupancy balance in production.

CONCEPT   Consider that all software structures' collective 3D geometrical volumes should not exceed the boundaries of a software architecture environment space.

Comparative Perspectives in a Software Architecture Space

Software implementations provide different ranges of solutions to business or technical problems. However, while some may execute many processes, others may offer limited functionality. In design terms, this implies that software implementations are affiliated with different levels of granularity.

For example, a monolithic implementation is known to be coarse-grained because it typically bundles many services and data. A microservice, on the other hand, is considered to be fine-grained because of the narrow scope of its operations.

So, should a runtime environment include software implementations at an approximate level of granularity? Or should the granularity levels of software not even be taken into account when deploying and integrating software? These questions represent dilemmas software architects typically grapple with when designing business products and hosting environments.

The rule suggests that a balanced software architecture ecosystem should not contain software implementations at extreme levels of granularity. Not only can such a configuration increase operational maintenance costs, but it would also be impractical to invest efforts in integrating software that does not equally scale in size, magnitude, and dimension. Acclimatize to the notion of *comparative perspective* to achieve such ecosystem parity.

CONCEPT   The term *comparative perspective* is all about the ability to compare the 3D geometrical volumes of software structures to promote effective software architecture equilibrium.

Again, an unbalanced software architecture space typically includes software implementations with exceedingly different granularity levels. This condition only increases architecture integration complexity, introduces software maintenance challenges, and raises the cost of their ownership. To mitigate such risks, consider integrating equal size software structures in production.

3D Software Structures in a Software Architecture Computing Space

Our ambition to view or understand an environment with higher dimensions, such as four or even beyond, introduces an intellectual challenge that is difficult to parse. Humans are trapped in a 3D space in which all objects possess three units of measurement: length, width, and height. However, despite our inability to live in a higher-dimensional world, we can still visualize a fourth-dimension ecosystem only when reflected as a three-dimension environment. Nevertheless, this reflection is typically represented on a flat computer screen representing a 2D display.

Despite the increasing number of movies and TV programs that depict higher dimensions than our natural 3D environment, viewers are being challenged to digest these fictional worlds that no one has ever physically visited. The movie *Interstellar*, for instance, brilliantly illustrates a mind-bending five-dimensional world in which the main character can view different points in time and perspective.

This section presents the software architecture computing space as a 3D ecosystem in which software structure volumes occupy individual spaces. Some structures comprise substructures that support programming logic. Others are fine-grained software formations, unbreakable constructs that merely host processes.

The software population in the 3D architecture space form collaborative and coordinated relationships to carry out transactions and share information. The structures are laid out in different styles to provide effective business and technological solutions to fulfill this mission. The term *styles* pertains to the arrangement and distribution of software in software architecture (refer to the section "Distribution Styles of Software Implementations in an Architecture Computing Space," which discusses software structure distribution styles).

The Impetus for Establishing a 3D Software Architecture Space

There is a dependency between geometrical software structures and their hosting 3D computing ecosystem. On the one hand, the impetus for devising a 3D software architecture space is accommodating the hosted 3D software structures and their related programming logic and processes. On the other hand, the 3D software structures' magnitude, volumes, and operations drive the requirements to shape a 3D software architecture space.

Consider the most common technological conditions necessary for supporting 3D software structures in a software architecture ecosystem:

Allocation of Computing Resources   Adequate computing resources to support the volumes of 3D software structures

Accommodation of Space   Satisfactory software architecture space to accommodate granularity levels of 3D software structures

Sustainment of Operations   Suitable software architecture ecosystem capability to sustain the operations (such as message exchange, business transactions, and information sharing) of a 3D software community

Control of Software Population Density   Mechanisms to control software population density to avoid overrunning a 3D software architecture space capacity

Positioning of Software   A coordinate system to locate the relative positioning of 3D software structures in a 3D software architecture space

Allocation of Software Architecture Space   Space allocation control system to guarantee the following: optimal utilization of software architecture space, and avoiding overlapping occupancy of 3D software structures in a 3D software architecture space

Balancing Software Architecture   Automated continuous deployment (CD) and continuous integration (CI) processes driven by comparative analysis to promote a balanced software architecture. The analysis should prioritize the deployment of comparable volumes of 3D software structures to a software architecture environment

Increasing Specificity of Software Design   A 3D geometrical space to increase the specificity of software design, such as software layering, structure volumes, capacity, space requirements, and more

Promoting Software Architecture Symmetry   Equally distributed software structures across a 3D software architecture computing space to fully leverage computing resources and data sharing capabilities in various deployment regions

While these environment essentials are vital to the survival of software structures, they can equally impact the hosting software architecture space. Therefore, this bidirectional dependency calls for establishing a balanced architecture driven by technological reconciliation, meaning give and take. For example, on the one hand, the 3D ecosystem should be able to sustain the density of a software population. On the other, each software should be given equal opportunities to provide business and technical services without being constrained by the architectural space they are deployed to.

Chief Features of Software Architecture Computing Space

A software architecture space is a demarcated 3D technological ecosystem, a geometrical topology that hosts 3D software structures and their corresponding business or technical functionality. Figure 7.17 illustrates a schematic software architecture computing space and 3D software structures. Note the software structures that occupy space in the 3D hosting environment.

A1: Atomic structure

A2: Atomic structure

A3: Atomic structure

M: Monolithic structure

C: Composite structure

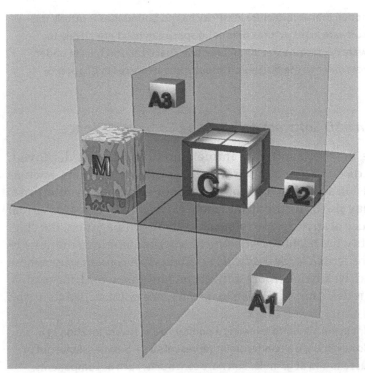

Figure 7.17: 3D Software Structures in a 3D Software Architecture Computing Space

Influences of Software Structures on Software Architecture Computing Space

An architectural computing space undergoes continuous deformation attributed to the behavior of the hosted software structures and their related software implementations. The term *continuous deformation* refers to the response of the computing space to the impact of software implementations. Gravitational, competing, and harmonizing software forces are examples of factors that influence the software architecture computing space as a whole (as discussed in Chapter 6, "Software Architecture Environment Construction"). Consumption of computing resources is another factor that may affect the software architecture space in its entirety.

The reaction of the software architecture computing space to these software behavioral events is rooted in the architecture properties that being assigned during design time by software architects. Software *architecture elasticity* for example, is a design property that enables the expansion and contraction of an architectural computing space. This continuous deformation can also occur due to the dynamic allocation of computing resources, such as the increase of data storage, memory, network bandwidth, and more.

CONCEPT   The notion that architecture elasticity has no boundaries is utterly misleading. Although a software architecture computing space can react effectively to the demands of software operations, the 3D architecture space can still buckle under extreme software forces (refer to the discussion about software forces in Chapter 6).

Relative Positions in a 3D Software Architecture Computing Space

There are no limits to where software implementations can be deployed. Organizations may disburse them to various geographical locations, such as regions or continents. In addition, they may be federated across an enterprise. Furthermore, they may also be distributed to mobile devices, desktops, or virtual environments. Because of such a wide range of software propagation, the chief challenge is to identify the *relative positioning* of software implementations in any environment. The term *relative positioning* pertains to a *point in space* where software can be found. Finally, in any 3D software architecture world, the relative position of software is determined relative to its reference point, called its *origin*.

CONCEPT   A point in the 3D world is merely a pointer to a software location in a deployment space. However, since a relative point represents a zero-dimensional dot in space, it can also be used to aim at granular software constructs, such as components, services, and processes.

Figure 7.18 depicts a 3D software architecture computing space with relative positions represented by points (shown as white dots). Note that each point in this geometrical space has no length, width, or height (refer to the discussion in the section "Software Architecture: Zero Dimension"). Their corresponding reference point, the *origin* (a dark dot), appears in the center of the computing space.

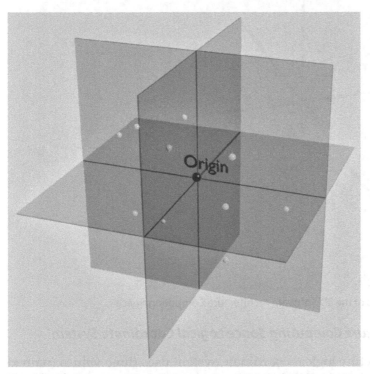

Figure 7.18: Points and Their Corresponding Origin in Software Architecture Computing Space

Coordinate Axes: Skeleton of a Software Architecture Computing Space

Direction, navigation, orientation, location, positioning, and volume are fundamental terminology vital to finding software assets in a computing environment. This lingo depicts the *logical positioning* of software in a runtime 3D space. Simply put, this logical addressability system identifies the space a software structure and its affiliated programming logic and processes occupy in a software architecture computing ecosystem.

Locating software in the logical world requires a skeleton in a software architecture computing space, as depicted in Figure 7.19. The skeleton contains three coordinate axes: X, Y, and Z. They meet at the origin (point O), the converging point at which the axes cross each other. Finally, the x- and y-axes are depicted as horizontal lines, and the z-axis points upward.

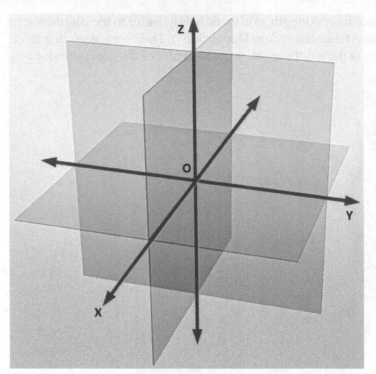

Figure 7.19: Three Axes of the 3D Software Architecture Computing Space

Software Architecture Computing Space Logical Coordinate System

A software architecture logical coordinate system uses three values (named *numerical coordinates*) to identify the locations of points or positions of software geometrical elements in a 3D software architecture computing space. Figure 7.20 illustrates a schematic presentation of a composite software structure in such an orientation system. The coordinate axis lines X, Y, and Z depict the skeleton of the system. As apparent, they go through a common point, the origin (O). As indicated by their arrows, each axis points in a different direction. Furthermore, the white demarcation bullets on each of them denote numerical units. And each white bullet represents one numerical coordinate value..

The numerical coordinate values for the software structure are shown in Figure 7.20. Generally, these three values can be associated with any of the structure's dimension length, width, or height. In this illustration, however, the coordinate lines X, Y, and Z represent these three dimensions of software structure with their corresponding values:

X (width) = 2

Y (length) = 4

Z (height) = 3

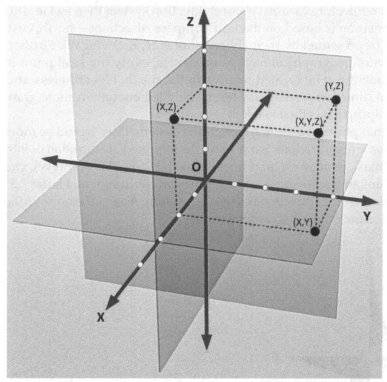

Figure 7.20: Software Architecture Computing Space Coordinate System

Moreover, not only do the values reveal the logical location of software in a software architecture computing space, but they also depict its size and help quantify its volume. Recall that the value of a 3D software structure's volume can be obtained by multiplying its numerical coordinates, X, Y, and Z. In Figure 7.20, this value amounts to (in any cubic metric system) 24 (2 × 4 × 3 = 24).

Cardinal and Intercardinal Physical Directions in Software Architecture Computing Space

As elaborated in the previous section, a software architecture *logical* coordinate system contributes to locating software assets in a given computing space. As shown, the numeric coordinate values (X, Y, and Z) indeed point to the 3D logical addressable locations in a software architecture environment. These coordinates, however, do not disclose the *physical* positions of software implementations in a runtime environment. They are merely used for spatial orientation, not for software's physical or geographical positioning.

The software architecture cardinal *physical* direction system then tackles this issue. This proposition is based on the four compass directions—north, east, south, and west (represented by their abbreviations: N, E, S, and W). Furthermore, as with every geographical navigation device, every physical point in a given environment can be located relative to the north. Nevertheless, this physical cardinal direction system may not be detailed enough. A more granular orientation approach is then needed.

The intercardinal physical direction navigation system, thus, would be more appropriate for some organizations. Simply put, the intermediate direction points, northeast, southeast, southwest, and northwest (NE, SE, SW, and NW), can better assist in depicting software assets in a physical environment. Figure 7.21 illustrates the intercardinal direction navigation system. Again, the north is the reference point for the other intercardinal points.

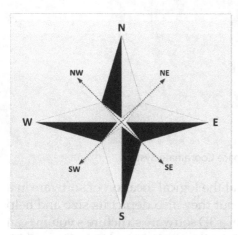

Figure 7.21: Cardinal and Intercardinal Directions in a Software Architecture Computing Space

Applying Cardinal and Intercardinal Directions to Software Architecture Computing Space

If necessary, a cardinal and intercardinal physical direction system can be shown in an illustration depicting a software architecture computing space (see Figure 7.22). Note that the physical direction system is at the bottom of the software architecture computing space.

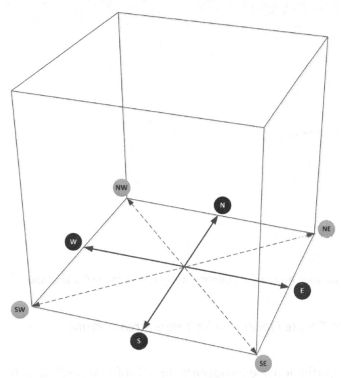

Figure 7.22: Applying an Intercardinal Directions System to a Software Architecture Computing Space

Marrying a Logical Coordinate System with Cardinal and Intercardinal Physical Directions System

Figure 7.23 represents a diagrammatic approach to marrying these two navigation systems (logical and physical). On the one hand, the logical coordinate system (shown with the x-, y-, and z-axes) is used to locate software implementations in a 3D space without any physical reference. On the other hand, the cardinal and intercardinal physical direction system panel is pasted on the bottom of the software architecture computing space.

Figure 7.23 illustrates an example of combining these two orientation systems. The x-axis (of the logical navigation system) corresponds to two possible cardinal physical directions: north and south. The y-axis (of the logical navigation system) conforms to the east and west cardinal physical directions. This configuration is not carved in stone, and there are no rules for aligning these two navigation systems. They can be aligned as it suits the need for software design.

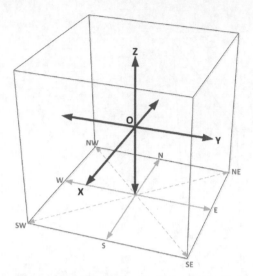

Figure 7.23: Combining the Software Architecture Coordinate System with the Cardinal and Intercardinal Directions Panel

Leveraging the Z-Axis to Create Floors in a Software Architecture Computing Space

We know that a logical coordinate system supports the 3D software architecture computing space, a navigation skeleton that includes the three axis lines: X, Y, and Z. In this 3D computing world, the z-axis represents its height. It can be used to horizontally slice a computing space into logical layers (floors).

Figure 7.24 illustrates this idea. It depicts a software architecture computing space sliced horizontally (in the middle of the z-axis) into two floors. The top contains a composite and two atomic software structures, and three atomic and composite software structures are featured on the bottom floor.

Software assets can be categorized into different layers in an integrated computing environment. Each layer represents a floor in the 3D computing space. Consider Table 7.6. The layer category column represents the group of floors listed under the floor column. For example, the layer category software deployment includes the business, utilities, middleware, and data floors (layers).

Table 7.6: Layering a Software Architecture Computing Space Example

LAYER CATEGORY	FLOOR
Software deployment	Business
	Utilities
	Middleware
	Data

LAYER CATEGORY	FLOOR
Criticality of software asset	Critical
	Medium
	Low
Line of business	Auto insurance
	Home insurance
	Life insurance

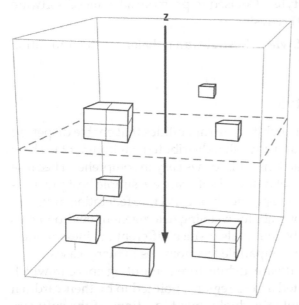

Figure 7.24: Two Floors in a Software Architecture Computing Space

Distribution Styles of 3D Software Implementations in an Architecture Computing Space

In a 3D computing space, software entities are distributed to either side of or on each coordinate line X, Y, and Z and positioned at particular points in space. This deployment scheme is driven by business, technical, social, financial, and other imperatives. Moreover, a software architecture computing space not driven by strategies (organically grown environments) typically spins out of control due to the arbitrary and unplanned distributions of software products in an unmanaged runtime ecosystem. Consequently, the implications are detrimental to the business and the production environment management.

The presented software distribution styles introduce opportunities to advance effective communication and information sharing between organizations, computer systems, and applications. In addition, they are devised to foster a balanced software architecture environment.

The following styles are discussed in detail in the sections that follow:

Federated Distribution Style   Discusses a generic software distribution style and the relationship between software entities in a 3D computing space

Flooring Distribution Style   Elaborates on positioning software implementations on different layers in a computing space

Symmetrical Distribution Style   Devised to promote a balanced software architecture space in a 3D ecosystem

Asymmetrical Distribution Style   Illustrates an unbalanced 3D computing space and how to avoid it

Federated Distribution Style

The concept of *federation* refers to architecture capabilities that enable dispersed organizations, lines of business, and any other distributed environment to share information and exchange transactions. This idea is easy to comprehend because reuse and redundancy reduction of data and software are simple best practices that most enterprises have adopted. Specifically, architecture federation promotes business and technological interoperability, enabling heterogenous environments to trade information. The chief benefit is clear since different business models drive these environments and incompatible technologies in many cases.

Figure 7.25 illustrates a 3D software architecture computing space in which software structures are distributed across regions, pointed to by their cardinal and intercardinal directions. Note the deployment locations of the software structures in relationship to their orientation:

Atomic A3: north

Composite C: northeast

Monolithic M: southeast

Atomic A1: west

Atomic A2: northwest

Furthermore, Figure 7.26 depicts a federated environment that demonstrates relationships between connected software entities (by connecting lines). Software architects should investigate the feasibility of such links and verify if they are practical and on equal footing.

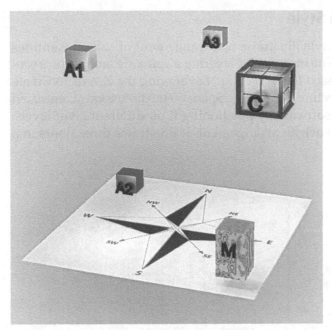

Figure 7.25: Three-Dimension Federation Style

CONCEPT The "equal footing" best practice calls for a verification process to ascertain if the connections between the federated software entities are based on their comparable criticality and granularity levels, volume, and other business and technical considerations.

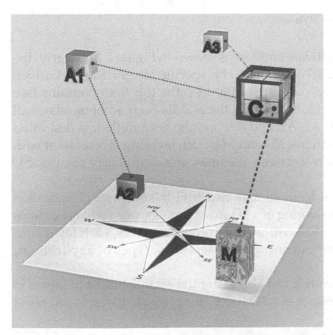

Figure 7.26: Federated Relationship Style in a 3D Computing Space

Flooring Distribution Style

The flooring distribution style illustrates an arrangement of software entities in a 3D computing space. The impetus for layering a software architecture ecosystem was initially discussed in the section "Leveraging the Z-Axis to Create Floors in a Software Architecture Computing Space." The discussion accentuated the need for categorizing software by positioning it on different layer levels. Figure 7.27 demonstrates such an arrangement. It illustrates three floors in a 3D computing ecosystem.

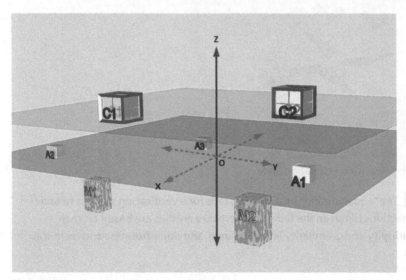

Figure 7.27: Flooring Distribution Style

The positioning of the software entities, as shown in Figure 7.27, clearly displays a compartmentalized 3D ecosystem. This specific categorization is driven by the type of the deployed software structures: the top floor contains two composite software structures, C1 and C2; the middle floor accommodates all atomic software structures, A1, A2, and A3; and the bottom floor is dedicated to the two monolithic formations, M1 and M2. Such layering is consistent with the requirement to keep software sizes, volumes, and granularity comparable on each floor.

Other organizational considerations may also drive this software classification method. As mentioned, the flooring of a 3D space can separate software entities by their business and technical criticality. In other instances, each layer contains different business lines, financial considerations, types of applications, and so forth.

The flooring distribution style can also foster the establishment of layers in a software structure that resides in a 3D space. Simply put, this style can assist software architects in compartmentalizing a particular software into different points of concern by promoting software isolation and modular design.

To better understand this concept, let's look at the example in Figure 7.28. Note that the three floors subdivide a composite structure into three layers: presentation, application, and data.

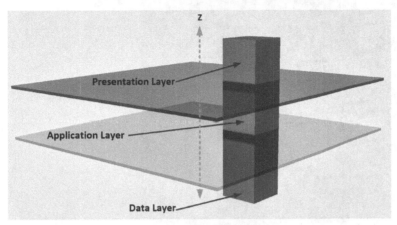

Figure 7.28: Layering a Software Structure in a 3D Computing Space

Symmetrical and Asymmetrical Distribution Styles

In essence, the absence of organizational best practices to promote a balanced software architecture in a computing space pertains to a 3D computing space that maintains a symmetrical software distribution scheme. In this context, "balance" calls for effective software architecture that guarantees business and technical continuity. A balanced architecture, for example, calls for sensible integration of software assets with comparable volumes and granularity levels and requires proper allocation of computing resources in a multidimensional ecosystem.

Symmetrical Distribution Style

In a symmetrical software architecture computing environment (as shown in Figure 7.29), software entities are distributed equally on either side of the 3D coordinate lines: X, Y, and Z.

This arrangement resembles a mirrored space in which software structures possess similar volumes and granularity levels and are equally spaced from each other. A completely symmetrical distribution would be hard to achieve because of business or technological constraints in production. Note that this guidance calls for sensible distribution to avoid a section in space that hosts a high-density software population that typically consumes computing resources that are hard to satisfy.

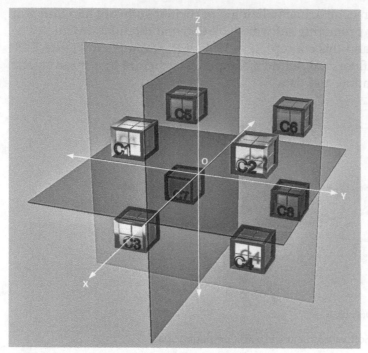

Figure 7.29: Symmetrical Distribution Style

In the symmetrical distribution style example illustrated in Figure 7.29,

- The composite software structures C1, C2, C3, and C4 are positioned on the positive values of the X-coordinate line.

- The C5, C6, C7, and C8 composite software structures are deployed along the negative numbers of the X-coordinate line.

- This symmetrical distribution style is also preserved along the Y-coordinate when C2, C4, C6, and C8 are positioned on the y-axis positive values, the composite services C1, C3, C5, and C7 deploy to the negative y-axis values.

- The same symmetrical arrangement applies to the composite software structures on both sizes of the z-axis. Note that C1, C2, C5, and C6 are deployed on the positive values of the Z-coordinate and C3, C4, C7, and C8 are located on the negative Z's values.

Consider the summary of software distribution guidelines that follow, devised to promote software architecture balanced in a 3D ecosystem:

Software Density   All regions in a 3D software architecture environment should be equally populated by software implementations.

Computing Resources   Evenly assign computing resources to all locations in a 3D computing space where the software population is equally spaced.

Spacing   Evenly space software entities in a computing ecosystem.

Information Sharing   Distribute data, messages, and transaction workload volumes in a software architecture runtime environment equally.

Asymmetrical Distribution Style

An asymmetrical distribution is formed when a software population is spread unequally across the x-, y-, and z-axes. Table 7.7 describes visible and invisible distribution attributes that negatively impact the equilibrium of a computing environment.

Table 7.7: Software Architecture Balance Tipping Factors

VISIBILITY	FACTOR	EXPLANATION
Visible	Software population	Ineffective containment of software population growth in a specific region of a computing space
	Software structure volumes	Distribution of incomparable software structure volumes
	Spacing	Unequal spacing between software entities in a software architecture ecosystem
	Software infrastructure	Saturation of software infrastructure platforms, such as middleware, at specific points in a 3D ecosystem
	Monitoring and security	Height concentration of monitoring and security facilities that occupy certain regions in a runtime environment
	Repositories	Repositories that are centered in specific locations in an architecture computing environment
	Software layering	An architecture that promotes excessive software layering
Invisible	Transaction volumes	A high volume of transactions executed in certain areas in the 3D computing space
	Computing resources	Extreme and uneven consumption levels of computing resources in different parts of a software architecture environment computing
	Software relationship	An integration scheme that supports excessive relationships in selected parts of a runtime ecosystem

Figure 7.30 shows an example of an asymmetrical software distribution style. Note the uneven positioning of the software structures in the three-dimensional software architecture computing space. Atomic software structures A1, A2, and A3 are deployed alongside the negative values of the coordinate line Y and the positive values of X. In addition, the C2 and C3 composite software structures

are located along the negative values of Y and simultaneously deployed beside the negative values of X. The C1 composite software structure is the only entity that occupies space adjacent to the positive values of X and Y.

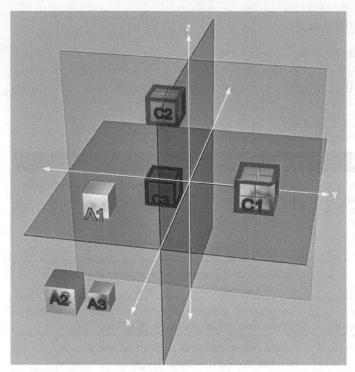

Figure 7.30: Asymmetrical Distribution Style

CONCEPT   An asymmetrical distribution style does not always represent an extremely unbalanced software architecture computing space. It depends on to which extent the overall deployment of software entities can tip the balance of a runtime environment.

Construction Life Cycle of Software Implementations

Software construction in a 3D computing world is driven by an iterative process, during which architects utilize tools and employ methods to achieve design equilibrium. And there is no limit to the number of iterations that can be pursued to achieve an optimal software construction. The term *design equilibrium* refers to a compromised architecture scheme that avoids radical business or technical solution choices.

As discussed in the sections that follow, software architects should seek a middle ground between two or more radical design solutions. For example, during the construction life cycle, architects may be called to opt for a design compromise between a software structure that contains too many or too few layers. Therefore, this determination should be driven by meticulous analysis and repetitive design cycles to achieve optimal software construction.

However, the challenges are even greater in a software architecture computing space, a 3D ecosystem. Namely, to achieve a balanced architecture in such a geometrical topology, the three axes—x, y, and z—that support the coordinate system must drive the software design. In the sections that follow, the x-axis is affiliated with the width of a software structure, y is related to its length, and z is associated with its height. Therefore, any manipulation of a software structure should be guided by these axes.

CONCEPT   The software construction life cycle requires iterative design activities in a 3D software architecture computing space. The ultimate goal of the design process is to promote an environment equilibrium by attaining optimal software formations that effectively interlock with each other.

Software Construction Process

The software construction process first calls for a pragmatic and gradual approach to understanding the nature of software structures in a 3D computing environment. Then, pursue an explorational design life cycle using powerful tools to build effective and feasible software structures.

To accomplish this, complete the following steps:

1. **Create a construction balance table**. Creating a software construction balance table involves developing a construction equilibrium list. Creating this allows one to understand enterprise strategies about best-practice design for formulating a balanced software architecture.

2. **Study the software construction design tools**. Become familiar with these tools and study their unique contribution to creating, altering, and optimizing software formations. This topic is discussed in section "Software Construction Design Activities."

Creating a Software Construction Balance Table

Before beginning the software construction life-cycle process, a list of design attributes can assist software architects in assessing the boundaries between extreme solutions. To better understand this idea, glance at Table 7.8, which exemplifies the range between two design propositions. the "Design Attribute I" and "Design Attribute II" columns represent radical design properties that should be balanced, with the "Software Design Activities" column offering best practices for achieving such equilibrium.

Table 7.8: Software Construction Balance Examples Table

DESIGN ATTRIBUTE I	DESIGN ATTRIBUTE II	SOFTWARE DESIGN ACTIVITIES
Impractical software distribution symmetry	Asymmetric software distribution	Find the golden mean between two extreme software entity distribution design symmetries.
Exceedingly coarse-grained	Highly fine-grained	Circumvent design solutions that promote extreme granularity levels of software structures (refers to the width of a software volume, as discussed in the section "Use Case I: Thicken and Contract Design Activities").
Radically layered	Extremely flat	Seek a construction balance between an extremely flat or radically layered software structure (refer to the discussion in the section "Use Case III: Layer and Delayer Design Activities").
Immense software structure volume	Excessively slight software structure volume	Foster a compromised software design that disfavors extremely large or excessively small software structure volumes.
Random deployment of software structure volumes	Incomparable software structure volumes	Promote a balanced software architecture in a computing space that calls for hosting comparable software structure volumes.
An unreasonably scaled software entity	Deficiently scaled software entity	Shun software design that disregards proper scalability and availability of software entities (discussed mainly in the section "Use Case II: Lengthen and Shorten Design Activities").
Overly thick software structure	Disproportionately thin software structure	Maintain a well-adjusted software design that sidesteps extremely thin or overly thick software structures (pertains to the width of a software volume as discussed in the section "Use Case I: Thicken and Contract Design Activities").

Software Construction Design Activities

The six unique design activities illustrated in Figure 7.31 ultimately drive the creation of optimal software construction. Note that these design tools are used to manipulate software structures hosted in a 3D software architecture computing space. Furthermore, every design activity should comply with the X-, Y-, and Z-coordinate directions. Specifically, as indicated previously in the introduction of this section, the x-axis is affiliated with changes to a software structure's width, the y is related to its length, and the z to its height.

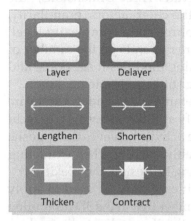

Figure 7.31: Software Construction Design Activities

Thicken   A design activity tool provided to solidify the width of a software structure (to be applied on the X-coordinate line)

Contract   Employed to optimize or reduce the width of a software structure (applies to the x-axis values)

Lengthen   Extends the range of software services and increases their availability to consumers by applying scaling mechanisms. This design activity refers to the modification of a software structure along the Y-coordinate

Shorten   Limits the range of software offerings and reduces its scalability and availability (pertains to the y-axis values)

Layer   Employed to add layers to a software structure (relates to the z-axis line)

Delayer   Used to reduce, eliminate, and deprecate layers of software structure (applies to the Z-coordinate line)

The sections that follow discuss in detail these software design activities that promote a balanced software architecture computing space:

Use Case I: Thicken and contract design activities

Use Case II: Lengthen and shorten design activities

Use Case III: Layer and delayer design activities

Use Case I: Thicken and Contract Design Activities

The thicken and contract design tools are all about manipulating the depth of a software structure in a 3D software architecture computing space. In this respect, depth is an attribute or quality primarily affiliated with a property of a software formation, such as width, range, breadth, magnitude, or thickness.

As discussed in the section "Software Architecture: Three Dimensions," the width of a software structure is influenced by the chief factors: granularity, modularity, structural complexity level, and source code complexity level. In a nutshell, the thickness of a software structure depends on the number of processes it possesses, the number of programming modules it supports, and the design complexity levels of its corresponding software implementation.

Furthermore, the thickened design tool can be employed to widen a software entity's solution scope or to add processes to satisfy additional business or technological requirements. In contrast, the contracting activity achieves the opposite results: the breadth of its services would inevitably narrow when extracting functionality from a software structure or reducing its design complexity.

Finally, the thicken and contract design activities should be used to apply changes to the width of a software structure. Remember that in the 3D computing world, these modifications should be visible on the X-coordinate line values (as we choose to relate the thickness of a structure to the x-axis). *The higher the X-coordinate values, the thicker the software formation, and vice versa.*

CONCEPT   Software architects ought to offer design solutions to promote balanced design regarding the width dimension of software structures. Namely, the balance between radically thick and fragile software formations must be sought to maintain an equilibrium of operations in the software architecture computing space.

When to Apply Thicken and Contract Design Activities

It is a common industry practice to apply software modifications throughout the development life cycle; this includes design, development, testing, deployment, integration, and operations. The most impactful software design changes typically occur early in product development. Specifically, adding or removing business or technical functionality during design time is the least costly effort. The later we augment software with additional processes and modules, the more we increase design complexity and maintenance expenditure.

The most challenging instances are when business and technical requirements call for changes later during the product life cycle. For example, there are instances when the business seeks to add functions, services, and product offerings. Marketing efforts can also necessitate additions to software products while they already operate in a runtime environment. In these cases, software architects are called to devise design modifications without hampering business and technical continuity.

Therefore, based on practical experience, *minor* thickening or contracting design activities on software structures should occur after the software construction phase is completed to minimize the risks to business operations. And in contrast, major modifications to software deployed, integrated, and already operating in production can disrupt the software architecture environment balance.

Thicken and Contract Design Methods

Consider Table 7.9, which elaborates on the chief design procedures employed to balance a software architecture environment. The "Design Activity" column includes the thicken and contract tools, the "Method" column lists four approaches for each design activity, and the "Task" column offers corresponding software design approaches.

Table 7.9: Thicken and Contract Design Methods

DESIGN ACTIVITY	METHOD	TASK
Thicken	Augmentation	Expanding software solution capabilities by adding more processes, services, and functionality to increase its granularity level
	Modularity	Migrating or adding programming modules into an existing software structure to simplify architecture and source code complexity, increase software reuse, and reduce maintenance cost
	Reinforcement	Combining fine-grained software structures into composite formations to promote software architecture balance when it comes to comparable volumes of software structures
	Consolidation	Merging two or more software structures (atomic, composite, or monolithic) into a single one to minimize redundancy of operations
Contract	Scope reduction	Reducing the solution scope of software by extracting or migrating out some of its services
	Architecture restructuring	Optimizing the composition of a software structure by removing related programming modules and reducing its granularity
	Deprecation	Retiring unused or dated software services and functionality
	Elimination	Removing redundant software functionality or programming modules

As shown, the thicken tool introduces four methods of software design: augmentation, modularity, reinforcement, and consolidation. These approaches can widen a software entity's solution scope, thereby affecting its structure's composition. Specifically, by adding more functions, services, and programming modules to the overall implementation, the supporting software structure expands accordingly.

In contrast, the contract design tool reduces the software implementation's solution range. There are four chief approaches to tackling this goal: scope reduction, architecture restructuring, deprecation, and elimination. These methods narrow the width of a software structure by removing its affiliated processes, programming logic, modules, and services. Finally, the architecture restructuring approach can be employed to streamline the design of a software structure and its related software implementation.

Software Structure Thickening and Contracting Process Outline

Figure 7.32 depicts the employment of the thicken and contract design activities. This example presents three design states: A, B, and C. As shown, by pursuing the presented design life cycle, the volume of the composite software structure is altered, and, evidently, its width shrinks and expands. Recall that this process affects the X-coordinate line values corresponding to the composite software structure's *width* in the context of a 3D software architecture computing world.

State A: Deficient Design   This design shows a composite software structure containing six composite and nine atomic substructures. This state results from the thickened design activity applied to state C and then B. A highly populated and coarse-grained software formation calls for narrowing its width by extracting its underlying functionality and services.

State B: Optimal Design   This state is presented as an optimal software construction state after applying the contract design activity on design state A and using the thicken tool on state C. As a result of the life-cycle process, state B is now regarded as a balanced design of the composite software structure that includes four composite and two atomic substructures.

State C: Deficient Design   This state is the outcome of the contract design activities applied to state A and then B. It is considered an impractical design solution since the composite software structure contains a single atomic substructure. Therefore, a fined-grained implementation does not always justify constructing a composite structure.

In addition, Figure 7.32 depicts the thickening and contract design activities that take place throughout the software construction life cycle. Here, the composite structure undergoes apparent modifications that result in each design state (A, B, and C). The ultimate goal of this exercise is to promote an optimal design balance as illustrated in design state B and can be achieved by iteration: pursuing design cycles until equilibrium has been achieved.

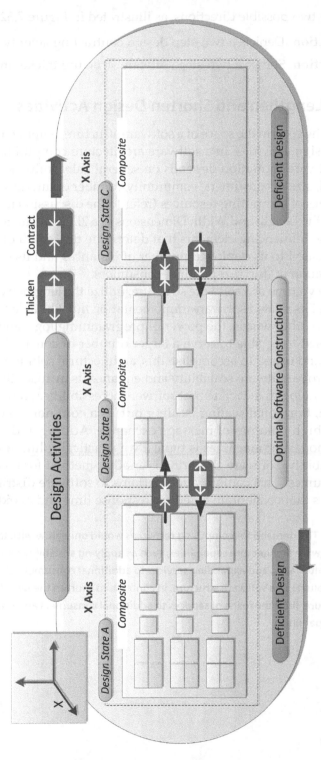

Figure 7.32: Thicken and Contract Life Cycle Design Activities Example

Consider the two possible directions, as illustrated in Figure 7.32:

A, B, C direction: Depicts a two-step design contracting activity

C, B, A direction: Shows a two-step software structure thickening activity

Use Case II: Lengthen and Shorten Design Activities

To manipulate the span in the space of a software structure, employ the lengthen and shorten design activities. In a software architecture computing space, the length of a software formation depends on several chief influencing factors: scalability level, size of consumers' community, number of interfaces, and consumption metrics of computing resources (refer to the discussion in the section "What Impacts the Length and Width Dimensions of a 2D Software Structure?"). In summary, the influencing elements that determine the length of a software structure are related to its deployed number of instances and its capability to serve its population of its corresponding consumers.

To extend the volume of a software structure, utilize the lengthen design tool. This implies that its related software implementation must be able to extend its service range. In other words, the power of programming logic and processes must be increased to be able to serve a larger number of consuming applications, systems, and users. To accomplish this, architectural solutions should be devised to improve software scalability and enhance its availability. There are a variety of technologies that can boost software accessibility and performance.

For example, horizontal scaling (scaling out) is a common mechanism to accommodate high volumes of message exchange. Adding additional computing space, nodes, or machines is typically a practical solution to increase software availability. Software clustering is another method for enabling high transaction volumes. This configuration pertains to software distribution to a group of servers that collaborate to reduce response time and avoid outages.

CONCEPT   The demand for computing resources would only grow with the increase of software architecture capabilities, such as applying scalability mechanisms, adding interfaces, and expanding services to additional consumers; this would lengthen the volume of a software structure. In contrast, to shorten the length of a software structure, limit the reach of services to additional consumers and scale down architecture capabilities.

Recall that the lengthened and shortened design activities should be applied to a software structure on the y-axis line in a 3D software architecture computing space. *The higher the Y-coordinate values, the longer the structure*. The opposite applies when shortening the structure.

When to Apply the Lengthen and Shorten Design Activities

Lengthening or shortening a software structure width may occur during all product planning, construction, deployment, and operations life-cycle phases. The solutions proposed during design time are conceptual or logical, not tangible or physical. And since manipulating a software structure is pursued only on paper, the cost would be minimal. However, the cost of changing a proposed architecture scheme climbs with time during the software development process and typically doubles or triples when the modifications are made during software deployment, integration, and maintenance.

As stated, the alteration to the length of a software structure is extremely pricy while it operates in production; this is due to new efforts calling for software architecture restructuring, reconfiguration, and reintegration. In addition, changing software formations in a runtime ecosystem may also require data migration, security mechanisms enhancement, and redeployment of monitoring utilities.

New business imperatives and renewed business strategies typically call for changes to software products after they have already been deployed to a software architecture computing space. Business requirements are then issued to reach new consumers, engage new customers, and establish partnerships with vendors. This transformation always impacts the 3D length of software structures. The only way to avoid the high cost of software modification is to apply gradual technological changes rather than initiating large-scale projects.

Lengthen and Shorten Design Methods

Table 7.10 lists approaches employed to manipulate the length of a software structure in a 3D computing space (the Y-coordinate line values indicate the length of the structure). Moreover, the lengthening and shortening tools are listed under the "Design Activity" column. The "Method" column specifies the approaches that each activity can pursue. Under the "Task" column, find a short description outlining the actual process that should be taken for each design approach.

Table 7.10: Lengthen and Shorten Design Methods

DESIGN ACTIVITY	METHOD	TASK
Lengthen	Software scaling	Increasing instances of the software to improve its high-availability capabilities and performance
	Interfacing	Improving software reuse by adding interfaces and adapters to engage additional consumers
	Extending service range	Extending the reach of services to broaden the consumer base
	Resource consumption	Boosting computing resources to accommodate higher demand for transaction volumes
Shorten	Software descaling	Optimizing or scaling back the number of software instances
	Minimizing relationship	Minimizing interactions, links, and communication between software entities, consumers, vendors, and partners
	Decreasing resource consumption	Optimizing computing resource consumption
	Decreasing service range	Reducing the number of consuming applications, systems, and customers

The lengthen activity shows four methods for software design: software scaling, interfacing, extending service range, and resource consumption. These design approaches, which impact a software structure's length, do not necessarily focus on adding functionality, processes, or services to a software entity. They are merely devised to extend the service range to reach more consumers, partners, vendors, applications, and systems. Accomplishing this requires software scalability, high availability enhancement, and boosted computing resources.

Conversely, the shortened design tool that can be used to scale down software outreach for consumers proposes four approaches: software descaling, minimizing relationships, reducing software consumption, and decreasing service range. These methods shorten the length of a software structure in a 3D architecture computing space. Moreover, the shortened design activity should be used to fine-tune a software structure to promote equilibrium in a runtime ecosystem when deploying comparable volumes (this topic is discussed in section "What Impacts the Length and Width Dimensions of a 2D Software Structure?").

Software Structure Lengthening and Shortening Process Outline

Figure 7.33 shows the utilization of the lengthening and shortening design tools. It illustrates a design process life cycle that spans three states: A, B, and C. In state C, there is only one composite formation. In design state A, the composite software has five instances; three are shown in state B. The latter is regarded as an optimal design obtained after the life-cycle iterative process. Remember that the values on the y-axis line indicate the length of a software structure.

State A: Deficient Design   A highly scaled composite software that spans five instances. This state results from applying the lengthened design activity to state C and then B. Software architects may consider pursuing more design iterations to avoid radical implementations. In certain environments, such extreme scalability may not be necessary.

State B: Optimal Design   An optimal software design showing three composite service instances. The state results from a compromise between the two radical design solutions apparent in states A and C. Therefore, to obtain a balanced design, the lengthening design activity is performed on state C, and the shortened tool is used to reduce the number of its instances shown in state A.

State C: Deficient Design   The outcome of the shortened design activities performed on state B; shows a single instance of a composite service. In many cases, such a lack of software scalability and availability mechanisms call for instantiating more instances to accommodate the high volume of transactions and maintain business continuity. In this respect, state C represents a radical solution that should be refined or architecturally restructured to increase its length.

Furthermore, Figure 7.33 emphasizes the need for pursuing design life-cycle iterations to obtain optimal software construction. The composite software structure is altered using the lengthened or shortened design tools in this use case. Again, the eventual objective of such a process is to foster an ideal design equilibrium, as is depicted in design state B. These activities result in the three apparent states, A, B, and C.

Consider these two possible directions, as illustrated in Figure 7.33:

A, B, C direction: Illustrates a two-step design shortening activity

C, B, A direction: Depicts a two-step design lengthening activity

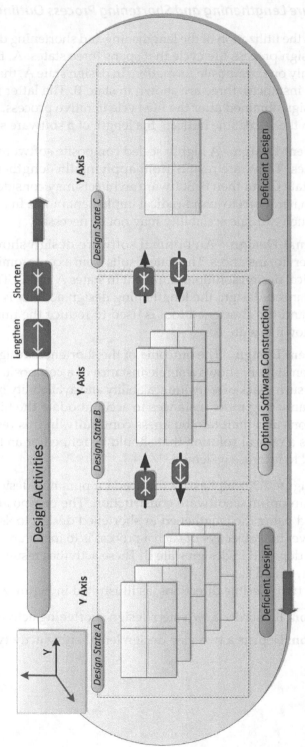

Figure 7.33: Lengthen and Shorten Life-Cycle Design Activities Example

Use Case III: Layer and Delayer Design Activities

The layer and delayer design tools can be utilized in a 3D architecture computing world to form or shape hierarchical software structures. Either of these design activities applies changes to the height of the software structure on the Z-coordinate line. Moreover, amassing software entities on top of each other is the art of layering. In contrast, delayering refers to removing layers from an existing software structure.

These activities are not only used to isolate, hide, eliminate, or protect processes and programming logic. They are also leveraged to separate or extract concerns. The activity of separating concerns refers to the task of breaking down software implementations into modules, each of which represents a solution in a specific area of expertise or knowledge. Some modules may be extracted if they do not significantly contribute to the business or technical solutions.

A conventional hierarchical software structure typically comprises three layers: the presentation layer, the application layer, and the data layer. These layers typically include routines and interfaces to exchange and persist data, process business logic, communicate with consumers, and pursue other vital functions. All structural hierarchy layers must work together to provide effective solutions. Each layer should communicate with its child, parent, or sibling to exchange information.

CONCEPT   Recall that piling up layers on top of layers, or removing ones, in an arbitrary fashion will never produce feasible outcomes. Therefore, the layer and delayer design activities must be accompanied by an analysis process driven by rational architecture decisions about the placement or exclusion of software layers.

So, what specifically is the recommended usage for the layer and delayer design tools? A broad array of design solutions can utilize the layered instrument. A software architect can employ it to add business functions or even technical procedures to an existing software structure. These may include programming modules embedded in layers, such as the presentation layer, persistence layer, data access layer, or data source layer. Conversely, the delayer design tool can be employed to detach these software layers from an existing software structure.

The correlation between layer and delayer design activities is easy to explain: extracting elements from a software formation is the opposite of adding them. By way of illustration, removing a layer from a hierarchical software structure is precisely the opposite of adding it back.

When to Apply Layer and Delayer Design Activities

Employing the layer and delayer design activities during the design-time phase is highly advised. However, when an architect intends to fine-tune a software structure and not drastically change it, the layer and delayer design activities can be applied during the software development phase.

But, what about utilizing the layer and delayer design tools during deployment, configuration, and integration in a software architecture environment? Software structures typically don't drastically change in a runtime ecosystem. Yet, there are instances when architects would recommend layering or delayering a software structure even when it's deployed in production. It is a prevalent practice to make small changes to structures even after they have been tested, approved, and deployed. For example, adding services, subtracting programming modules, adding business processes, or adding more components to a structure—all in the name of fine-tuning performance and quality of services.

Layer and Delayer Design Methods

Software architects must have specific objectives in mind before making use of the layer and delayer design tools. They ought to be cognizant of the consequences when employing these design approaches because the attributes and functionality of a software implementation, such as an application, can be altered if its supporting structure is modified.

Table 7.11 displays the various layer and delayer design activity methods and tasks. Each layer and delayer activity introduces four methods, supporting how software architects can fulfill their goals.

Table 7.11: Layer and Delayer Design Methods

DESIGN ACTIVITY	METHOD	TASK
Layer	Stacking	Increasing the solution scope of software by stacking additional layers on top of its existing structure to include more modules and components
	Insertion	Augmenting software capabilities by inserting layers in an existing layered software structure
	Reinforcement	Reinforcing a software structure by adding to its base layers to support the layers above (such as the data layer)
	Replacement	Adding a layer of a software structure to substitute for an existing one that has been deprecated or removed
Delayer	Unstacking	Reducing the height of a software structure by restructuring its composition
	Unification	Unifying redundant layers in software structures
	Deprecation	Retiring unused legacy layers from a software structure
	Elimination	Removing a layer from a software structure

The layered activity introduces four design methods: stacking, insertion, reinforcement, and replacement. These are employed to augment, add, or replace existing layers of a software structure. In this context, the layer activity is used to increase, refine, enhance, or strengthen the operations of software implementation.

Conversely, the delayer design activity is chiefly about reducing layers of a software structure. Table 7.11 lists these four approaches: unstacking, unification, deprecation, and elimination. These design methods justify the removal of layers for different reasons, such as eliminating or consolidating redundant layers.

Layer and Delayer Process Outline

Figure 7.34 illustrates an example of three layering and delayering design activities, each yielding three distinct states (A, B, and C). During this design life cycle, each state manifests the result of the layer and delayer activities.

State A: Deficient Design   Exhibits a hierarchical software structure that comprises eight layers: Data, data source, persistence, business, application, control, presentation, and user interface. Such a highly stocked structure only increases architecture complexity and introduces operation maintenance challenges in production. This state is the outcome of the layer design activity applied to state C and then B.

State B: Optimal Design   Recognized as an optimal software architecture construction that includes data, persistence, application, and presentation layers. This design state reflects a balanced design achieved by the delayer design activities performed on state A, or layer activities on state C.

State C: Deficient Design   A radical design state that depicts a flat software structure that consists of data and application layers. The design demonstrates weak conceptual design that limits consumer reusability and software modularity. This state is the outcome of the delayer design activities that are applied on state A and then B.

Figure 7.34 also illustrates two design activity directions. The transition between each design state is driven by layer or delayer activities. In the context of the shown design life cycle, software architects may choose to deliver a solution that starts from any design state, then continue to refine the architecture until an optimal software construction has been achieved.

Consider these two possible directions illustrated in Figure 7.34:

A, B, C direction: Shows a two-step design delayering activity

C, B, A direction: Illustrates a two-step layering activity

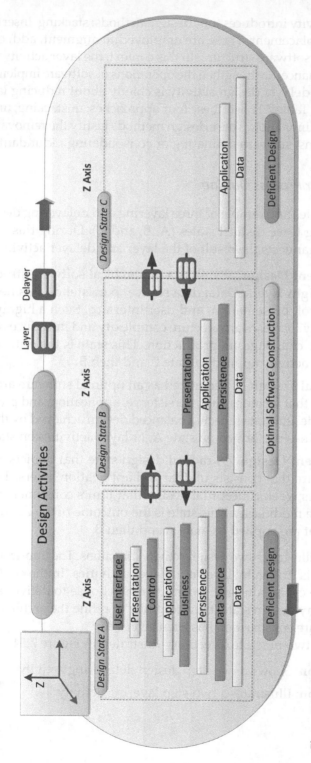

Figure 7.34: Layer and Delayer Design Activities Example

Governing Laws for Software Construction in a 3D Computing World

The governing laws for software construction in a 3D architecture ecosystem set the boundaries for design activities. They identify the attributes of a hosting runtime geometrical space, define the structural properties of a software formation, and outline the impact of the construction life cycle on software implementations.

Software Architecture Solids   Software solids are the most rudimentary computing structures, a type of skeleton employed to support business and technical processes.

Structure Geometrical Formation   A software structure is a geometrical formation established by its width, length, and height dimensions; it occupies space in a software architecture computing topology.

Software Structural Support   Every software implementation, such as programming logic, business, or technical processes, is supported by a 3D software structure.

Software Architecture Space Coordinate System   The 3D software computing environment possesses a coordinate system skeleton based on three axes: x, y, and z.

Software Structure Dimensions   A software structure possesses up to four geometrical properties: zero, one, two, and three dimensions.

Collective Occupancy of Software Structures   The collective volumes of deployed 3D software structures may exceed the geometrical boundaries of their hosting architecture computing environment.

Software Construction Life Cycle   The construction is an iterative design process to create and/or manipulate structures that ultimately impact software behavior.

Software Construction Designing Activities   Software construction is about making, shaping, or manipulating software structure styles and patterns by employing designing tools.

Architecture Symmetry   Software architecture symmetry always promotes software reuse, consolidation of assets, deployment of comparative software structure volumes, and equal distribution of software products and data across a 3D computing space.

Software Architecture Elasticity   There are limits to architecture elasticity in a 3D world.

Best Practices for Constructing Software Implementations

The list that follows outlines 16 best practices for constructing software implementations. They accentuate building, manipulating, and optimizing software structures in a 3D software architecture computing space. These best practices also address software distribution aspects that promote a balanced software architecture:

Software Construction Elements   Start a construction process by employing software architecture solids.

Composite Software Construction   Do not overpopulate a composite software structure with substructures. Conversely, there is no justification for developing, deploying, and integrating a composite structure that encompasses a single substructure.

Software Architecture Computing Space   One of the chief software construction goals is to integrate and distribute 3D software structures in a 3D software architecture computing space.

Software Architecture Symmetry   To achieve architecture symmetry, distribute software entities equally to all regions of a software architecture computing space.

Volumes of Software Structures   Deploy comparable volumes of software structures to a 3D computing space.

Software Granularity   Deploy software with comparable granularity levels to a 3D software architecture computing space.

Population Density   Do not overpopulate a software architecture computing space with software products. Carve out capacity planning strategies to determine the adequate population density that a particular computing space can sustain.

Collective Software Structure Volumes   The collective geometrical volumes of all deployed software structures should not exceed the boundaries of a software architecture computing space.

Software Architecture Elasticity   Architecture elasticity is not limitless in a 3D computing space.

Computing Space Logical Coordinate System   Use the computing space coordinate system to specify the logical positioning of software implementations in a 3D computing space.

Cardinal and Intercardinal Physical Direction System   Use the cardinal and intercardinal direction system to specify the physical positioning of software products in a software architecture computing space.

Combination of Space Navigation Systems   Combine the computing space logical coordinate system with the physical cardinal and intercardinal direction system.

Flooring   Leverage the z-axis to establish layers in a 3D software architecture computing space.

Equal footing   Verify if the relationships created between federated software implementations are based on their granularity level, business or technical criticality, volume, and other architecture attributes that are considered vital to software design.

Software Construction Balance Table   Develop a balance table containing organizational best practices and guiding principles to drive a balanced design for software architecture.

Software Construction Tools   To create, manipulate, or optimize a software structure, employ the six software design tools: thicken, contract, lengthen, shorten, layer, and delayer.

Software Architecture Interview Preparations

In This Part

Part 4

Preparing for a Software Architecture Interview: A Winning Strategy

It's never a clever idea to show up for a software architecture job interview unprepared. The chance to ace the interview without performing due diligence is near zero. Not only is a considerable amount of time wasted on a failed attempt to get a desired position, but also the candidate's reputation could be damaged.

NOTE Therefore, never attend an interview before carving out a coherent strategy that will increase the odds of receiving a job offer. Never settle for less!

Interviewers and interviewees typically understand the undocumented job interview survival rule: at the end of the day, it's a zero-sum game. Simply put, only one candidate will be offered a single software architecture position, the others will be rejected. Nevertheless, flubbing an interview is not the end of the world. There are umpteen software architecture positions on the market. There is no defense, however, against being sloppy or not preparing adequately.

The term *preparation* pertains here to meticulous research and study conducted before a job interview in a field of expertise. The software architecture practice, in particular, covers a broad range of disciplines in which a candidate must demonstrate mastery. By showing up to an interview without laying the proper groundwork, a candidate might fail miserably.

So, how should one prepare ahead of an upcoming software architecture interview? There is no limit on the range of queries thrown at a candidate who is already under daunting pressure. The answer to this question brings us to a simple idea: carve out an interview strategy that could yield a lucrative job offer.

The sections that follow discuss a winning strategy and tactical approaches that must be mastered before attending a software architecture job interview.

Software Architecture Job Interview Strategy

The software architecture job interview strategy should include two different plans: *defense* and *attack*. These devices introduce approaches to help applicants overcome eight common challenges both before and during the interview, as indicated in the list that follows:

Attend to the job requirements.   Do not get sidetracked: always focus on the job requirements that are part of the job description. These vital requirements must drive the preparations for the job interview.

Tackle surprise.   Handle unexpected interview circumstances or difficult questions.

Demonstrate knowledge.   Provide professional, relevant, and satisfactory answers.

Make leadership capabilities clear.   Prove interpersonal and management skills.

Think strategically.   Show strategic and technological leadership.

Communicate self-confidence.   Withstand interview pressures.

Focus on substance.   Avoid trivial topics of discussion.

Be proactive.   Take charge on interview communication.

Let's explore now the defense and attack plans of the software architecture job interview strategy.

Preparing a Job Interview Defense Plan

The defense plan should simply shield a candidate against the failure to answer *basic* software architecture questions. The term *basic* implies that an architect must demonstrate rudimentary architecture knowledge to build instant trust with interviewers.

For example, elementary knowledge in the field of software architecture may pertain to design patterns, the software development life cycle, best practices, development and testing tools, design approaches, and others (refer to Chapter 9, "An Outline for Software Architecture Job Interview Questions," for the architecture questions model). Without the job candidate demonstrating such basic architecture knowledge, an interviewer would be able to quickly discover the interviewee's competency gap. This would definitely end the interview more quickly than expected.

Obviously, it's not hard to grasp the idea that attending a software architecture job interview requires proper preparation to boost a candidate's confidence. Consequently, the defense plan portion of the job interview strategy should consist of research and study to *supplement candidates' base knowledge before an interview*. If there is any lack of understanding of what enterprise integration patterns[1] are, for example, then buy books, search the topic on the Internet, ask peers, and even undertake adequate training.

Finally, filling in the *personal knowledge gap* should be pursued only after studying the corresponding job requirements outlined in every job description. These prerequisites are always published before any job interview.

Preparing a Job Interview Attack Plan

The other part of the interview strategy is the attack plan. It should encourage applicants to arm themselves with an arsenal of comprehensive knowledge about anticipated interview topics. This valuable information could supplement answers to the presented questions—demonstrating wide-ranging and exceptional knowledge in the field of software architecture. Furthermore, the attack plan could lessen an interviewer's appetite for launching a new round of challenging queries. An attack plan could also send a clear signal that the candidate is prepared, knowledgeable, and motivated to face interview challenges.

Strategically, the goal of an interviewee would then be to take the reins of control over interview communication to avert painful setbacks. This implies that a candidate should come forward with impressive knowledge, perhaps food for thought for the interviewers. For example, if a query calls for defining the term SOLID,[2] it would be probably sufficient to specify in broad strokes that the term represents principles to foster software flexibility, simplicity, and maintainability.

But with a wise attack plan, an interviewee would be able to achieve more. It would propel a candidate to demonstrate additional knowledge of the topic in question. For example, in addition to a brief introduction to SOLID, a candidate could also raise the bar by naming its principles: open-closed principle, interface segregation principle, single-responsibility principle, Liskov substitution principle, and dependency inversion principle.

Last, avoid lengthy and overwhelming answers. Do not feed an interviewer trivial information that is not related to the question at hand. Testing

---

[1] Recommended enterprise integration patterns material: www.enterprise integrationpatterns.com/
[2] Watch this video about SOLID tenets: www.youtube.com/watch?v=A6ZqNQdJPjc

an interviewer's patience is a grave mistake that is typically hard to repair. The attack plan, therefore, must add value to interview discussions rather than jeopardize the prospects for getting hired.

Software Architecture Job Interview Preparation Model

Prior to a looming job interview there is nothing more important than to prepare for it in a meticulous fashion. This process must follow a tidy method, a step-by-step study to handle the forthcoming interview challenge. Hence, the proposed interview strategy model offers a study and research approach that would not only broaden an applicant's software architecture knowledge base, but also introduce the proper tools to familiarize candidates with the hiring organization. It simply implies that supplementing the architecture knowledge would not be enough. The study process should also include a deep dive into the business model, services, and industry of the recruiting institution.

There are other preparations that must be pursued before an interview. Some are affiliated with adopting an effective communication approach to convey clear ideas and demonstrate soft skills.[3] Others are related to developing a software architecture lingo to present coherent concepts and methodologies.

All in all, the interview strategy model presented in Table 8.1 encompasses a checklist for success. Treat these items as tasks to accomplish prior to an interview. Take as much time as possible to rehearse likely interview scenarios.

> **NOTE**   Unleash the power of the strategic defense plans when needed and launch the attack plans to beat the competition.

Table 8.1: Software Architecture Job Interview Preparation Model

PLAN TYPE	AREA OF RESEARCH AND STUDY
Defense	Study and analyze the job description.
	Create a software architect skill competency model for the job description.
	Assess whether the next software architecture job is a strategic career move.
	Conduct software architecture mock interviews.
Attack	Study the hiring organization's business.
	Understand the hiring organization's technology.
	Adopt a software architecture lingo.
	Remember software architecture tools.
	Get familiar with software architecture analysis and evaluation methods.
	Talk about software architecture analysis standards.

---

[3] An individual's social interaction and communication skills that enable one to interact and collaborate effectively with others.

The sections that follow bring light to the software architecture job interview preparation model. They elaborate on the contribution of the defense and attack plans to a candidate's job interview.

Software Architecture Job Interview Defense Plan

One of the aims of every software architecture job interview defense plan is to fully prepare applicants to provide satisfactory answers to the hiring organization's rudimentary screening questions. These basic queries are always presented at the onset of a job interview. Without successfully mastering this interview stage, an applicant is doomed to failure.

But the software architecture job interview defense plan is not only about preparing for basic interview queries. The crux of this plan is to assist applicants in discovering any gaps in architecture knowledge that they need to fill in. Compensating for a lack of software architecture experience calls for study, research, and an understanding of what the job requirements are all about. As a result, this meticulous analysis uncovers a range of software architecture proficiencies that must be honed to perform well in a technical interview.

To carve out a potent defense plan, follow this simple process:

1. Study and analyze the software architect job description.
2. Understand its underpinning job requirements.
3. Construct a software architect skill competency model for the job description.
4. Discover the gap in software architecture knowledge.
5. Conduct a software architecture mock interview and score the quality of the preparation efforts.

From here, the hard work begins.

Study and Analyze the Job Description

Studying job requirements before an interview simply means doing the homework. Without inspecting, understanding, and analyzing job descriptions there is not even a slight chance of getting hired. Despite the accuracy or detail level of the requirements, preparations are exceedingly encouraged. Do not take this issue lightly because every step of career growth is highly dependent on job opportunities.

NOTE   Opportunities are not awarded to applicants without job interviews.

Start with Identifying the Scope of the Software Architecture Job Requirements

A software architecture job interview is one of the most challenging stages in the hiring process. It's difficult because nowadays a growing number of organizations prefer applicants who demonstrate broad technological knowledge. Frequently, the candidates must prove their capability of mastering numerous disciplines that span most phases of the product development life cycle. Consequently, many job requirements indicate that a candidate must possess not only *vertical* but also *horizontal knowledge*.

The term *vertical knowledge* relates to a narrow scope of expertise. For example, an application testing architect whose responsibilities include functional and nonfunctional performance assessment is confined to a specific discipline. This architect, however, may possess *deep* knowledge about capacity planning tools and platforms. But the expertise purview of the testing architect is still narrow. In contrast, horizontal knowledge pertains to *broader* technological skills that may span multiple software architecture disciplines, such as integration, cloud migration, cybersecurity, and even database design.

Another example that explains the difference between the vertical and horizontal knowledge scopes is the common comparison between the duties of an application architect and an enterprise architect. The deliverables of an application architect typically focus on a narrow solution scope. These artifacts may include software modeling diagrams for a specific application, database design, or even an application user's guide. But job requirements for an enterprise software architect characteristically call for a broader range of knowledge. These may include skills such as middleware integration, data aggregation, and the ability to devise interoperability strategies for an enterprise environment.

> **NOTE**   Architecture talents with combined horizontal and vertical knowledge are hard to come by. But more important, job requirements that fail to specify the scope of architecture expertise are typically confusing and unfeasible.

Consider these recommendations:

Knowledge scope   No applicant should consider a job proposition if its requirements fail to indicate the scope of software architecture expertise and duties.

Generic or unclear requirements   Shy away from an opportunity if its job requirements are unclear or too generic.

Architecture skill verification   Applicants should verify job skill requirements match the scope of their architecture knowledge and capabilities.

Practicality   Be aware of whether the vertical and horizontal architecture skills required by an organization are typically impractical.

Dive Deep into the Software Architect Job Description

After discovering the software architect's scope of duties in the job requirements, as explained in the previous section, the time has come to explore if the position is a good fit for the applicant. To accomplish this, let's begin with a detailed analysis to shed light on what type of talents the hiring organization is actually seeking to employ. Furthermore, the job requirements may also give us some hints about the specific expertise that a candidate must possess.

Before moving to the detailed analysis of the job requirements, review first the "Software Architect Job Description" sidebar, an example that contains three parts.

Summary   The job description synopsis typically includes the justification for hiring a software architect. But this information may not always be readily apparent. An applicant's analysis task would then be to understand the organization's business imperatives, organizational initiatives, or planned or ongoing projects. A summary portion of a job description may also indicate what type of architecture talent is needed.

Responsibilities   The responsibilities part is related to the chief deliverables that the software architect will be required to fulfill.

Skills   The skills portion of the job description identifies the desired areas of expertise of the software architect.

SOFTWARE ARCHITECT JOB DESCRIPTION

Summary

Our home loan division currently is seeking an experienced application architect for our new cloud-based borrower portal. The selected candidate will be in charge of application design tasks for our home loan portal project. In addition, technical leadership will be required to provide guidance and practical direction to the development teams. This is an excellent career opportunity for a motivated individual with an impressive architectural design talent and outstanding interpersonal skills.

Responsibilities

- Provide technological leadership and mentorship to guide our development teams
- Oversee application cybersecurity to ensure data integrity
- Conduct commercial off-the-shelf (COTS) product selection and evaluation and deliver related product technical requirements, product evaluation documents, and product installation manuals to promote state-of-the-art technological capabilities

Skills

- Master's degree in computer science or computer engineering

- Experience of seven or more years in application design and the capability to deliver conceptual, logical, and physical architectural models

- Proven knowledge of cybersecurity and the ability to devise application vulnerability models, security controls best practices, and penetration testing guidance

- Excellent knowledge of the software development life cycle (SDLC) and vast experience in delivering design verification checklists, testing requirements, and application integration models

To sum up, by asking these rudimentary questions, attempt to understand what the job requirements actually entail:

Justification Why is the hiring organization seeking to employ a software architect?

Software architect type What type of a software architect are they looking for? Data architect? Security architect? Integration architect? Application architect? Enterprise architect?

Business necessity What is the business imperative that compels the organization to hire an architect?

Deliverables If employed, what will the software architect be asked to deliver?

Expertise What kind of architecture expertise is the recruiting organization looking for?

Start with Analyzing the Summary Portion of the Job Requirements

So, what should a software architect applicant discover in the job description summary portion? Three simple pieces of information ought to be revealed.

Project Attempt to understand the hiring organization's motivation for employing a software architect. This company's incentive may be driven by projects or by other, larger, business initiatives.

Type of Software Architect Next, find out what kind of a software architect the recruiting company is seeking to bring on board, such as a data architect, a cybersecurity architect, or a cloud architect.

Software Architecture Expertise Discover the areas of knowledge, fields of expertise, specialties, or architecture disciplines the software architect applicant must possess. For example, a cybersecurity architect may be required to perform vulnerability and penetration testing, conduct risk analyses, and accomplish security assessments.

Consequently, as shown underlined in the "Job Description's Summary Segment" sidebar, our analysis rendered these three findings:

Type of Software Architect Application architect

Expertise/Architecture Discipline Application design

Project Home loan portal

JOB DESCRIPTION'S SUMMARY SEGMENT

Summary

Our home loan division is currently seeking an experienced *application architect* for our new cloud-based borrower portal. The selected candidate will be in charge of *application design* tasks for our *home loan portal project*. In addition, technical leadership will be required to provide guidance and practical direction to the development teams. This is an excellent career opportunity for a motivated individual with an impressive architectural design talent and outstanding interpersonal skills.

Create a Findings Table Version I for the Job Description

Now create a table akin to Table 8.2. Let's start here with the information discovered in the job description summary portion that was analyzed in the previous section. Fill in the table with this information:

- In the very top row of the of the table, type **Application Architect**.
- In the Project column, insert **Home Loan Portal**.
- In the Expertise/Architecture Discipline column, type **Application design**.

Table 8.2: Job Description Analysis Findings Version 1

APPLICATION ARCHITECT		
Project	**Expertise/Architecture Discipline**	**Deliverables**
Home Loan Portal	Application design	

Next, Analyze the Responsibilities Portion of the Job Requirements

Let's ask the same question again: what might a software architect applicant possibly discover in the responsibilities part of the job description? Devote attention to these possible findings:

Software architecture deliverables   Software architects are typically required to provide a wide range of design artifacts, issue development guidance documents, devise best practices, and provide other deliverables.

Software architecture expertise   The recruiting companies employ software architecture talents with specific domain knowledge, fields of expertise, specialties, or architecture disciplines to provide solutions to organizational problems. These skills, for example, may include cloud security, big data[4] design, and application integration.

Subsequently, our analysis rendered these findings, as shown underlined in the "Job Description's Responsibilities Segment" sidebar:

- Expertise/Architecture Discipline: cybersecurity
- Expertise/Architecture Discipline: COTS product selection and evaluation
- Deliverable: product technical requirements
- Deliverable: product evaluation documents
- Deliverable: product installation manuals

JOB DESCRIPTION'S RESPONSIBILITIES SEGMENT

- Provide technological leadership and mentorship to guide our development teams
- Oversee application <u>cybersecurity</u> to ensure data integrity
- Conduct <u>COTS product selection and evaluation</u> and deliver related <u>product technical requirements, product evaluation documents</u>, and <u>product installation manuals</u> to promote state-of-the-art technological capabilities

---

Then, Update the Findings Table Version II of the Job Description

Recall that the findings table version I has already been created (see Table 8.2). The task at hand then is to update this table with the information discovered in the Responsibilities portion of the job description. We rename the table "Job Description Analysis Findings Version 2." Note that all *updates are highlighted*.

---

[4] Big data is a computing environment that includes substantial volumes of structured and unstructured information that it's impossible to process, manage, and manipulate with the traditional software data tools and platforms. Advanced technologies have been developed to benefit from big data environments.

Table 8.3: Job Description Analysis Findings Version 2

APPLICATION ARCHITECT		
Project	**Expertise/Architecture Discipline**	**Deliverables**
Home Loan Portal	Application design	
	Cybersecurity	
	COTS product selection and evaluation	Product technical requirements, product evaluation documents, product installation manuals

Follow this quick guidance:

- To the "Expertise/Architecture Discipline" column, add the value **cybersecurity**.

- Add another value to the "Expertise/Architecture Discipline" column: **COTS product selection and evaluation**.

- In the column named "Deliverables," insert these deliverables for the "COTS product selection and evaluation" is an expertise / architecture discipline. The deliverable for this discipline is "product technical requirements, product evaluation documents, and product installation manuals".

Last, Analyze the Software Architect Skills Portion of the Job Requirements

We conclude here our software architecture job description analysis with the inspection of the skills segment. This portion is depicted in the "Job Description's Skills Segment" sidebar.

It's common to find in this segment a mix of key words and key phrases that might be valuable to the analysis process. But the most important ones are related to software architecture expertise that the hiring organization may be interested in. In addition, more software architecture deliverables are likely to be unveiled.

Our analysis of the skills portion of the job description resulted in these findings:

1. **Expertise/Architecture Discipline**: application design

2. **Deliverables**: architectural models

3. **Expertise/Architecture Discipline**: cybersecurity

4. **Deliverable**: application vulnerability models

5. **Deliverable**: security controls best practices

6. **Deliverable**: penetration testing guidance

7. **Expertise/Architecture Discipline**: software development life cycle (SDLC)

8. **Deliverable**: design verification checklists

9. **Deliverable**: testing requirements

10. **Deliverable**: application integration models

JOB DESCRIPTION'S SKILLS SEGMENT

Skills

■ Master's degree in computer science or computer engineering

■ Experience of seven or more years in <u>application design</u> and the capability to deliver conceptual, logical, and physical <u>architectural models</u>

■ Proven knowledge of <u>cybersecurity</u> and the ability to devise <u>application vulnerability models</u>, <u>security controls best practices</u>, and <u>penetration testing guidance</u>

■ Excellent knowledge of the <u>software development life cycle (SDLC)</u> and vast experience in delivering <u>design verification checklists</u>, <u>testing requirements</u>, and <u>application integration models</u>

Do Not Forget to Update the Findings Table of the Job Description

This will be the third update to the job description analysis findings table version III. Here, the software architect applicant should add the key words and key phrases discovered in the *skills* segment. To realize these additions, take a look at Table 8.4. *Note that all updates to the table are highlighted.*

To accomplish this, follow these quick instructions:

■ Add **software development life cycle (SDLC)** to the "Expertise/Architecture Discipline" column.

■ Insert **architectural models** in the "Deliverables" for the "application design" entry in the "Expertise/Architecture Discipline" column

■ Insert these deliverables in the "Deliverables" column for the "cybersecurity" entry in the "Expertise/Architecture Discipline" column: **application vulnerability models**, **security controls**, **penetration testing guidance**.

- Insert these deliverables in the "Deliverables" column for *the software development life cycle (SDLC) entry in the "Expertise/Architecture Discipline" column* **verification checklists**, **testing requirements**, and **application integration models**.

Note that there is no need to add application design or cybersecurity as an expertise because they have been added previously.

Table 8.4: Job Description Analysis Findings Version 3

APPLICATION ARCHITECT		
Project	**Expertise/Architecture Discipline**	**Deliverables**
Home Loan Portal	Application design	Architectural models
	Cybersecurity	Application vulnerability models, security controls best practices, penetration testing guidance
	COTS product selection and evaluation	Product technical requirements, product evaluation documents, product installation manuals
	Software development life cycle (SDLC)	Design verification checklists, testing requirements, application integration models

Create a Software Architect Skill Competency Model for the Job Description

Table 8.4, completed in the previous section, was designed to collect vital information from the job requirements published by the hiring organization. In essence, the table represents an abbreviated software architect skill competency model that was largely discussed in Chapter 1, "Software Architect Capability Model."

Now we have all the needed information for creating a full version of the skill competency model for the job description. This process is going to be easy to accomplish. Ambitious applicants would find it utterly useful. By doing this, software architecture candidates will better understand what architecture talents an organization is seeking to employ. Moreover, finding out any personal shortfall in knowledge would encourage applicants to better prepare for an interview.

Time to review the full version of the skill competency model for the job description depicted in Figure 8.1. Again, we have populated this model with all the information collected from Table 8.4. The sections that follow depict its breakdown.

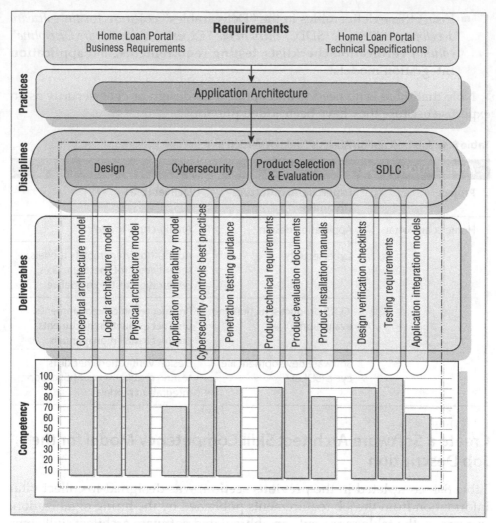

Figure 8.1: Skill Competency Model for Job Requirements

Skill Competency Model's Requirements and Practices

Presented in Figure 8.1, the top of our software architect skill competency model presents two sections:

Requirements Shown are two types of requirements: Home Loan Portal Business Requirements and Home Loan Technical Specifications. Both refer to the project name entered in Table 8.4.

Practices Discovered in the job description, the architect type was revealed as a software architect. Therefore, the practice in this model is named *software architecture*.

Skill Competency Model's Disciplines

As apparent in Figure 8.1, the areas of expertise—namely, the architecture disciplines—that the applicant architect must possess are shown as *design*, *cybersecurity*, *products selection and evaluation*, and *SDLC*. Right beneath, find the corresponding deliverables for each discipline as elaborated on in the sections that follow.

Design Discipline's Deliverables

According to the job description, there are software design artifacts that the employed application architect will be required to deliver. These deliverables are captured in the software architect skill competency model illustrated in Figure 8.1.

Conceptual architecture model   Diagrams specifying the overarching decomposition of an application components and their internal and external relationship with other software implementations

Logical architecture model   Charts that typically depict software behavior, message exchange, interaction, and data flow between internal application components and external software entities

Physical architecture model   This deliverable refers to the deployment scheme of an application in a related production environment. It may include physical components, such as servers, network topology specifications, routers, and gateways.

Cybersecurity Discipline Deliverables

Cybersecurity is another field of expertise that a software architect candidate must possess consistent with the job requirements. These are the expected deliverables shown in the skill competency model:

Application vulnerability model   This deliverable refers to features (security controls) that protect the confidentiality, integrity, and availability of an application. The vulnerability model may include data encryption mechanisms, application access control methods, potential threat handling, and authentication and authorization policies.

Security Controls Best Practices   The application architect candidate with cybersecurity expertise will be required to deliver security controls to guide IT professionals about how to mitigate risks to systems and applications. The guidance may include methods, plans, actions, solutions, and techniques. Some of these solutions may include the installation of security monitoring and surveillance platforms, firewalls, and anti-malware software.

Penetration Testing Guidance   This cybersecurity deliverable pertains to documents guiding IT professionals to simulate cyber-attacks against applications and systems to discover their operational vulnerabilities.

Products Selection and Evaluation Discipline's Deliverables

If an application calls for using products that are unavailable in the organization's software library, architects may choose to utilize COTS products[5] to compensate for the absence of functionality. As recalled, the job description calls for candidates' capabilities to provide these deliverables:

Product technical requirements   Before selecting an off-the-shelf product, the technical requirements must outline its chief features, such as functionality, attributes, performance, integration capabilities, and anticipated computing resources.

Product evaluation documents   During the product selection process, the architect is required to provide an assessment document. This would not only depict a comparison between similar products on the market but also justify the ultimate selection.

Product installation manuals   Every adopted third-party product must come with manuals that include environment compatibility requirements, installation procedures, and other technical guidance to ease integration. An application architect must then verify that such manuals indeed exist and are updated with the current product's features.

SDLC Discipline's Deliverables

The software development life cycle calls for software architects to technically guide and supervise the development teams. The application architect candidate, therefore, will be commissioned to contribute these deliverables:

Design verification checklists   Every software development life cycle should include verification sessions to confirm that the source code complies with the design specifications. For this deliverable, the architect signs off on a design verification checklist that certifies the implementation.

Application testing requirements   Implementation testing is mandatory to ensure compliance with functional and nonfunctional requirements.[6] To

---

[5] Commercial off-the-shelf (COTS) products are packaged and ready-to-use software implementations, such as applications, services, or middleware acquired by organizations to avoid in-house software development efforts.

[6] The term functional pertains to business processes and user interface activities. Nonfunctional requirements are about application performance, interface respond time, computing resource capacity, and more.

prepare for the testing, the software architect candidate will be commissioned to provide proper requirements. These documents will outline testing methods, procedures, milestones, and goals.

Application integration verification   Most applications typically integrate with repositories and data sources, peer applications, and middleware. Thus, this deliverable is an official signoff on the integration aspects of an application.

The Competency Part of the Skill Competency Model

The last segment of the skill competency model shown in Figure 8.1 is labeled "Competency." This section is all about quantifying the necessary skills that an applicant must possess for certain architecture disciplines and their related deliverables. But how would such a competency scale be determined if the required skill level is not specified in the job requirements?

When creating a skill competency model for job requirements, a software architect candidate should rely on personal experience. If there is an absence of knowledge, the applicant should conduct research to complete the skill competency section. Furthermore, even speculation could help to roughly assess the required skill levels for certain disciplines and corresponding deliverables.

For example, as illustrated in Figure 8.1, the skill competency levels for the three deliverables of software design discipline are 100 percent. This deduction is based on an assumption that an application architect must possess the highest possible capability level to be able to provide conceptual, logical, and physical architecture models. Note that the same skill competency measurement method applies to the cybersecurity, product selection and evaluation, and SDLC deliverables.

Discover the Personal Knowledge Gap Before Attending a Job Interview

Now that the skill competency model for the job description is completed, applicants should be able to discover any areas of expertise they lack. Simply put, before attending the interview, the applicant is encouraged to understand what gaps in knowledge should be filled.

To uncover any lack of architecture knowledge, an applicant should simply follow these easy steps:

1. **Personal skill competency model**. Create a personal skill competency model as devised in Chapter 1.

2. **Personal skill competency pattern**. Create a skill competency pattern for the individual skill competency model as instructed in Chapter 1.

3. **Job requirements skill competency pattern**. Create a skill competency pattern for the job requirement skill competency model.

4. **Pattern comparison**. Compare the two skill competency patterns to uncover the knowledge gap for each architecture discipline and its associated deliverables.

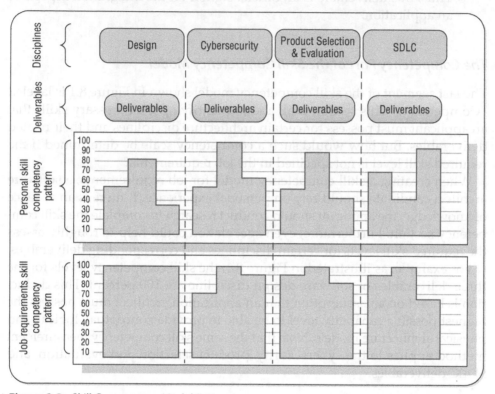

Figure 8.2: Skill Competency Model Patterns

Figure 8.2 demonstrates the outcome of this process. The illustration shows the two skill competency model patterns. The personal pattern is displayed on top, and the job requirements pattern is shown on the bottom. This visual comparison clearly reveals lack of software architecture knowledge and the capability to provide solutions in all four disciplines (software design, cybersecurity, products selection, SDLC) and their related deliverables.

Assess Whether the Next Software Architecture Job Is a Strategic Career Move

Applicants are always being challenged to determine whether a software architect occupation depicted in a job description is a good match for the next step in their career. Not all job requirements descriptions are detailed enough to convey what the exact talents are that the hiring organization is seeking to hire.

The rule of thumb suggests, however, that an applicant should be utterly *practical* before applying for software architecture work. The term *practical* implies that every job move must be a *strategic* endeavor—not a tactical venture. Underemployment,[7] for example, typically slows down career progress. This may result in steep income losses and, most dangerous, cessation of software architecture skill development.

Consider these, "warnings and recommendations" before applying for a software architecture job:

Alignment   A job description must be aligned with a candidate's career strategy—not the other way around.

Underemployment   Be patient. Never choose underemployment if the current market offers better career opportunities for software architects.

Compensation   Only accept fair compensation. Do not settle for undercut wages. Compare the software architecture job offer with salary information provided by market research salary survey companies.

Hasty career decisions   Job descriptions do not always reflect the actual work challenges. Never make hasty job moves, therefore, before meticulously studying the job requirements.

Mixed bag of IT practices   Be practical. Do not apply for a software architect position that also involves other unrelated IT practices, such as source code development, desktop support, and network maintenance tasks.

Conduct a Software Architecture Mock Interview

A good job interview defense plan should include a mock interview. The term *mock interview* refers to preparation activities that not only increase software architecture applicants' confidence in their ability to handle unexpected circumstances that induce pressure. This groundwork should also enable applicants to focus on effective and persuasive answers to interviewers' queries.

Showing up for a software architecture job interview without having a clear and defined agenda for expressing ideas and elaborating on technological strategies would most certainly result in a failure. Candidates must prepare talking points—predefined topics for conversation—to smooth the interaction with interviewers; to demonstrate technological leadership; to come across as a subject-matter expert (SME) in the field of software architecture; and to be

---

[7] Pertains to a job that is beneath one's skill level, with a compensation offer that is below what this individual should earn

able to take charge of the interview. Bottom line: it's all about proving superb and authentic architecture practice expertise.

The sections that follow introduce simple mechanisms to conduct useful software architecture mock interviews.

Prepare a Software Architecture Interview Cheat Sheet

It would be impossible for software architecture applicants to cheat on a technical job interview if they show up unprepared. In just a few minutes it would become apparent that they had not done all the necessary due diligence to formulate a presentation strategy. So, the cheat sheet is actually not a cheating mechanism to compensate for preparing the essential homework. It's simply a compiled list of discussion points, deduced from a job description, to be able to provide fitting answers to queries.

Table 8.5 exemplifies software architecture notes that applicants should compile according to the job they're applying for.

Table 8.5: Cheat Sheet Notes Examples

NOTE CONTEXT	WHEN SHOULD BE USED	EXAMPLES
Complex concept simplification	Keywords and key phrases to simplify complex software architecture concepts or elaborate on approaches and principles	Tightly coupled implementation, environment interoperability, asset federation, data access layer, data aggregation, interface segregation principle (ISP[8])
Software architecture implementation mechanisms	Keywords, key phrases, and terms that will help explain architecture and software development implementations	Single sign-on (SSO[9]), message orchestration, service discovery and binding, service registration, software as a service (SaaS), microservices, Representational State Transfer (RESTful) application programming interface (API)[10]
Software architecture environments	Depicting deployment and integration technological environments	Public cloud, hybrid cloud, data warehouse, server farm, virtual servers, disaster recovery, and high-availability sites

---

[8] The ISP is a SOLID principle that not only promotes the reduction or optimization of interface redundancy, but also advocates to eliminate unutilized methods.
[9] Organizations employ a single sign-on (SSO) authentication mechanism that enables consumers to use multiple applications and systems with a single set of security credentials.
[10] The RESTful API is a commonly used programming interfaces to connect software components that operate on a network in a client-server architecture ecosystem.

NOTE CONTEXT	WHEN SHOULD BE USED	EXAMPLES
Software architecture integration	Providing examples of integration facilities, middleware, and infrastructure	Data transformer, language translator, data merger, message hub, gateway, data migration, enterprise service bus

Prepare for Possible Software Architecture Interview Questions

Chapter 9 is fully dedicated to the topic of software architecture questions. It offers a number of query categories that candidates will likely encounter during a job interview. This categorization approach would help carve out a potent strategy to simplify difficult topics of discussion. Applicants would then be able to prove technological leadership by generalizing the answers and talking more about architectural solutions to address a wide array of problems. This idea goes hand in hand with what a software architect should actually be doing for living.

NOTE Generalize specific problems to effectively provide overarching solutions.

Therefore, attend to Chapter 9's recommendations. Understand the provided question. Learn how to respond effectively to challenging software architecture interview questions.

And then, start the rehearsal.

The Software Architecture Mock Interview

The word *rehearsal* pertains to the simple concept of conducting a software architecture mock interview. This simulation idea calls for setting up a quiet place resembling a small interview office. Then:

- Answer the toughest questions possible by simplifying complex software architecture concepts.
- This exercise should be driven by the presented query categories in Chapter 9.
- Recall that each category obviously contains an array of context related questions.
- Stay calm and answer these queries methodically.
- Avoid jumping from one topic to another. Stay persistent!
- Long answers should be avoided.
- Accentuate strategies, approaches, principles, standards, best practices, policies, and development life-cycle aspects.
- Generalize answers, and, only when asked, drill down into the details, such as technologies, source code of applications and services, and database structures.

- Employ the power of exchanging ideas with interviewers. Turn answers into engaging technological discussions.

- Raising problems is an insufficient interview strategy. Always demonstrate technological leadership by introducing software architecture solutions.

And Then, What After the Software Architecture Mock Interview?

When the show is over, restart a new mock interview. Again, and again, ask the hardest questions. Never skip over challenging queries. Push yourself to the limit. With each self-challenging interview iteration evaluate your answers. Score them. The self-scoring should give a clear indication if an applicant is indeed ready to put on the best suit and wear the shiniest shoes found in the closet.

NOTE   If there is a need for conducting extra research, then, again—pursue it. But never accept the feeling of dissatisfaction; never settle for a self-score of less than 100 percent.

Software Architecture Job Interview Attack Plan

An attack plan is a strategy that enables applicants to demonstrate outstanding software architecture knowledge and technological leadership during a job interview. To carve out such an emphatic plan, applicants ought to conduct thorough research and studies to elevate their proficiency levels beyond those that are called for by the job requirements.

To score even more points during an interview, applicants must be familiar with the hiring organization's business model, technologies, projects, and vision and strategy. Moreover, substantial insight into the company's technological challenges and solutions would only increase applicants' ability to communicate persuasive software architecture solutions.

A job interview attack plan is even more powerful when applicants use the software architecture lingo to communicate ideas, strategies, and implementations. The vocabulary includes a wide array of language-specific technical terminology, such as *design patterns, best practices, principles, and policies*. Through the power of this winning approach, interviewers will be assured that an applicant is indeed fluent in software architecture jargon. And to a large extent, it affirms the applicant's vast experience with devising potent software architecture solutions to mitigate organizational issues.

Before diving deep into the details of the software architecture job interview attack plan discussed in the sections that follow, consider its fundamental building blocks:

Business view   Learn everything possible about the business of the hiring organization.

Technology view   Understand the hiring organization's technology and production environments.

Lingo   Learn how to communicate in the software architecture language.

Tools   Use software architecture tools examples to depict solutions.

Analysis and evaluation   Be ready to answer questions about software architecture analysis and evaluation methods.

Quality   Use software architecture analysis standards to discuss architecture quality topics.

Study the Hiring Organization's Business

One of the most powerful interview attack plan approaches is to demonstrate deep knowledge of the hiring organization's business. Applicants may wonder why it's so necessary to acquire this information. Undeniably, learning about the business may sound as if it's a tedious task and even time-consuming. But the benefits may turn out to be utterly effective.

Equipped with this vital business information, an applicant may prevail over other candidates by gaining the confidence of the interviewers. There is nothing more persuasive than demonstrating familiarity with the business model, culture, sources of income, clients, competitors, the background—and even the history—of the company.

In addition to meticulously studying the business, the candidate should also explore how the hiring organization employs software architecture to promote its vision and strategy. The sections that follow, then, focus on both business and technological aspects.

Start by Finding Information About the Hiring Organization

This pivotal data about the recruiting company typically reveals analytical insights and commercial information instrumental to understanding the business. Fortunately, there is an abundance of data sources offered by numerous information providers that specialize in an in-depth analysis of companies' data.

The type of business-related material that an applicant can find on websites, in libraries, and in databases could shed light on organizational structures and management. This data is characteristically associated with type of industries, annual revenue, number of employees, financial statements, credit reports, and even business activities.

A software architect applicant, therefore, should query as many research resources as possible to obtain valuable business information before an interview. Such a wealth of business domain knowledge and understanding could demonstrate the candidate's ability to provide valuable solutions to organizational challenges.

Review Table 8.6. It includes a number of leading institutions that offer business data repositories for commercial and research purposes. One way of accessing these databases is from public or university libraries.

Table 8.6: Business Information Providers Examples[11]

INFORMATION PROVIDER	LINK	OFFERED BUSINESS INFORMATION
Reference USA/ Reference Solutions	`www.nypl.org/ collections/ articles-databases/ reference-usa`	Basic information on more than 25 million companies and 270 million consumers
	`dataverse.harvard.edu/ dataset.xhtml?persistent Id=hdl:1902.1/22281`	Job listings
Mergent Intellect	`www.nypl.org/ collections/ articles-databases/ mergent-intellect`	Directory database with information about 100 million businesses
	`libguides.colostate .edu/c.php?g=481949& p=3295824`	Data about 6,000 U.S. public companies
		200 million residents and local businesses
D&B Hoover's	`www.nypl.org/ collections/articles- databases/hoovers`	43,000 directory entries for private and public companies
	`www.dnb.com/products/ marketing-sales/dnb- hoovers/dnb-hoovers- free-trial.html`	Data for 600 industries
	`www.dnb.com/marketing/ media/dnb-hoovers-free- trial.html`	
D&B	`www.dnb.com/about-us/ data-cloud.html`	D&B cloud data offers comprehensive business data and analytical insights
	`www.dnb.com/solutions/ analytics.html`	More than 300 million business records
		375 million data records

[11] Adapted from The New York Public Library/`www.nypl.org/collections/ nypl-recommendations/guides/company-research`. Last accessed November 30, 2022.

INFORMATION PROVIDER	LINK	OFFERED BUSINESS INFORMATION

Standard and Poor's Capital IQ	`www.nypl.org/ collections/ articles-databases/ standard-and-poors- net-advantage`
	
	`www.spglobal.com/ marketintelligence/en/ solutions/sp-capital-iq- platform`
		Companies' financial information
		
		Corporation records
		
		Stock reports

Plunkett Research Online	`www.nypl.org/ collections/articles- databases/plunkett- research-online`	Market research reports Analytics reports for 500 industries Benchmark reports that include 3,800 corporations

Business Insights: Essentials	`www.nypl.org/ collections/ articles-databases/ business-insights- essentials`
	
	`www.gale.com/c/ business-insights- essentials`
		Company profiles
		
		Industry profiles
		
		Product and brands data
		
		Financial reports

Library of Congress	`guides.loc.gov/ company-research`	Business reference services

Leveraging Business Knowledge During an Interview

So how should business knowledge be leveraged during an interview? Successful responses to software architecture questions should embed examples that bear a resemblance to the hiring institution's business model, culture, size, revenue, and even industry.

What then would be a software architect candidate's convincing answer to an interview question about addressing production environments' communication and information sharing challenges? In this case, a winning interview strategy would be to tackle this query by *using business knowledge acquired about the hiring organization*. For example, if its business is based on the restaurant franchise model, then the candidate's most satisfying answer would depict the approach by which applications across the different franchise regions exchange data.

An interviewer would be further impressed to hear more details about the deployment of the business applications across the dispersed production environments. A candidate then may include technical specifications for protocols, middleware, and infrastructure that enable the applications to talk to each other.

Recall that the driving strategy for answering technical questions should rely heavily on the candidate's business knowledge of the hiring organization.

Understand the Business Model

Vital business information that a software architect candidate should obtain before an interview is the business model of the hiring organization. A business model typically includes strategic aspects that a company must embrace to withstand harsh market competition.

By understanding the recruiting organization's business model, a software architect candidate could learn about the company's vision, strategy, structure, and lines of business. This information could shed light on the specific technology in place to promote the business. It also reveals what types of applications are in use and the method by which they are deployed locally or remotely.

To establish a solid business model and survival plan, enterprise executives must define the model components as shown in Table 8.7. In addition, it depicts the correlation between these components and the technologies that a candidate can use for conjecture.

Table 8.7: Company Business Model and Software Architecture Candidate's Discovery

BUSINESS MODEL COMPONENT	EXPLANATION	CANDIDATE'S DISCOVERY	CANDIDATE'S TECHNOLOGICAL INTEREST
Offerings	Type of services and products the company provides to its client base	Type of data the company utilizes to promote services.	Data formats, data source providers, data protocols
		Data examples: Insurance, equity trading, banking, healthcare records	Data exchange protocol examples: HL7,[12] ACORD XML,[13] FIX[14]

---

[12] Health Level Seven (HL7) is a messaging protocol standard that enables clinical applications to exchange data.

[13] The Association for Cooperative Operations Research and Development (ACORD), a nonprofit organization that operates in the insurance industry, established electronic data exchange standards (supported by Extensible Markup Language, XML) to be used between collaborating companies and consumers.

[14] The financial information exchange (FIX) is an international data exchange protocol employed for securities transactions.

BUSINESS MODEL COMPONENT	EXPLANATION	CANDIDATE'S DISCOVERY	CANDIDATE'S TECHNOLOGICAL INTEREST
Industry[15] and sector[16]	Industry and sector classification	Company's primary business engagements Sector examples: Financial, energy, healthcare Industry examples: Banking, insurance, air transportation, accommodation	Type of systems and applications supporting the company's industry and sector Examples: Trading system, banking portal, healthcare, home insurance application
Customers	Customer segmentation[17]	Targets clients by learning about their geographic locations, demographics (age, income, gender), social preferences (entertainment, travel, etc.,), and product consumption habits and history	User experience technologies, applications, and customer interface mechanisms Examples: Web, social media platforms, cloud community, online stores, consumer portals
Business process	The means by which services are provided to clients	Type of systems, applications, or technologies employed to deliver business services	Service-oriented architecture (SOA), microservices, Business process modeling (BPM), business orchestration, service lookup, SOAP,[18] REST[19] Implementation examples: Web applications, software as a service (SaaS), desktop applications

Continues

[15] The North American Industry Classification System (NAICS) is a U.S. federal statistics classification system used to group corporations based on their business affiliations and operations.
[16] A business category that identifies common business products or services
[17] Market research typically offers customer segmentation data that identifies consumers' social interests, product consumption habits, and more.
[18] Simple Object Access Protocol (SOAP) is a structured message exchange protocol for web services, used for sharing data on computer networks.
[19] Representational State Transfer (REST) is an application programming interface (API) employed to exchange data between consumers and web services.

Table 8.7 (*continued*)

BUSINESS MODEL COMPONENT	EXPLANATION	CANDIDATE'S DISCOVERY	CANDIDATE'S TECHNOLOGICAL INTEREST
Structure	Geographical (regions, states, continents, etc.) distribution of company's workforce and lines of business	Deployment of company's applications across geographical locations	Integration patterns, message-oriented middleware (MOM[20]), interoperability model
Policies	Company's business practices and policies employed to provide quality services	Company's applications maintaining government and industrywide regulations for conducting business Examples: Sarbanes-Oxley,[21] employment and labor law,[22] anti-trust law[23]	Integration of COTS or modifiable off-the shelf (MOTS[24]) products with company's production environment
Infrastructure	Supporting technologies	Company's chief production environment technologies	Cloud, middleware, messaging model, security model, network protocols, infrastructure as a service (IaaS)

Get Familiar with the Hiring Company's Culture

Before attending an interview, software architecture applicants might want to get a glimpse of the hiring organization's culture. The term *culture* refers to company's business code of conduct, rules of behavior, believes, and policies.

---

[20] Infrastructure (software or hardware) deployed to a production environment to support message exchange between distributed applications, services, and systems

[21] The Sarbanes-Oxley Act (section 404) requires public institutions to provide annual assessments of internal control over their financial status.

[22] State and federal laws that govern the employment of employees and contractors anti-trust law

[23] U.S. federal laws established to govern business conduct to promote fair competition

[24] An off-the-self product that enables companies to modify its source code and configuration to meet business and technical requirements

Studying the company's culture, however, would not necessarily reveal much about how software architecture practices promote the business. But acquiring such knowledge may shed light on the company's social attributes, such as internal communication between employees. Other cultural aspects are related to interaction with the outside world. This pertains to applications and systems used to interface with company's vendors and clients.

The most important cultural facet for software architecture applicants to discern is if the hiring company's approach to addressing business challenges is by leveraging technology. Case in point, technology-driven solutions are being adopted by institutions that typically promote automation over human intervention in business processes. This organizational determination is aligned with proactive technological initiatives designed to avert business calamities before they hit the shore. Therefore, such cultural preferences may shed light on the company's commitment to invest in their IT organization. As a result, this investment would certainly support software architecture projects.

So, what specifically should a software architect applicant learn about the hiring organization's culture? Whether the company is

- willing to invest in technology to promote business initiatives

- committed to sponsor IT projects

- dedicated to investing in IT professionals' careers

Conduct a Quick SWOT Analysis

Applicants who are eager to learn more about the hiring organization's operations, potential business perils, avenues for growth, and competition should conduct the well-known business analysis named SWOT (stands for strengths, weaknesses, opportunities, threats).

This exercise is typically a strategic endeavor. It enables executives, business analysts, research personnel, and others to learn about the positioning of the company in the market. The term *positioning* applies to the company's capability to withstand industry and operational challenges.

Once conducted, the SWOT analysis offers four different business perspectives.

Strengths   Reveals the company's advantage over its competitors in terms of technology, investment resources, quality of services, dedicated and trained staff, and more

Weaknesses   Uncovers the company's disadvantage in relationship to other organizations because of shortfalls in strategy and business execution

Opportunities   An analytic view that divulges the company's prospects for growth, client acquisition, and operations expansion

Threats   Depicts business perils that may result in loss of revenue and mounting risks to survival

The upshot of the SWOT analysis becomes handy when the aim is to learn about current market conditions and identify competitors in the same sector and/or industry. Getting to know the clients is another advantage that should not be overlooked.

This analysis, though, should prompt software architecture candidates to focus more on a different perspective. Here, we're required to observe the SWOT's technological view by asking these questions:

- What technologies does the company possess to maintain its advantages over the competition?
- Why does the company fail to adopt a potent technological strategy, leaving it at a disadvantage against some of its competitors?
- How could technological superiority empower the company to grow?
- How could a leading technological capability diminish business threats?

Understand the Hiring Organization's Technology

Software architecture applicants should be familiar with the hiring organization's technology. Generally speaking, the term *technology* encompasses numerous practices, disciplines, processes, techniques, and methodologies that are affiliated with computer science. These technological aspects are the underpinning factors that support the business. In other words, nowadays, without technology no institution can survive and prosper.

In the quest to understand how the hiring organization utilizes technology to promote its business strategy, applicants may face two obstacles: typically, there is not much time to prepare for a job interview, and there is not much information about technology that can be easily scooped out from an abbreviated job description. At this point, therefore, the applicants' obligation is to look at alternative sources of information to fill in the gaps in the knowledge needed for a successful interview attack plan.

Technological Information Sources

Since time is of the essence, the quickest way to obtain information about the hiring organization's technology and architecture is by searching the Internet or even visiting the library. A great deal of knowledge can be drawn from a company's public press releases, in which it typically announces its project accomplishments. For example, applicants may be able to learn about successful data migration to the cloud. In other press releases, companies may reveal their partnerships with data source providers and others and may even give clues about the type of data they consume.

An abundance of a company's technological information also can be found in technology reviews and innovation and scientific magazines. Applicants could subscribe online to this professional literature and receive periodic technology coverage. Furthermore, specific information for software architects could be acquired from software development magazines, software development news,[25] software architecture journals, cybersecurity[26] magazines, and network computing[27] publications. Some of these sources even offer free subscriptions.

Another way of learning about the hiring organization's technology is to search for its virtual trade shows[28] online or visit trade shows in person. Many organizations are motivated to participate in trade shows because of the opportunity to present their offerings directly to potential customers and address arising questions. Applicants could also leverage the opportunity to acquire information at trade shows and learn more about the company's products, services, and supporting technologies.

Finally, there are many other sources of information on the Internet that a software architecture candidate could use to learn about companies' technologies. Follow them on social media, subscribe to their email newsletters, listen to videos posted by their executives, and watch their online training.

The list that follows provides only a partial list of information sources from which a candidate may learn about the technologies of the hiring institutions:

Libraries City libraries, university libraries

News platforms Press releases, software development news, electronic newsletters

Magazines and publications Innovation publications, technology reviews, scientific magazines, software development magazines, software architecture journals, cybersecurity magazines, and network computing publications

Trade shows and conferences Virtual and in-person trade shows, conferences, convention centers

---

[25] sdtimes.com and www.eweek.com or t3technologyhub.com/fidelity adds-new-self-service-capabilities-in-its-open-architecture-digital-store-integration-xchange

[26] www.scmagazine.com/

[27] www.networkcomputing.com

[28] www.vfairs.com/solutions/virtual-trade-shows

Training and education   Virtual training, training facilities, podcasts, seminars, continuing education classes, undergraduate and graduate studies

Social media and information exchange platforms   Marketing platforms, photo and video-sharing platforms, chat and messaging applications, friends and family communication platforms

Never miss an opportunity to gather more information about the driving technology of the hiring institution. So, what type of information should an applicant search for? The sections that follow provide software architecture principal points that applicants should focus on.

Discover the Environment's Technology Stack

Demonstrating knowledge about the recruiting organization's technological environment during a job interview would certainly impress interviewers and even add extra points to an applicant's evaluation. The term *technological environment* pertains to the landscape in which the organization deploys its systems and applications—namely, the production environment.

There is so much to know about an organization's technological ecosystem and its empowering infrastructure. The information about the components of such an operation production environment is not easy to obtain. But candidates could employ some common sense to figure out what type of technology such a business would require to execute its strategy.

For example, a hiring organization that provides data analytics services for the auto industry to its clients would more likely base its production environment on large data repository capabilities, such as big data technologies. Furthermore, direct access to data could breach security policies. In this case, architecture best practices typically call for middleware products to manage safe data access.

Other than middleware and repositories, many information-providing organizations also employ cloud architecture. This technology capitalizes on computer resource elasticity[29] to accommodate enough computing capacity to address future growth of data and client base.

A software architecture applicant should then study the technological environment of the hiring organization by using similar discovery points, as shown in Table 8.8. It lists the chief technology components that an applicant ought to explore before a job interview.

---

[29] Cloud elasticity pertains to the capability of a cloud environment to automatically provide growing computing resources to demanding applications, services, and systems.

Table 8.8: Environment Technology Stack Discovery

TECHNOLOGY STACK	EXAMPLES
Cloud computing	Amazon Web Services (AWS), Microsoft Azure, Google Cloud
Language platforms	Python, Java, C++, PHP
Operating systems	Linux, Windows
Middleware	Data access layer, message orchestrator, service discovery, data aggregator, service bus
Data repositories	MySQL, MongoDB, Hadoop
Frameworks	Flask, Ruby on Rails, Swift, Django, Objective-C
Servers	NGINX, Apache
DevOps[30] tools	Jenkins, Chef, Git, Puppet, Ansible
Container platforms	Docker, Kubernetes
Communication and collaboration	Slack, Microsoft Teams
Monitoring	AppDynamics, Splunk
IT ticketing	ServiceNow

Learn About the Development Technology Stack

Application-level and even enterprise-level software architecture applicants should be knowledgeable about the hiring organization's development technology stack in advance of a job interview. This should include a list of the technologies—also known as *technology stacks*—employed to construct and operate applications and services in production. More specifically, the technology stack should encompass a list of servers, languages, databases, and operating systems that developers leverage for software development.

As a part of the preparation for an impending job interview, construct a development technology list, comparable to the example shown in Table 8.9. It depicts two frequently used development stacks for web development: LAMP (Linux, Apache, MySQL, PHP) and MEAN (MongoDB, Express.js, Angular, Node.js). The former is typically adopted for developing dynamic websites and web applications. The latter, on the other hand, is more suited for building applications with one language only. In this respect, a single programming language is used for developing both the server-side and client-side application modules.

---

[30] DevOps refers to best practices, standards, and policies chiefly related to IT operations. The driving DevOps concerns are affiliated with the continuous delivery and continuous integration of applications and systems.

> **NOTE** Software architecture applicants: build a technology stack based on the knowledge acquired about the hiring organization's production systems.

Table 8.9: Industry Common Development Technology Stacks

STACK NAME	TECHNOLOGY	TYPE
LAMP	Linux	Operating system
	Apache	Web server
	MySQL	Database
	PHP	Programming language
MEAN	MongoDB	Database
	Express.js	Server-side web application framework
	Angular	Client-side application framework
	Node.js	Server-side environment

Study the Applications

When it comes to understanding the supporting technology of a hiring organization, there is always a compelling correlation between the related industry and the type of applications supporting its business. Accordingly, common sense suggests that a banking institution typically supports banking applications. This wide range of related banking implementations may include applications for business loans, bill pay, money transfers, and account statements.

In the same fashion, it would be reasonable to assume that an asset management firm would more likely operate numerous applications related to the investment industry. These implementations may include portfolio management, trading, and market data applications.

Organize the discovery of business implementations by creating a simple list of the hiring institution's industry and its related applications. Follow the structure shown in Table 8.10. In this respect, the listed applications support the insurance process and its related product life cycle.

Table 8.10: Hiring Institution's Industry-Related Applications

INDUSTRY	RELATED APPLICATIONS
Insurance	Customer questionnaire
	Insurance customer profiling
	Underwriting
	Claims processing
	Insurance pricing
	Credit analysis

Identify Specific IT Projects

Recruiting companies often post job descriptions that include some hints about ongoing or imminent business and technological initiatives. Doing this does not mean that the hiring institution intends to employ software architects for a short period of time. Nor does the organization intend to bring applicants on board for a narrow-scoped project. In most cases, the aim of the job posting is to attract software architecture talents who are familiar with the recruiting company's specific industry, line of products, and services.

For example, a job description may indicate that the hiring organization is seeking to employ software architects to design an insurance client portal. This requirement typically calls for a long development life cycle budgeted by large business investments.

In other instances, organizations may not reveal the specific business intent behind hiring software architects. Instead, their job descriptions may indicate that the positions require skills and experience for a particular product or environment. This may include, for instance, software architecture talents who specialize in a particular document management system, cloud architecture, or middleware product.

As a part of the preparation for a job interview, software architecture applicants should gather as much information as possible about the hiring institution's current and imminent projects or initiatives. Here are the chief directives:

- Understand the scope of the software architecture work
- Become familiar with the specific lines of business
- Learn about the business strategy and vision
- Study the hiring organization's sector and industry

Demonstrate Enterprise Architecture Knowledge of the Hiring Organization

An effective job interview plan of attack would be to demonstrate substantial knowledge about the hiring organization's enterprise architecture, even if the applicant is applying for an application or solution architecture position. Although this information is not always included in a job description, software architecture applicants should be motivated enough to study the architectural landscape by searching other sources of information. To accomplish this, circle back to the section "Technological Information Services" presented previously in this chapter to search for and explore the architectural environments of specific companies.

Once this information has been unearthed, software architecture applicants should narrow their study to only a few aspects of the hiring organization's architectural environment. The focus of this exercise should not be dedicated mostly to the functional requirements of the deployed applications. The term *functional requirements* chiefly refers to business processes and services. Here, software architecture applicants should direct the bulk of their attention to the organization-empowering infrastructure in production and, most important, to understanding how the enterprise architecture is devised to provide solutions on an organizational level.

To understand how the technological environment delivers tangible solutions for the hiring institution, decompose the enterprise architecture into the fundamental elements, which are shown in Table 8.11. When pursuing this, list the driving architecture components in the "Architecture Elements" column. Then, describe in the "Function" column what each element contributes to the enterprise deployment environment. Lastly, list in the "Mechanisms/Capabilities" column the infrastructure (software or hardware) solutions employed by the hiring organization. This column could include, for instance, COTS products, software or hardware development concepts, or any other technology that facilitates architecture solutions.

Table 8.11: Enterprise Architecture Environment Decomposition Example

ARCHITECTURE ELEMENTS	FUNCTION	MECHANISMS/CAPABILITIES
Message-oriented middleware (MOM)	Infrastructure (software or hardware) supporting message exchange between service providers and consumers	Enterprise service bus (ESB), message bus, message queueing, message broker
Asset integration	Infrastructure (software or hardware) mechanisms deployed to link assets in production	Customer data integration (CDI), workflow automation, service discovery, service binding, service orchestration
Interoperability	Infrastructure (software or hardware) that enables seamless communication between heterogeneous computing environments	Message gateway, message hub, message routing, data transformation, message transformation
Data management	Data persistence, routing, filtering, and conversion capabilities	Data repositories, data warehouse, data access layer, data hub, data abstraction layer, data transformation, CRUD[31]
Architecture styles, Architecture patterns, design patterns	Design solutions, akin to templates, that can be applied to solving repeatable problems	Integration patterns, messaging patterns, data management patterns, message bus pattern, data access pattern

---

[31] CRUD: Create, Read, Write, Delete

Adopt Software Architecture Lingo

Many practitioners, such as brain surgeons, airline pilots, and family physicians use a professional vocabulary to communicate and exchange information about discipline procedures, daily activities, and information. Similar in concept, a unique jargon with an inimitable lexicon has been developed by software architects. This language of technological terminology enables the software architecture community to describe design concepts, ideas, and software implementations that otherwise would be hard to express in plain language.

More than we might assume, astute interviewers are attentive to the lingo the software architect candidate uses to convey strategies and concepts. Therefore, prepare for a job interview by memorizing and practicing the software architecture vocabulary. Speaking this inherited language fluently would affirm candidates' experience in the field and the ability to understand architecture-specific terminologies.

Recall that the software architecture lingo includes countless key words, phrases, and expressions that would be impractical to cover in this book. An applicant, however, should prepare for an impending job interview with a number of flashcards related to specific job requirements. If a recruiting organization, for example, is seeking to hire a talent with vast experience in design patterns, then the flashcards should include related architecture vocabulary. The jargon in this case may contain architecture patterns used to describe a software implementation scheme, such as *façade,*[32] *controller,*[33] *and hub and spokes distribution model.*[34]

The sections that follow offer examples for software architecture lingo grouped by a number of language interests, such as best practices, principles, ideas, implementation patterns, concepts, and processes. Again, based on the provided examples, software architecture candidates should prepare their own vocabulary to use during an interview.

Use Design Patterns Vocabulary

Design patterns have contributed immensely to the software architecture lingo's terminology. By using this vocabulary, software architects can describe technological solutions, depict deployment environments, and offer templates for rectifying future problems with no special need for submitting lengthy documentation.

---

[32] A façade is a front-end interface that conceals or shelters complex structural architecture or source code.

[33] A controller is a software implementation that manages the flow of data and messages between consumers and software components.

[34] The hub and spoke distribution model refers to the centralization of message exchange controlled by a hub that communicates with related consumers.

Interviewers typically expect short and to-the-point answers, rather than lengthy descriptions of software architecture solutions. When responding to their queries, using software architecture lingo could simplify complex design concepts that an applicant might be required to communicate.

To illustrate this concept, imagine that an applicant is being asked to describe an architecture style that uses a central connection point to link and integrate applications. A prudent answer would then satisfy this query by using an architecture lingo that describes such a message mediation design scheme. The star topology or hub and spoke architecture style would be the correct vocabulary to use for illustrating this environment. In such a configuration, the hub would signify the central point of message integration, while the spokes are the message routes that connect the applications.

Before attending an interview, read the job description carefully. Then prepare software architecture vocabulary that may be used for answering interviewers' questions. Review Table 8.12 and construct a similar one for listing the the lingo's key words and the potential talking points to use during the job interview.

Table 8.12: Design Patterns Vocabulary

VOCABULARY	TALKING POINTS
Façade	Provides a central interface to an application or service
Front Controller	A central service that handles all consumer requests for a website
Proxy	A software intermediary that controls access to a target application or service
Model-View-Controller (MVC)	Defines the interaction between three components: the model (manages application data), the view (renders presentation of the model), and the controller (interacts with the user and manipulates the model)

Use the Software Architecture Guidelines Lingo to Communicate Solutions

Software architecture *best practices*, *principles*, *standards*, and *policies* are all *guidelines* that facilitate product development life-cycle tasks and milestones. They promote the development, deployment, and maintenance of organizational assets, such as applications, services, and systems. Furthermore, these guidelines foster the *strategy and direction* of enterprise projects and initiatives. Without them, a *transition* to new business phases and the adoption of advanced technologies may render organizational chaos that would be arduous to overcome.

NOTE   During a job interview, adopt this software architecture lingo. Talk about software architecture best practices, principles, standards, and policies when there is a need to elaborate on approaches, strategies, and software design directions.

Give Architecture Principle Examples to Explain Impact on Software Development

The term *software architecture principles* refers to a set of *decision-making* design *rules*, typically affecting application development and their operating environments. For example, *separation of concerns* is a well-known design principle that guides developers to avoid the construction of tightly coupled applications (also known as the *low cohesion effect*). Differently put, this principle characteristically advocates separating the application's business logic from its user interface, infrastructure, or any other related functionality. The separation of these components typically allows easier source code maintenance, reuse, and testing.

The principle of least knowledge (recognized as Law of Demeter, LoD) is another example of a decision-making design rule that promotes implementation loose coupling and protection. This rule calls for a software component to hide most of its private data without sharing it with other unrelated components.

Give Software Architecture Best Practice Examples to Demonstrate Problem-Solving Skills

Most institutions devise best practices to reduce expenditure, boost quality of services, and accelerate time to market. Generally speaking, these business imperatives call for establishing *problem-solving processes*. Once adopted, they render the *best solutions possible* for an organization. Simply put, best practices are formulated by the enterprise as the most suitable approaches and processes for "doing things" to tackle organizational problems—in other words, best practices are all about the "*how.*"

In the same way, software architecture best practices are founded to provide implementation *guidance* for product design and development, software acquisition, deployment, integration, and operations. One of the most common software architecture best practices is *buy versus build analysis*. This practice implies that an IT organization should determine *how* to meet business requirements: should the company acquire software or build in-house products? Design verification best practices are formulated to guide software architects on how to confirm that the programming source code adheres to architecture blueprints and models.

Furthermore, when it comes to the quality of business products, best practices typically offer general guidance that can improve the excellence of applications, services, and systems. *Knowledge of how to conduct source code reviews during milestones of the software development life cycle is one example of how best practices can improve applications, services and systems.* Application and system testing are related to other best practices, devised to guide developers and analysts on how to ensure operation stability in production.

The following questions summarize the need for organizational best practices to promote solid software architecture environments:

- How should software be designed?
- How should software architecture be tested?
- How should applications be integrated in production?
- How should applications utilize messaging infrastructure capabilities in production?
- How should enterprise architecture patterns be employed to enable environment interoperability?

Give Software Architecture Standards Examples to Demonstrate Technological Standardization Capabilities

There are vast number of standards that pertain to almost any software architecture practice and discipline. There is also no shortage of literatures, research, and publications that provide guidance for software design, development, deployment, and integration. Furthermore, many organizations, especially nonprofit institutions, embark on the mission to train, educate, and guide professionals who seek to advance their careers in the computer field. In addition, these companies pledge to standardize technologies, methodologies, disciplines, and practices across the software architecture industry. Their mission is then to promote the industry's common language and expand the market's vocabulary.

Consider the list of architecture standards examples in Table 8.13.

Table 8.13: Software Architecture Standard Examples

ORIGINATING ORGANIZATION	STANDARD
ISO/IEC/IEEE: `ieeexplore.ieee.org/document/6129467`	Standard 42010:2011: Architecture terminology, concepts, frameworks, and definitions
The Open Group: `www.opengroup.org/togaf`	The Open Group Architecture Framework (TOGAF): Governance and development of enterprise architecture
The Open Group/Archimate: `www.opengroup.org/archimate-forum/archimate-overview`	Enterprise architecture visualization and documentation
Department of Defense (DoD): `dodcio.defense.gov/library/dod-architecture-framework/`	DoD Architecture Framework (DODAF): viewpoints for the development of architectures and architecture artifacts

NOTE Software architecture standards and frameworks drive the architecture and software development life cycle. Therefore, remember to accompany answers to interviewers' questions with a couple of standards to increase credibility and demonstrate deep understanding of the software architecture industry.

Give Software Architecture Policies Examples to Demonstrate Pragmatic Software Design Approaches

Enterprise management often devises *pragmatic protocols* and *codes of implementation and behavior* for addressing organizational challenges. Software architects then must comply with institutional business and technological policies to promote business continuity in production.

Consider the policy examples in the following list:

- Software architects must be responsible and accountable for the design and deployment of software products to production.
- No copies of an authoritative data source should be deployed to production.
- Software implementation must be accompanied by system design documents (SDDs) and operation manuals.
- Before embarking on a software development project, business requirements and technical specifications must be presented to construction teams.
- The business and IT organizations must apply safeguards mechanisms to protect the confidentiality of personally identifiable information (PII).
- All corporate data must be protected and backed up in a secure location.
- Business requirements must indicate the acceptable recovery time of a system after it has been halted (known as *recovery time objective*, RTO).

Moreover, when it comes to software architecture *governance*, policies focus on the *responsibilities and roles* of software architects. These guidelines define their *authority, accountability,* and *scope of operation* to institutionalize software products and provide tangible solutions to organizational problems. Policies also formulate software architecture *management structures* and *hierarchies* intended to respond effectively to business requirements.

Use Software Architecture Guidelines Lingo

It's always helpful to generate a lingo table for software architecture guidelines before attending an interview. It should include best practices, principles, and policies that could help an applicant to respond eloquently to interviewers' questions. These queries may be about development processes, design solutions, problem-solving standards, and more.

Table 8.14 provides examples that applicants could follow to build their own lists based on the job descriptions for the positions they apply for.

Table 8.14: Software Architecture Guidelines Lingo

GUIDELINE TYPE	GUIDELINE	EXPLANATION
Principle	Separation of concerns	A design principle that promotes implementation loose coupling by advocating decomposition of capabilities
Best practice	Buy versus build analysis	A software architecture best practice that calls for IT management to determine if software acquisition outweighs the benefits of in-house development efforts
Policy	Role and responsibilities	Policy that defines the role and responsibilities of software architects in the organization
Standard	Software modeling	A software design standard that enables software architects to visualize and describe software implementations

Remember Software Architecture Tools

The utilization and the contribution of software architecture tools are often important topics of discussion during a job interview. Frequently, applicants are asked to name a number of tools, utilities, and platforms employed during the architecture life cycle. It would be almost impossible to perform well in a software architecture interview if such knowledge were absent. It's an applicant's responsibility, therefore, to be prepared for these questions, not only by reviewing past project notes, but also by conducting appropriate research.

The space of architecture tools is vast. And there is a myriad of tools on the market addressing different phases of the product development life cycle. These phases include the disciplines of business architecture, architecture strategy, architecture visualization, software modeling, business analysis, architecture validation and evaluation, software deployment and integration, and production operations.

Moreover, software architecture tools are designed for different architecture levels. The term *level* refers to the target architecture range, such as application architecture or enterprise architecture.[35] Application architecture tools that focus on a narrower solution purview may not be suited for enterprise-level utilization.

---

[35] Enterprise architecture tools examples: www.gartner.com/reviews/market/enterprise-architecture-tools

Classification of Software Architecture Tools

To demonstrate technological superiority and capabilities to provide organizational solutions, software architecture candidates must be familiar with tools that facilitate the product development life cycle. Not only is it important to bring forth tool features during interview discussions, it also is vital to understand which category the tools are affiliated with.

Before an upcoming job interview, prepare an architecture tools list that is related to the job description. For instance, if the hiring organization is seeking to employ a software architect who possesses modeling and diagraming skills, then, accordingly, the table should include an architecture visualization category.

Table 8.15 lists only a few examples of tool categories. Applicants should not only indicate the tools' features and capabilities, but also list actual tools that are affiliated with the "Category" column.

Consider the following list of software architecture tool categories:

Business domain   This category includes tools promoting organizational strategy and vision. It groups a variety of tools facilitating a large number of business activities, such as business analysis, digital transformation, business architecture, risk analysis, and business value proposition analysis.

Architecture visualization   This segment is related to diagramming, architecture modeling, and software simulation.

Architecture strategy   To lead an organizational architecture direction and address software design decisions, this category tackles a number of crucial technological strategies. Examples include migration of assets, software modernization and transformation, architecture analysis, and architecture evaluation.

Architecture discovery   Prior to any technological initiatives, software architects ought to discover the production environment, application dependencies, and network topology.

DevOps and DevSecOps[36]   This is another software architecture key category that focuses on operations' processes—often named *pipelines*. These production operation activities include security controls, monitoring, continuous integration (CI), and continuous deployment (CD) of implementations to production.

Repositories   This category includes a diversity of tools and platforms that offer document management, source code versioning and repositories, knowledge sharing, and metadata management.

---

[36] DevOps is a collection of agile software development and production operation practices. DevSecOps, on the other hand, pertain to common industry security practices added to the existing DevOps operation practices.

Table 8.15: Architecture Tools Category, Features, and Capabilities

TOOL CATEGORY	TOOL FEATURES	TOOL CAPABILITIES
Business domain	Business concepts management	Establishing ideas and concepts for products and launching business initiatives
	Business analysis	Identifying business problems, providing business solutions, assessing business progress and evolution, monitoring business changes, providing business requirements
	Digital transformation	Facilitating business process automation, promoting business innovation, fostering business agility and efficiency
	Application portfolio management	Aligning business and IT vision and strategies, managing application inventories, cultivating asset reuse
	Business risk analysis	Identifying business perils and providing solution alternatives
	Business transformation	Promoting business growth, tracing business evolution and change
	Business architecture	Discovering and tracing business problems and needs, defining business strategies, founding business goals, providing business solutions, performing business process modeling
	Business value proposition analysis	Tracking return on business investments, realizing business value proposition
Architecture visualization	Diagramming	Providing visual presentations of technical solutions
	Modeling	Designing software solutions
	Simulation	Analyzing software behavior in mock-up environments

TOOL CATEGORY	TOOL FEATURES	TOOL CAPABILITIES
Architecture strategy	Architecture conceptualization	Promoting technological innovation through establishment of ideas and concepts
	Technological modernization and transformation	Promoting technological change by adopting advanced development methods, facilities, and devices
	System interoperability	Enabling information exchange between technological heterogenous environments
	System integration	Linking organizational applications, systems, and data to deliver joint technological implementations
	Architecture analysis	Performing architecture evaluation and validation adhering to technological best practices, assessing architecture feasibility, performing technical gap analyses
	Asset migration	Planning and facilitating the migration of organizational assets from legacy environments to next-generation environments
	System security	Forming security best practices and facilitating security controls
	Architecture verification	Confirming implementation adherence with architectural models
Architecture discovery	Application discovery	Siting the deployment of organizational applications in production
	Network topology discovery	Studying the structural composition of a network, ascertaining topographical links of nodes on a network
	Application dependency mapping	Identifying the dependency and relationship between deployed applications

Continues

Table 8-15 (*continued*)

TOOL CATEGORY	TOOL FEATURES	TOOL CAPABILITIES
DevOps and DevSecOps	Pipeline automation	Automating continuous deployment (CD) and continuous integration (CI)
	Capacity planning and performance analysis	Monitoring implementations in production environments, creating performance dashboards, performing current and predictive computing capacity modeling
	Cybersecurity tools and platforms	Applying security controls, monitoring, vulnerability and penetration testing
Repositories	Architecture knowledge sharing repository	Sharing information about architecture implementation methods, design solutions, utilization of tools and platforms
	Source code repository and version control	Enhancing source code integrity, enabling source code sharing, fostering implementation reuse
	Document management	Data indexing, cataloging, storing, version tracking
	Meta data management	Analyzing, understanding, evaluating, facilitating the discovery and management of data
	Data management	Data modeling, data sharing mechanisms, data protection technologies, data integrity approaches, data access techniques

Especially Prepare for Architecture Visualization Tools Questions

One of the most common topics of discussion during job interviews is about the arsenal of tools that software architects employ to communicate end-state design solutions. Moreover, applicants are often asked to name some tools and explain how they are being utilized.

Fortunately, the market is saturated with architecture visualization tools and platforms[37] with capabilities for creating design charts, graphs, and illustrations. But merely mentioning them during an interview would not be enough. Proper preparations, therefore, should include a list of design diagrams that might be

---

[37] Examples of architecture visualization tools and platforms: www.gartner.com/ reviews/market/enterprise-architecture-tools

beneficial to discuss when appropriate, as shown in Table 8.16. The "Design Perspective" column identifies three architecture views, each of which represents the related diagrams and the benefits of their utilization.

Table 8.16: Design Diagrams Example

DESIGN PERSPECTIVE	DIAGRAM	WHAT IS IT	BENEFITS
Conceptual	Reference architecture	A typical enterprise-level architecture environment abstraction with interacting functions and/or components that collectively provide solutions	Promotes environment interoperability, fosters software reuse, introduces organizational design vocabulary to improve stakeholders' communications
Logical	Component diagram	Depiction of system-level or application-level linked elements and their relationship to provide business or technical solutions	Offers a common language between various project stakeholders, introduces design intent and solution roadmap
	Activity diagram	A flowchart containing data flows, processes, and activities	Shows an overarching step-by-step path to a solution, assists developers with visualizing algorithms and program procedures
Physical	Deployment diagram	A physical deployment of implementation elements to testing and production environments	Visualizes a runtime environment with implementation elements on a network

Get Familiar with Software Architecture Analysis and Evaluation Methods

In simple terms, architecture evaluation[38,39] is an analysis task that renders conclusions about how well the design meets business or technical requirements. This

---

[38] Architecture evaluation tools or platforms are typically based on scenario development driven by simulations that include algorithms with mathematical modeling, and experience-based reasoning.

[39] P. Shanmugapriya and R. M. Suresh, "Software Architecture Evaluation Methods - A Survey," *International Journal of Computer Applications* (0975–8887), Volume 49, No.16, July 2012.

examination focuses on studying software architecture properties, architecture styles, and design patterns. Moreover, the analysis discovery process is devised to ensure software quality, implementation stability, and compliance with functional and nonfunctional requirements.[40] Although this assessment is not as popular as the design visualization practice discussed in the previous section, a growing number of institutions have been making inroads into establishing such a process.

The architecture assessment may take place during any time of the application or system life cycle. To avoid unnecessary development expenditure, the early architecture evaluation takes place at the onset of a product life span—even before the design phase. On the other hand, the late architecture evaluation occurs after the product has been installed in production to determine if a design is effective enough.

Be Aware of Early Architecture Evaluation Methods

Popular early evaluation approaches are the Scenario-based methods,[41] as shown in Table 8.17. These approaches are devised to uncover issues in software architecture from different viewpoints, such as those of business stakeholders, users, and partners.

Table 8.17: Early Architecture Evaluation Methods Examples

METHOD	GOAL
Scenario-based Software Architecture Analysis Method (SAAM[42])	1) Count the number of components affected by a scenario, 2) Test functionality of components, 3) Examine scenario results, 4) Estimate architecture remediation cost.
Architecture-Level Modifiability Analysis (ALMA[43])	1) Predict software architecture maintenance cost, 2) Conduct failure and risk assessment for software architecture.
SAAM for Complex Scenarios (SAAMCS[44])	1) Determine if the software architecture is too complex to implement, 2) Increase architecture simplicity and flexibility.

---

[40] P. Shanmugapriya and R. M. Suresh, "Software Architecture Evaluation Methods - A Survey," *International Journal of Computer Applications*, (0975–8887), Volume 49, No.16, July 2012.

[41] M. A. Babar and I. Gorton, "Comparison of Scenario-Based Software Architecture Evaluation Methods," *Asia-Pacific Software Engineering Conference*, pp. 584–585, 2004

[42] R. Kazman, G. Abowd, and M. Webb, "SAAM: A Method for Analyzing the Properties of Software Architectures," *16th International Conference on Software Engineering*, pp. 81–90, 1994

[43] P. Bengtsson, N. Lassing, J. Bosch, and H. V. Vliet, "Architecture-Level Modifiability Analysis," *Journal of Systems and Software*, vol. 69, 2004.

[44] N. Lassing, D. Rijsenbrij, and H. v. Vliet, "On Software Architecture Analysis of Flexibility," Complexity of Changes: Size Isn't Everything, 2nd Nordic Software Architecture Workshop, 1999

The scenario invocation process is about testing the execution of software components that may include important algorithms, processes, procedures, modules, or services. Modification to the software architecture then would be required if a scenario fails to perform. In this case, the architecture remediation cost should be communicated to the business sponsors.

Be Aware of Late Architecture Evaluation Methods

One of the most common failures in production is caused by ill-designed systems. Performance degradation, for example, may occur by deploying tightly coupled implementations, evading nonfunctional requirements, or employing improper architectural patterns. Clearly, it's not only performance problems that should be investigated in production and testing environments. Architects tend to conduct late latency architecture evaluations to rectify other design issues. These problems may be affiliated with lack of database capacity or even inadequate network bandwidth.

Consider the approaches in Table 8.18. These are devised to address performance, adherence to nonfunctional requirements, and compliance with design principles.

Table 8.18: Late Architecture Evaluation Methods Examples

METHOD	GOAL
Tvedt, et al.[45]	Improving system performance by ensuring architecture adherence to functional and nonfunctional requirements
Murphy, et al.[46]	Validating the compliance of implementation source code to design artifacts
Lindvall, et al.[47]	Assessing software maintainability by confirming its compliance with component-based design principles

Talk About Software Architecture Analysis Standards

During a job interview, applicants are often given software architecture analysis questions. These queries characteristically require deep knowledge in *architecture quality* standards, approaches, and models. Most of these industry

[45] R.T. Tvedt, M. Lindvall, and P. Costa, A Process for Software Architecture Evaluation Using Metrics, 27th Annual NASA Goddard/IEEE, pp. 191–196, 2002

[46] G. C. Murphy, D. Notkin, and K. Sullivan, Software Reflexion Models: Bridging The Gap Between Source And High-Level Models, 3rd ACM SIGSOFT symposium on Foundations of Software Engineering, pp. 18–28, 1995.

[47] M. Lindvall, R. T. Tvedt, and P. Costa, An Empirically Based Process For Software Architecture Evaluation, Empirical Software Engineering 8(1): 83Y108, 2003

norms call for validating that the design and implementation indeed comply with the functional and nonfunctional requirements.

But the software architecture analysis process is not only about the implementation itself. It also calls for examining whether an architecture is suitable to operate in certain production environments with the allocated infrastructure and computing capacity. The analysis discipline then entails a 360-degree study of the deployment landscape to ensure business continuity and operational stability.

To give satisfactory answers to software architecture analysis questions, applicants should study the international standards for systems and software quality. Table 8.19 provides an abbreviated list as a base for applicants to expand their studies.

Table 8.19: Systems and Software Quality Standards Examples

STANDARD	FOCUS	REQUIREMENTS
ISO/IEC 25010:2011[48]	Systems and software quality model	Functional suitability, performance efficiency, compatibility, usability, reliability, security, maintainability, portability
Consortium for IT Software Quality (CISQ[49])	Evaluating and benchmarking IT software	Reliability, security, performance efficiency, maintainability
ISO/IEC 25023:2016[50]	Measurement of system and software product quality	External measure of system and software quality, internal measure of software quality

---

[48] www.iso.org/obp/ui/#iso:std:iso-iec:25010:ed-1:v1:en
[49] www.it-cisq.org/standards/code-quality-standards/
[50] www.iso.org/obp/ui/#iso:std:iso-iec:25023:ed-1:v1:en

An Outline for Software Architecture Job Interview Questions

Preparing for potential software architecture questions increases the odds of acing an interview. Never attend an interview without compiling a list of queries that could help you focus on specific software architecture topics. This approach falls under the interview defensive strategy concept covered in Chapter 8, "Preparing for a Software Architecture Interview: A Winning Strategy."

The more questions an applicant can anticipate before an interview, the better the chances of standing out among the competition. To accomplish this, first carefully study the job description and understand the business and technological imperatives of the hiring organization before speculating on the questions an interviewer might ask.

The purpose of this chapter is to provide a framework for possible interview questions in different categories, as shown in the list that follows. A software architecture candidate should feel free to expand on these topics as needed.

Behavioral questions   These questions prepare software architecture candidates for demonstrating communication, interpersonal relationship, and leadership capabilities.

Skill assessment questions   The answers to these questions typically reveal the competency level, experience, and training history of applicants.

Architecture attributes questions   These are questions about functional and nonfunctional requirements for applications and systems.

Software architecture life-cycle questions   These are queries about software architecture activities and milestones during the software development life cycle.

Software architecture concepts questions   This topic covers software design concepts, architecture environment design concepts, business concepts, and consumer concepts.

Architecture and design pattern questions   These are queries about architecture patterns, design patterns, and architecture styles.

Problem-solving and decision-making questions   This section elaborates on the problem-solving process that software architects should embark on before making decisions and providing solutions.

Data-related questions   These queries focus on data topics that may be asked during an interview. Data access, data integrity, data transformation, and others alike are common subjects for discussion.

Production environment questions   These queries are designed to discover applicants' understanding of the impact of a software architecture environment on production. Refer to the definition of a software architecture environment in Chapter 6, "Software Architecture Environment Construction."

Software architecture frameworks questions   Questions about frameworks are popular during interviews as they reveal candidates' knowledge about software architecture best practices, standards, policies, and principles.

Behavioral Questions

Interviewers typically tend to catch a glimpse of applicants' personalities and behavior. The ability to withstand work-related pressures, handle challenging projects, and communicate eloquently are certainly desirable skills in an applicant. A software architecture job applicant is more likely to score high points during an interview by providing persuasive responses to these revealing personality queries.

It's not only the software architect's style of *interaction* with business and development teams that can determine the success of a project. Social and cultural factors, such as promoting productive *teamwork*, may also affect information technology (IT) initiatives. The term *teamwork* pertains to the collaboration between various project stakeholders to ensure the deployment of high-quality software products.

NOTE   Applicants who are able to demonstrate leadership and strong ethics are in high demand. Their ability to foster fruitful interpersonal relationships and mitigate arising conflicts between development teams is a big plus. Undoubtedly, these software architect leadership characteristics often contribute to providing potent business and IT solutions.

Attend to possible behavioral questions that may impact the outcome of the software architecture job interview. Understand the motivation behind these queries and prepare to answer them with examples of personal experiences.

Communication

A software architect should dedicate a considerable amount of time to communicating effectively with a project's stakeholders. The term *communication* refers to the capability to broadcast and keep business and IT professionals informed about product development progress, challenges, and risks.

But communication is not only about circulating crucial information among managers and development teams. It's also about the software architect's ability to sell an architecture vision and mission. Moreover, in many cases, persuading sponsors to pledge software development budgets requires special talents. Therefore, superb communication skills characteristically result in organizational commitment to technological innovation.

NOTE Good organizational communication culture enables the exchange of technological ideas that subsequently drive business success. Good communication is also about the ability to embrace differing software architecture approaches. And it's definitely about encouraging teamwork to promote productive conversations.

Prepare for such communication questions as shown in the list that follows:

Buy-in   How do you achieve buy-in for your architecture vision from peers, executives, project managers, and team members?

End-state architecture   How do you persuade management to accept your end-state architecture implementation?

Sponsorship   How do you coax business executives to sponsor architectural initiatives?

Progress information   How do you keep stakeholders abreast of software development projects' progress?

Architectural decisions   What tools and communication platforms are you using to disseminate vital software architecture decisions?

Alerts   In what circumstances do you alert management about technological or business risks?

Architecture complexity   How would you explain complex software architecture implementations to nontechnical stakeholders, such as business sponsors and business executives?

Architecture vision   How do you handle communication with professionals who disagree with your software architecture vision?

Interpersonal Relationships

In the context of this chapter, the term *interpersonal relationships* is all about the *interaction* between individuals who collaborate on accomplishing software architecture goals. To attain these vital objectives, a software architect, therefore, must possess soft skills to interact harmoniously and effectively with peers, development teams, and management.

Soft skills refers to a slew of social traits that a software architect must have to promote *collaborative teamwork* within an organization. One of the most important skills is the capability to *negotiate* technological solutions with development and operations teams. The ability to *resolve conflicts* when disagreements arise is another talent that a software architect should be endowed with.

> **NOTE**   In addition to the ability to negotiate, a software architect must also be able to inspire, encourage, and motivate project teams to collaborate on providing outstanding software solutions. Empathy for others, listening to team members, and caring for staff are extra capabilities that could only empower the leadership of software architects.

Prepare to answer questions similar to these in the list that follows:

Interpersonal skills   What are the most important interpersonal skills that a software architect must possess to successfully facilitate software implementations?

Conflicts   What methods do you typically employ to resolve interpersonal conflicts among software development team members? Provide examples.

Personal agendas   How do you make certain that development team members do not pursue personal agendas that may derail software implementation and deployment projects?

Acceptance of leadership   How do you deal with team members who refuse to accept your software architecture leadership?

Architecture goals   How do you inspire and motivate professionals to work together and fulfill your end-state architecture goals?

Software Architecture Leadership

The ability to lead is a skill that hiring organizations are actively seeking. Without leadership talents, a software architect would face difficulties in promoting architecture vision and mission. Without leadership skills it would be hard to achieve buy-in from business executives who typically sponsor software development projects.

NOTE It's the leadership talent that entices followers, impacts organizational culture, fosters high ethical standards, and, as a result, promotes business goals.

Furthermore, software architecture leadership is about the aptitude for identifying problems. It's also about making appropriate technological decisions to cultivate suitable business solutions. With the power of their leadership skills, software architects can save projects and avoid software development and integration failures.

Prepare for software architecture leadership questions similar to these:

Managers vs. leaders What's the difference between a technology manager and a leader?

Technological leadership How would you, as a software architect, demonstrate technological leadership?

Challenging project What has been your most challenging project problem, and what initiative did you take to resolve it?

Project saving Have you ever rescued a software development project from failing? Why was the project about to fail, and how did your architecture leadership save it?

Time-to-market Have you ever applied changes to software architecture for the purpose of accelerating time-to-market? What were these design changes, and how did they impact organizational expenditure?

Advisory role In which instances did you use your software architecture advisory talents to guide development, integration, and operations teams?

Skill Assessment Questions

During a job interview there is not much time to assess the skill competency levels of software architecture applicants. But queries of such nature often arise. The responses to these queries, however, could unveil the levels of project difficulties and challenges applicants have faced. They also could give a clue about candidates' leadership skills and their ability to withstand deadline pressures.

Despite tight interview schedules, applicants should be prepared to outline their career paths and share compelling project experiences.

NOTE During an interview, describe the technological challenges when led software architecture projects. Share software design mistakes that resulted in production failures. Elaborate on the remedies applied to mend application performance issues. This self-exposure will shed light on candidates' talents and their ability to offer first-rate technological solutions.

Prepare for skill assessment interview questions similar to these:

Training   What professional training classes have you attended?

Certificates   Have you been granted any architecture certificates?

Architecture skills   Describe the most complex project you have worked on and how your software architecture skills impacted its outcome.

Design mistakes   What kind of design mistakes have you made, and how did you employ your software architecture talents to correct them?

Decision-making mistakes   What have you learned from your decision-making mistakes, and what actions have you taken to avoid them in the future?

Software Architecture Attributes Questions

Applicants should devote substantial effort to preparing for interview questions about architecture attributes.[1] The term *architecture attributes* describes characteristics of deployed applications and systems in a software architecture environment that is hosted in production. Availability,[2] scalability,[3] accessibility,[4] and elasticity[5] are some examples of architecture attributes. When an architecture is established upon these traits, it habitually contributes to implementation stability, acceptable application performance rates, business continuity, and security.

But applications and systems do not operate in a vacuum. They are hosted by production environments that must support the required software architecture attributes. Put differently, a production environment with proper infrastructure must maintain the characteristics of a software architecture environment.

So, where could these requirements for architecture attributes be found? They are often specified in nonfunctional requirements at the inception phase

---

[1] Refer to the ISO/IEC 25010:2011 standard for architecture attributes examples, such as reliability, operability, performance, efficiency, security, and compatibility.

[2] The term *availability* pertains to the capacity of a software implementation, such as an application, to be accessible and responsive to service consumers' (peer software or users) requests.

[3] Scalability is a software environment's capability to supply enough computing resources and maintain operational continuity without changing the underlying structures of software implementations. This ability is typically promoted by horizontal and/or vertical scaling (out and up), clustering, etc.

[4] In technical terms, *accessibility* refers to mechanisms that enable consumers to find, reach, and use software services, functionality, and processes withing the boundaries of security policies.

[5] Elasticity is an architecture attribute that enables a deployment environment to meet the fluctuating demand of software implementations for computing resources.

of the software development life cycle. These documents establish benchmarks devised to facilitate smooth operations in a production environment. Software recovery from fatal outages, high-volume exchange of transactions, adequate computing capacity for process consumption, and circumvention of security threats are only a few concerns that nonfunctional requirements aim to address.

The questions that follow are examples of questions related to architecture attributes that an applicant might encounter during an interview. These are devised to foster architecture best practices and promote business continuity in production.

Scalability   As a software architect, how would you devise to increase the *scalability* of a web application if its performance fails to meet the nonfunctional requirements?

Availability   What mechanisms should be employed to ensure applications and systems *availability* in production?

Recoverability[6]   Outline a disaster recovery (DR) strategy to guarantee application and data recovery in production. Specify the tools, infrastructure, and approaches to enable *recoverability*.

Adaptability[7]   What are the technologies and mechanisms that can boost application intelligence and *adaptability*?

Reusability[8]   Name at least three methods to advance organizational software *reusability*.

Portability[9]   How can a software architect devise architecture *portability* across technological heterogenous environments?

Elasticity   What is *elasticity*, and how can this architecture characteristic address the deficiency of computing resource capacity?

Software Architecture LifeCycle Questions

During the system development life cycle (SDLC), business and technical professionals are engaged in a slew of application development activities. Architects

---

[6] The capability of an application, service, or system to restore its services in a timely manner, as specified in the service-level agreement (SLA).
[7] The capability of a software implementation to effectively respond to business and technological changes. These modifications include environment transformation, business modernization, and market trends.
[8] *Reusability* refers to mechanisms that enable software functionality reuse, data reutilization, and information repurposing.
[9] Portability is a software architecture attribute that describes the ability of a computer program to run on different platforms and environments without applying major changes to its composition and/or structure.

not only facilitate the development process, but also pursue their own wide range of tasks that are in line with software architecture practices and disciplines (refer to Chapter 1, "Software Architect Capability Model," to learn more about architecture practices and disciplines). So far, many organizations have recognized the contribution of software architecture processes to the SDLC. Consequently, this realization has helped establish the software architecture life cycle that has become an integral part of the SDLC timeline.

So, what are the most significant software architecture activities to be performed during the software architecture life cycle? Unfortunately, there is no industry-wide standard that defines common goals, milestones, and tasks for software architecture duties. The absence of a universal software architecture process, therefore, incentivizes organizations to develop proprietary ones to satisfy their own enterprise imperatives.

Nevertheless, the good news is that there are numerous propositions[10] that outline the various responsibilities and methodologies for software architects during the SDLC. Applicants should study carefully these publications to prepare for software architecture life-cycle questions during an interview.

> **NOTE** Recall that interviewers may query applicants about software architecture activities. Therefore, be prepared to outline a rudimentary software architecture life-cycle model to address the process-related queries.

In simple words, should the opportunity arrive during an interview, propose a general pattern of duties that architects could be engage in, similar to the one depicted in Figure 9.1. As shown, this illustration identifies four chief software architecture life-cycle stages, each of which may consist of related activities, as indicated in Table 9.1.

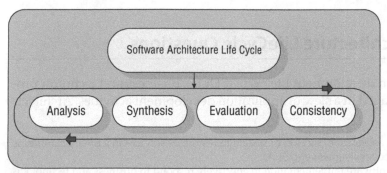

Figure 9.1: A Conceptual Model for Software Architecture Life Cycle Stages

---

[10] Example: Rick Kazman, Robert L. Nord, and Mark Klein, A Life-Cycle View of Architecture Analysis and Design Methods, Carnegie Mellon, September 2003: `apps.dtic.mil/sti/pdfs/ADA421679.pdf`

Table 9.1: Software Architecture Life Cycle Stages and Proposed Activities

STAGE	PROPOSED ACTIVITIES
Analysis	Problem domain analysis,[11] business requirements analysis, analysis of software architecture life-cycle cost,[12] total cost of ownership (TCO),[13] return on investment (ROI), architecture solution feasibility analysis.[14]
Synthesis	Facilitate the development of architecture themes,[15] develop user-related stories and epics,[16,17] deliver application and/or system design for software development efforts, offer technologies and devise integration patterns for application and systems, facilitate data modeling and data architecture, apply security policies, formulate capacity planning for computer resource utilization.
Evaluation	Verify if the implemented software architecture complies with the proposed application and/or system design, test architecture assumptions and goals in preproduction environments by planning proof of concepts (POC) activities.
Consistency	Ensure business and technical continuity by monitoring applications and systems in production, apply design and integration changes to boost software architecture efficiency in production.

Finally, consider the possible questions that may come up during a software architecture interview. Again, provide an elementary model for software architecture life cycle and elaborate on possible related activities.

Software architecture life cycle   Identify software architecture life-cycle stages.

Software architecture tasks   What should be the chief tasks to accomplish during the software architecture life cycle?

Architecture and design activities   What is the difference between design and architecture, and how do these activities differ?

---

[11] Problem domain analysis calls for discovering organizational challenges and risks before authoring business and technical requirements.

[12] Total cost of software architecture life cycle. This includes business and technological expenditures to provide firm-wide solutions.

[13] Total cost of ownership includes business products and infrastructure sponsorship, management, and maintenance typically after software solutions have been deployed to production.

[14] The process of validating the practicality and return on investment of design solutions.

[15] An architecture theme pertains to a unifying motif, concept, abstraction, or idea that drives the design of software implementations. Such themes can be typically spotted in requirements and design documents.

[16] A user story depicts in a simple language the software capability requirements of application and system users.

[17] An epic is a collection of users' stories.

Architecture and design evaluation   How do software architects ensure that application and/or system implementations adhere to architecture blueprints?

Business consistency   How do software architects guarantee business continuity in production?

Technical consistency   How do software architects avoid the deployment of ill-designed applications and/or systems to production?

Software Architecture Concepts Questions

Applicants are asked to demonstrate knowledge and explain software architecture concepts in almost every job interview. These queries are not randomly selected by interviewers. They are typically affiliated with the job requirements that outline present projects and the software architecture skills that the hiring organization is seeking to acquire.

Then why are software architecture concepts fundamental to every software architect? The answer to this question is rooted in the notion that technological solutions emanate from ideas. And when these ideas mature, they become architecture concepts. These concepts are the driving forces of every software development initiative.

> **NOTE**   Without concepts, software architects would not be able to see the big picture.

This means that without concepts, software architects are incapable of generalizing overarching solutions for organizational problems. Without technological concepts, development teams tend to dive directly into the source code. As a result, they typically disregard software reuse principles, ignore componentization,[18] and neglect architecture decomposition[19] best practices.

> **NOTE**   The link between technological ideas and enterprise solutions is the crux of the software architecture thinking process. And the most necessary software architecture tools used to facilitate organizational solutions are architecture concepts.

---

[18] Componentization is the process of devising software components to increase software reuse and promote Loose-coupling design.

[19] Architecture decomposition is the process that calls for breaking down complex software and environment design to isolate problems and focus on providing solutions.

Applicants ought to prepare for software architecture concepts questions that are associated with these four categories, as shown in Figure 9.2: design, environment, business, and consumer. The sections that follow elaborate on these concepts that might be presented during a job interview.

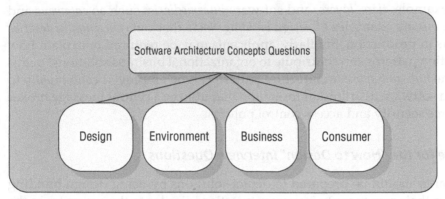

Figure 9.2: A Model for Software Architecture Concepts

Design Building Blocks Concepts

Under time constraints and the burden of interview pressures, applicants are often asked to provide a solution to a business problem. The "how" types of questions are especially challenging when design solutions must be put into a few words without delving too deep into specific business requirements.

> **NOTE** One of the most effective ways to come up with a satisfying answer without even fully understanding the array of problems that the hiring organization is facing would be to outline a solution by employing design building blocks concepts. In doing so, a candidate could employ a set of abstractions to demonstrate effective software architecture problem-solving skills.

Recall, the software architecture practice is driven by design building blocks concepts employed to facilitate the construction of executables deployed to production. These concepts embody ideas and abstractions essential to every software development project.

Employ Design Building Blocks Concepts to Depict Solutions

Moreover, experienced architects typically use design concepts to characterize *building blocks* of software applications and systems. These building blocks pertain to a large number of software entities, such as classes, components, modules, services, application programming interfaces (APIs), databases, and others.

> **NOTE**   Remember, almost every architecture artifact, component, pattern, method, process, principle, and best practice can be used during an interview as a design building block concept to illustrate a solution. And these concepts should be employed to satisfy the "how to design" questions.

For example, *tiers*, *layers*, and software *intermediaries* such as *gateways* and *message bus* are examples of *design building blocks* that can *conceptually describe solutions* in production. Similarly, applicants may be required to explain how integration patterns can contribute to organizational business solutions. In this case, the *hub-and-spoke* architecture pattern can be employed *conceptually* to depict a software distribution formation that utilizes a central message broker to enforce security and access control policies.

Prepare for the "How to Design" Interview Questions

Applicants should be prepared to depict solutions by using design building blocks in their responses to interview questions similar to the examples in the list that follows. These solutions should correspond to the jobs that they are applying for. One of the best places to find clues about these design building blocks concepts is obviously in the corresponding job description.

Federated architecture[20]   Name software architecture components that could be employed to describe a federated architecture.

High cohesion[21]   Describe the design building blocks of architecture components that promote high cohesion.

Tiers[22] **and layers**[23]   Describe an implementation that consists of tiers and layers.

Hub-and-spoke architecture pattern   Provide a design outline for a hub-and-spoke software architecture that promotes a balanced centralized software architecture environment.

---

[20] Federated architecture is an architecture style that enables information sharing data transfer between heterogenous computing environments that are based on different technologies and business models.

[21] High cohesion is a design term related to the loose coupling practice that advocates breaking down software into smaller structural components to increase reusability and reduce architecture complexity and maintenance costs.

[22] Tiers depict the separation of software into components (each of which represents a different concern) that are physically deployed to a production ecosystem. In this context, software refers to applications, services, or systems.

[23] Layers represent the conceptual or logical arrangement of software into a hierarchy of components that collaborate with each other to provide a business or technical solution.

Componentization[24]   Why does software componentization ultimately enable software reuse? Provide an example.

Containerization[25]   What are the drawbacks of utilizing software containers? Illustrate an architecture that utilizes containers.

Interoperability[26]   Describe architecture building blocks that enable interoperability between heterogenous systems.

Encapsulation[27]   What is the purpose of encapsulating data and source code? Describe building blocks of an architecture that enables data encapsulation.

Software Architecture Environment Concepts

Too often interview questions call for *characterizing and describing software architecture environments*. Applicants then are required to illustrate a deployment landscape in which architecture components collaborate and exchange messages to meet technical requirements. Rather than focusing on architecture solutions, the answers to these questions should demonstrate deep knowledge about the architecture parts that make up a run-time environment.

Characterizing and effectively depicting a software architecture environment not only requires demonstrating verbal visualization skills. The capability to lay out a clear technological environment could land a lucrative software architecture job.

So, what are the examples of those software architecture components, the building blocks of a production environment? The list is indeed long, and the technical vocabulary used to describe them is vast. Here are a few to consider: applications, systems, services, cloud computing, containers, middleware platforms, and network devices such as switches, firewalls, load balancers, and routers.

Fortunately, today's technology jargon offers a great deal of conceptual terms and language that represent computing environments and facilities on a larger scale. For example, a *database farm* is a term that refers to server clusters and empowering infrastructure for information retrieval. Correspondingly, *private cloud* is another conceptual term that depicts a deployment environment, computing capabilities, and data storage for an organization. A *demilitarized zone* is

---

[24] Componentization is a software development logical method that calls for breaking down software into pieces that are independently developed. Once deployed to production, they are linked to provide collaborative technological and business solutions.

[25] Containerization is a process of populating virtual entities, named containers, with packaged software services that can operate on any deployment environment.

[26] The ability of separated and heterogeneous computer systems to exchange information.

[27] Encapsulation is a design method that calls for hiding source code to avoid exposure of implementation details to consuming applications, services, or systems.

yet another term applied to illustrate a perimeter environment created to protect an organization's internal network from unauthorized external consumers.

As is apparent, examples of technology jargon attest that the industry has already developed a common language and a conceptual vocabulary used to depict deployment environments. Software architecture applicants should embrace this conceptual language and use its lexicon during an interview to demonstrate knowledge about organizational production landscapes and their components.

> **NOTE** During an interview, attend to the principles of technical language simplicity: employ concepts and metaphors to describe a deployment environment and avoid delving into implementation specifications. Shy away from trivial details, such as programming languages, development platforms, and deployment life cycle. Focus only on integration and architecture patterns, middleware products, software intermediaries, network topology, gateways, interoperability principles, server clusters, disaster recovery and high-availability facilities, and even data access layers. Bottom line: stay strategic!

Prepare for interview questions, similar to those in the list below, that call for the description of an organizational production environment. Stay focused, however, on software architecture components that make up a production environment. Again, utilize technical concepts that depict software architecture elements.

Cybersecurity   Depict an architecture environment that is designed to protect systems against cybersecurity attacks. Give examples of security controls to address environment vulnerability.

Disaster recovery   Identify the necessary software capabilities of an effective DR site. Focus on software mechanisms that provide data transfer and synchronization.

Scalability   Recommend software architecture elements that could be utilized to boost application scalability.

Reusability   Identify integration patterns that promote service reusability.

Layered architecture   What are the elements and the structure of a layered architectural style?

Message bus   Describe an architectural environment in which a message bus offers routing and orchestration capabilities.

Middleware   How does middleware foster business and technological interoperability? Describe an architectural environment in which a message bus offers routing and orchestration capabilities.

Business Concepts

Every software architect must be mindful of business terminology and concepts that influence software design decisions. These concepts are typically affiliated with the fundamental business vocabulary, such as business model, vision, strategy, and mission.

Business concept queries during an interview typically uncover whether applicants understand the influence of business strategies on software development. How a business model bears upon technological solutions is another popular topic of the questions that interviewers often ask. A similar query might be related to the applicant's awareness that business requirements drive the software architecture life cycle.

Business concept questions are characteristically associated with the business terms in the list that follows:

Survival Business revenue, profits, and return on investment

Industry The industry that the business is related to

Products Organizational line of products that is dictated by the business vision and strategy

Competitors Market competition and business risks

Applicants should be ready to explain business concepts related to the software architecture job description. The example questions that follow are often presented by hiring organizations:

Business architecture What is the business architect contribution to business strategies, vision, and mission?

Business analysis What are the benefits of business analysis?

Business model How does a business model influence software design decisions?

Time to market How can a robust software architecture accelerate the construction of a software product?

Total cost of ownership How can software architecture reduce organizational TCO?

Business mission and strategy Why must a software architect adhere to an organizational mission and implement business strategies?

Customer experience Why is customer experience technology vital to business marketing?

Competitive advantage[28] How can software architecture best practices enable organizational competitive advantage?

Segmentation What is the difference between product segmentation, market segmentation, and client segmentation?

---

[28] Competitive advantage pertains to aspects that allow an organization to offer efficient services and cheaper products than its competitors.

Consumer Concepts

How do business requirements influence software architecture that ultimately affects systems and application behavior? The answer to this question is rooted in the business activities that take place at the outset of the software development life cycle. This preliminary business requirements gathering process is conducted to find out what software functionalities users need. A common practice employed to discover these imperatives is to compile a set of user stories.

The term *stories* pertains to an analysis method—a *predominately conceptual business exercise*—performed by various stakeholders, such as business sponsors, executives, managers, business analysts, and even developers. This process is all about asking *customers* to describe in simple words what applications and systems functions they would like to utilize; what are their preferences; and how should user interfaces be simplified. In short, user stories are confined to the personal requirements of individuals.

For example, a story may capture a particular user's needs and expectations from a banking portal:

- "As a banking customer, in addition to my checking account, I'd also like to open a new savings account so that I can earn some interest on my money."

- "As a savings account holder, I'd also need to receive instant text messages when money is withdrawn from my account, so that I can be notified promptly."

- "As a banking customer, I'd like to have 24/7 online access to my savings account so that I can avoid waiting for my monthly account statements."

NOTE Remember, tell stories from a user's perspective to simplify interview answers related to business requirements and application capabilities.

Each story should allude to four fundamental pieces of information that could inevitably influence software development goals.

- Consumer identification
- Related business requirements
- Software implementation functionality and capabilities
- Justification for embarking on a particular software development initiative

Finally, be prepared for questions similar to those in the list that follows:

User requirements   Why do users' necessities drive business and technical requirements?

Application capabilities   How can users' needs manifest themselves in application capabilities?

Business requirements   Give examples of consumers' needs that drive business requirements.

Technical Specifications   Tell a personal user's story that influences technical specifications.

Software Architecture Decisions   Tell a personal user's story that drives software architecture decisions.

Software Development Scope   How does a user's story set boundaries for software development scope and goals?

Architecture Style, Architecture Pattern, and Design Pattern Questions

Architecture and design patterns are employed mostly to provide solutions. They are thought of as reusable remedies for solving recurring business and/or technological problems. Moreover, patterns typically reveal a great deal of information about application and system design decisions. These choices are made chiefly by architects to determine the formation of application deployment in production, integration patterns, system federation, interoperability, and more.

Architecture Patterns vs. Design Patterns

The terms *architecture patterns* and *design patterns* are often used interchangeably. Be aware, however, that a growing number of professionals claim that these terms differ. Their assertion is that architecture patterns represent solutions for enterprise-level challenges, and enterprise-level architecture patterns are devised to address large-scale business and technical solutions. These solutions are related to problems with deployment to production environments, such as middleware capabilities, integration of applications and systems, messaging patterns, and more.

On the other hand, according to these claims, design patterns are subsets of architecture patterns and employed to provide solutions on smaller scales. They are confined merely to application-level solutions that include implementations of software modules, packages, and APIs.

> **NOTE**   In a nutshell, an architecture pattern is devised to offer broad solutions for organizational problems. On the contrary, a design pattern typically satisfies a smaller scale of requirements and is a subset of an architecture pattern.

Table 9.2 supports the notion that design patterns are subsets of architecture patterns. Note the relationship examples between these two types of patterns.

As shown for the Microservices[29] architecture pattern, there are three affiliated design patterns: API Gateway,[30] Aggregator,[31] and Saga.[32] In the same fashion, the Master Data Hub[33] architecture pattern consists of three design patterns: Registry Hub,[34] Centralized Hub,[35] and Consolidated Hub.[36]

Table 9.2: Architecture Patterns vs. Design Patterns

ARCHITECTURE PATTERN EXAMPLES	RELATED DESIGN PATTERN EXAMPLES
Microservices	API gateway
	Aggregator
	Saga
Master data hub	Registry hub (virtual hub)
	Centralized hub
	Consolidated hub

[29] A microservice is a loosely coupled and fine-grained service that operates from within a system or an application utilizing technology-agnostic protocols, such as HTTP. Microservices refers also to an architecture pattern that calls for grouping microservices working together to provide solutions.

[30] An API gateway is a design pattern that calls for the utilization of an intermediary or a hub for intercepting messages exchanged between consumers and microservices, applications, or systems. Similar to reverse proxies, an API gateway implementation may possess more capabilities than message mediation. These may include message filtering, security enforcement mechanisms, etc.

[31] The aggregator design pattern refers to an implementation that upon a consumer's request collects data from a variety of sources, such as repositories, information providers, applications, and systems. Then the collected data is combined, processed, and packed into a response to the requesting consumer.

[32] Saga is a microservice design pattern that depicts a sequence of transactions that involve two or more microservices. Each microservice in the chain processes and then passes the data to the next microservice inline.

[33] The master data hub is an architecture pattern that refers to a centralized implementation that provides data services to consumers. It's typically utilized to protect data sources from unauthorized exposure and standardizes data access mechanisms across an organization.

[34] The registry hub design pattern depicts a software entity that maintains a virtual index of pointers to physical data in an authoritative repository. Upon a consumer's request, the registry hub retrieves the corresponding record from the repository, delivers it, and then stores it for future transactions.

[35] The centralized hub design pattern refers to an intermediary that stores data retrieved from an authoritative database. By doing this, it essentially becomes the system of record for all consumers' read/write requests. Ingestion mechanisms then update the authoritative database based on predefined schedules.

[36] The consolidated hub refers to a central broker that aggregates data from a number of data sources and stores the information locally for read-only purposes. This is not a viable solution since the aggregation process does not ensure real-time ingestion of information.

Understand Architecture Styles

Simply put, an *architecture style* is a catalog that includes a collection of architecture patterns. Cataloging and grouping architecture patterns by their attributes, capabilities, and features would contribute immensely to understanding how each architecture pattern can be employed to provide a business or technological solution.

Find three examples of *architecture styles* in Table 9.3. They are well known for characterizing unique deployment environment formations. As indicated in the Characterization column, the Layered Architecture style is known for separating various concerns into layers, such as user interface, business logic, data, and possibly other application elements. Moreover, each of these layers may be driven by a group of related architecture patterns, as indicated in the Related Architecture Patterns column. Along these lines, the *Monolithic Architecture style* may be driven by the related group of *architecture patterns* too. And this logic also corresponds to the Service-Oriented Architecture (SOA) style.

Note that there may be common architecture patterns for two or more architecture styles. For example, the layered architecture, monolithic architecture, and SOA may implement the microservice architecture pattern.

Table 9.3: Architecture Styles Examples

ARCHITECTURE STYLE	CHARACTERIZATION	RELATED ARCHITECTURE PATTERNS
Layered architecture	Layers represent different architecture concerns, compartmentalizing and componentizing software implementations.	Related group of architecture patterns
Monolithic architecture	Business and/or technical processes along with related data data forming a single, tightly-coupled, self-sufficient distributed software implementation.	Related group of architecture patterns
SOA	Architectural style driven by autonomous, fine-grained, and reusable services that promote business and technological goals.	Related group of architecture patterns

Remember Contextual Hierarchy of Patterns

The most effective way to tackle architecture and design pattern questions would be to accept the notion that patterns are indeed arranged in hierarchical formations. In other words, an architecture style is located at the top of the pyramid. Then architecture patterns are found beneath each architecture style. Positioned at the very bottom of the hierarchy are the design patterns. This concept is illustrated in Figure 9.3.

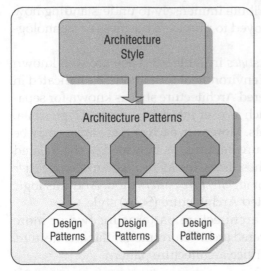

Figure 9.3: Style and Pattern Hierarchy

Why Interviewers Ask Architecture and Design Pattern Questions

To a large extent, patterns are software architecture solutions, employed to provide repeatable remedies to similar business or technical problems. Interviewers, therefore, typically ask architecture and design pattern questions to reveal how effectively a candidate would make use of these patterns. It's not only about assessing the applicant's decision-making process; the intention is also to evaluate the candidate's judgment when it comes to tackling organizational challenges.

Often interviewers ask candidates to provide examples for organizational challenges and how should they be rectified. Recall that the term *challenges* pertains to business and technical problems. From a technical point of view then, the term *challenges* is related to a large variety of operational problems. They may include issues with application reuse, scalability, performance, disaster recovery, and response time. On the business level, challenges may be related to boosting sales, offering compelling products, and improving user interfaces and experiences.

> **NOTE**   When architecture and design pattern questions come up during an interview, remember to emphasize that patterns are in essence reusable solutions to recurring organizational problems. The answers then should accentuate the strategic contributions of patterns. And never forget to accompany responses with corresponding examples.

Prepare for Architecture and Design Pattern Questions

There are a myriad of architecture and design patterns to learn about. It would be impractical, however, to memorize randomly hundreds and hundreds of patterns before an interview. Instead, study carefully the software architecture job description and adhere to the process that follows:

1. Understand what talents the hiring organization is seeking to employ.

2. Learn about its technologies and environments.

3. Devote attention to the duties that the future architect will be required to fulfill.

4. Understand the problems that the hiring organization is facing.

5. Then hypothesize possible solutions to these issues.

6. Come up with architecture and design patterns to provide adequate solutions.

NOTE   To provide compelling answers to architecture and design pattern questions, embrace the claims that architecture patterns and design patterns differ. Remember the contextual hierarchy between architecture styles, architecture patterns, and design patterns discussed so far.

The list that follows represents common architecture and design pattern queries that typically surface during a software architecture interview:

Microservice patterns   Mention at least three microservice-related patterns that you'd employ to provide a business solution for your organization. Explain how these patterns would meet specific business requirements

Integration patterns   Which integration patterns would you utilize to shield and isolate an organizational master database?

Application design patterns   You're being asked to carve out a strategy for building a banking application that enables customers to open checking and savings accounts. Which design patterns would you employ to facilitate the software development efforts?

Interoperability   Reference architecture patterns to promote interoperability between two organizational production environments.

Federated and centralized architectures   What is the difference between centralized and federated types of architectures?

Single sign-on (SSO)[37]   What would be the most compelling design patterns to enable organizational SSO capabilities?

---

[37] SSO is a mechanism that authenticates users only once with multiple applications and systems without repetitive credential checking.

Architecture styles, architecture patterns, and design patterns   What is the difference between architecture styles, architecture patterns, and design patterns? Provide styles and pattern examples.

Problem-solving and decision-making Questions

Problem-solving and decision-making questions are often challenging, not just because they are complex queries. The interview time constraints and, in many cases, applicants' lack of problem-solving experience may derail the chances of getting hired. No matter how technically competent a software architect candidate may be, providing compelling and persuasive answers to these types of questions can be difficult for some.

There is nothing better than rigorously preparing for problem-solving questions. Even if there are no clues to organizational problems found in the job description, there are always ways to dodge failure. One of the best approaches is to get acquainted with the problem-solving process outlined in the next section.

NOTE   Study the mechanisms that can be applied to providing software architecture solutions, and demonstrate good judgment when it comes to technological decision-making.

Embrace the Software Architecture Problem-Solving and Decision-Making Process

An applicant must master the problem-solving and decision-making processes to prepare for a software architecture interview. Without adequate groundwork, it would be difficult for applicants to prove their ability to deliver organizational solutions. Without demonstrating such competencies, there would be no chance to ace an interview.

NOTE   Ultimately, the software architecture problem-solving process must conclude with technical decisions. But even before taking such stands, problem-solving activities must start with inspecting the business.

Identifying Business Problems

Consequently, the software architecture problem-solving process must begin with studies and analyses. These activities are necessary to understand the business vision and strategy of the organization. But the most important task is to fully comprehend the specific problems that the enterprise is facing. Every challenge that requires solutions must be further investigated to identify the immediate cause of the problem.

Moreover, to be able to provide a suitable technological response to a business problem, the software architect must also study the business requirements. They typically reflect business solutions that must be met. At this point in time, the software architecture problem-solving process goes into high gear.

So, what is next? Nothing is more compelling for a software architect than to study the scientific evidence of a specific organizational problem. And nothing is more important than studying the actual data that introduces the business challenge. For example, if a vital application shows sluggish response time, a root-cause analysis should spur architectural decisions.

Attend to the Problem-Solving and Decision-Making Process

Not matter how difficult a problem-solving and decision-making query might be, always keep in mind that answers should be driven by a logical train of thought, a line of reasoning, and good judgment.

> **NOTE** During a software architecture interview, an applicant's compelling thought process can demonstrate the capability to provide potent software architecture solutions.

Study this problem-solving and decision-making process in preparation for possible challenging questions.

Problem domain analysis   Start with studying the business problem domain.

Root-cause analysis   Conduct a root-cause analysis to understand what has triggered the specific organizational problem.

Scientific evidence   Never make software architecture decisions without studying the scientific evidence and its related data.

Business solutions   Never make software architecture decisions without understanding the business solutions reflected in the business requirements.

Technological solutions   Next, provide a number of technological solutions and lean toward strategic approaches rather than tactical ones.

Choose the best one   Then select the best solutions. Do not procrastinate; there is no time for "analysis-paralysis."

Agnostic solutions   Promote an agnostic solution. Never be locked into a vendor's offerings.

Prepare for Problem-Solving and Decision-Making Questions

There are a vast number of potential problem-solving and decision-making questions that an applicant may be required to address. Take a look at the queries that follow. Similar ones may be asked during a software architecture interview.

Problem-solving and decision-making process   Describe the step-by-step software architect problem-solving and decision-making process.

Problem severity   What is an organizational problem, and how would you assess its severity?

Strategic and tactical solutions   What is the difference between software architecture strategic and tactical solutions? Provide an example.

Software architecture decision   What is a software architecture decision, and how does it ultimately impact a technological implementation? Provide an example.

Solution alternatives   How would you choose the best software architecture solution alternative?

Stakeholders   Who would be the business and technology stakeholders who may be involved in providing a software architecture solution?

Data integrity   How can architectural decisions ensure data integrity?

Security   How can architectural decisions promote systems security?

Data-Related Questions

In the course of a software architecture interview, data-affiliated questions are common. Although there may be a vast number of data queries to prepare for, applicants must prioritize their studying efforts. The groundwork, therefore, should be devoted to data aspects that are chiefly reflected in the job description.

Remember, narrow down the preparation scope of data topics by focusing on these activities:

- Understand what type of data the hiring organization is using.
- Study the mechanisms and protocols by which their applications and systems exchange information over the network.
- Learn about the type of the repositories the organization is hosting.
- Understand how the organizational data is manipulated, interpreted, and transformed in a production environment.

Focus on Data Aspects Related to Software Architecture

The focus on data aspects that are mostly associated with software architecture narrows down the scope of interview questions that an applicant must prepare for. With this reduction in scope, applicants should be ready to explain how software architecture capabilities can provide various data solutions for an organization. These solutions are typically related to the fundamental questions that follow:

- How is data shared and distributed in a production environment?
- What are the organizational data storage facilities?
- How is the data manipulated to meet business requirements?
- How is the data exchanged between applications and systems?

NOTE   Before attending a software architecture interview, compile a list of data-related topics similar to the one shown in Table 9.4. And get ready to explain how software architecture disciplines can satisfy business requirements related to organizational data.

Table 9.4: Preparation Data Topics for a Software Architecture Interview

DATA TOPIC	POTENTIAL INTERVIEW QUESTION
Data access	What mechanisms should a software architect employ to protect and isolate application data?
Data integrity	What architecture patterns should a software architect devise to maintain application data integrity?
Data storage	What types of repositories or data platforms are you familiar with?
Data sources	Provide examples of various data sources that an organization may be utilizing.
Data types	What types of data are you familiar with?
Data manipulation	What is CRUD (create, read, update, and delete)?
Data transformation	In which circumstances is data transformation necessary?
Data delivery	Which mechanisms and protocols are you familiar with that facilitate data exchange between applications and systems?

More Data-Related Interview Questions

The previous section raises the importance of software architecture to facilitate organizational data needs. But applicants should not be caught by surprise if interviewers go beyond the software architecture paradigm to assess applicants' general data knowledge. In this case, experience does count. And for those who seek to enter the software architecture field, meticulous preparation is required.

> **NOTE** Always remember to carefully inspect the software architecture job description to discover clues to what data-related questions may be in store.

- What is the difference between data integrity and data quality?
- Why do organizations tend to isolate data sources?
- How does technological interoperability foster information sharing? Provide an example.
- Why do organizations support data hubs?
- Describe scenarios for data filtering, augmentation, and formatting.
- What is the importance of data cleansing?
- What is data mining?
- Who in the organization benefits the most from data analytics?
- What are the types of data collection?
- How does the process of data collection work?
- Why is data aggregation needed?
- What is data mapping?
- What is data integration?

Production Environment Questions

When questioned, you have many ways to describe a production environment, and there are so many manners in which you could depict a deployment ecosystem that hosts applications and systems. Nevertheless, the most compelling answer always comes from an applicant who dares to wear a software architect hat; from an applicant who is adept in software architecture disciplines; from an applicant who underscores the contribution of software architecture and its environment to production; from an applicant who understands the vital role of architecture in facilitating effective distribution of software, integration, and interoperability.

> **NOTE** In brief, a software architecture environment hosted by a production environment is where organizational applications and systems are deployed, installed, configured, secured, and maintained to provide business and technological solutions.

Characteristics of Software Architecture Environment Hosted in Production

Roles and responsibilities of production environment assets, such as applications and infrastructure, have never been radically altered: nowadays applications continue to execute business functions, and infrastructure still supports systems operations. In contrast, a production environment as a whole continues to grow and change as time goes by. It's a living ecosystem whose never-ending transformation calls for constant software architecture efforts to enable flawless execution of applications and systems.

So, why are software architects often commissioned to remediate production environment problems? The answer to this question is rooted in the *changing characteristics of environments over time*. For example, multiple deployments of infrastructure and systems tend to degrade production agility and even erode application performance. Furthermore, myriad installations and configurations in production tend to impair environment scalability.

NOTE Interview questions affiliated with production environment characteristics are common. They are related to software architecture environment imperatives that must be met to maintain business continuity. A candidate then should prepare to demonstrate profound knowledge of software architecture environment needs. Most important, be able to explain the impact of software architecture environment on production operations.

Before attending a software architecture interview, prepare a table of software architecture environment characteristics similar to the one shown in Table 9.5. As closely as possible, deduce these features from the software architecture job description.

Table 9.5: Software architecture Environment Features

FEATURE	EXPLANATION
Elastic	An environment that meets workload changes by increasing or decreasing computing resources
Agile	An environment that adapts promptly to market trends and customer demands
Scalable	An environment that enables the *increase* in computing resources to maintain effective system performance
Interoperable	An environment that enables heterogenous systems to exchange and share information
Secured	An environment that promotes confidentiality, integrity, and availability security policies

Production Environment-Related Questions

Take time to prepare for software architecture interview questions similar to those in the list that follows. These queries are related to the capabilities, features, and elements of a production environment. Always remember to embed software architecture views in the provided answers.

Although the presented questions seem random, a software architect should prepare to demonstrate rudimentary knowledge of related production environment technologies.

- What is a subnet?
- What is a network hop?
- What is a load balancer?
- What is continuous integration and continuous deployment?
- What is a DR environment?
- What is high availability?
- Define middleware.
- How can a software architect devise system elasticity?
- What is the difference between message orchestration and message choreography?
- What is an enterprise service bus?
- Define infrastructure.
- What is the difference between an application and a system?
- What is a router?
- What is a reverse proxy?
- What is a firewall?
- What is the difference between Internet Protocol (IP), IPv4, and IPv6?
- What are network nodes?
- What is network topology?
- What is a gateway?
- What is a portal?
- What is a CIA (confidentiality, integrity, and availability) triad?
- What is a security control?
- What is capacity planning?
- What is a synthetic transaction?

- What is containerization?
- What is the difference between the public and private clouds?
- What is architecture federation?
- Define scalability
- What is configuration management?
- What is a denial-of-service attack?
- What is ransomware?
- Name production environment monitoring tools.
- What is SSO?
- What types of quality assurance tests are you familiar with?
- Name a number of testing tools and their utilization in production.
- What is protected health information (PHI) and personal identifying information (PII)?
- What is the difference between authentication and authorization?

Software Architecture Framework Questions

The absence of a common industry software architecture *best practices, standards, policies,* and *principles* gave rise to the establishment of proprietary frameworks. Some organizations privately develop guidelines for governing software architecture life cycles. Others exclusively devise software design approaches. Several institute internal architecture best practices. Although these frameworks were created by different organizations, their ultimate goal is to provide *guidance and methods* for software architecture disciplines.

> **NOTE** To maintain governance uniformity across multiple lines of business, organizations tend to enforce sweeping regulations for software architecture. These guidelines typically include best practices, standards, policies, principles, methodologies, and conventions.

Focus on Array of Framework Contributions

Not all existing software architecture frameworks devised by different organizations offer equal value or comparable guidance. During an interview, therefore, emphasize that each prevailing framework serves the software architecture practice in a different manner.

NOTE   In an interview, the applicant should stress that a software architect typically employs various frameworks to describe applications and systems in pursuit of business and technological solutions.

The list that follows identifies chief software architecture framework contributions utilized to tackle business and technological problems:

Architecture governance   Methods and best practices devised to institute software architecture centers of excellence to promote business and technological objectives. In addition, it offers guiding policies and principles to help promote organizational architecture governance

Life cycle   Processes, milestones, and goals to govern the software architecture life cycle

Business analysis   Tactics provided to conduct business problem domain analyses, understand business solutions, and analyze business requirements

Designing methods   Approaches, development tools, best practices, and principles for designing applications and systems. Moreover, these methods provide architecture decomposition guidance to foster loosely coupled deployment environments

Artifacts   Rules and best practices for delivering software architecture artifacts, such as design specifications, diagrams and charts, reference architecture, and more

Architecture evaluation   Methods for verifying if application and system implementations indeed meet software architecture blueprints

To provide satisfactory answers to software architecture interview questions, consider the list in Table 9.6.

Table 9.6: Examples of Software Architecture Frameworks

FRAMEWORK	CONTRIBUTION
The open group architecture framework[38] (TOGAF)	Enterprise architecture framework offering architecture standards, architecture development methods, and processes for the software architecture life cycle
Kruchten's 4+1 view model[39]	A software architecture method driven by logical, physical, process, developer, and scenarios views

---

[38] www.opengroup.org/togaf
[39] P. B. Kruchten, "The 4+1 View Model of architecture," in IEEE Software, vol. 12, no. 6, pp. 42-50, Nov. 1995, doi: 10.1109/52.469759.

FRAMEWORK	CONTRIBUTION
U.S. department of defense (DoD) architecture framework[40]	An architecture framework devised to promote effective management decisions by sharing vital information among DoD organizations
U.S. federal enterprise architecture framework (FEAF)[41]	An architecture framework comprised of reference models describing six subarchitecture domains: strategy, business, data, applications, infrastructure, and security

Software Architecture Framework Questions

Software architecture framework questions are typically challenging and therefore require laborious preparations. These interview queries pertain to a wide range of organizational policies. They also encompass a rainbow of business and IT governance guidelines.

Study carefully the questions that follow and prepare for similar ones. Understand the driving motivations and contributions of the various frameworks to application and system development. Finally, remember that there are widely recognized software architecture stand-alone best practices, principles, policies, and principles that are not necessarily supported by prevailing industry frameworks. Dedicate attention to these as well to ensure successful interviews.

- What are the chief contributions of software architecture frameworks to technological solutions and decision-making?

- Which framework's best practices would you adhere to for providing architecture descriptions[42]?

- How would you utilize the 4+1 view model to provide architecture solutions? Provide at least one example.

- What types of TOGAF diagrams are you familiar with?

- What is the benefit of the TOGAF's Architecture Development Method (ADM) to software design and development?

- What does the International Organization for Standardization[43] (ISO)/ International Electrotechnical Commission[44] (IEC)/ Institute of Electrical and Electronics Engineers[45] (IEEE) 42010[46] international architecture standard offer to software architecture practices? What do the International

---

[40] dodcio.defense.gov/Library/DoD-Architecture-Framework
[41] obamawhitehouse.archives.gov/sites/default/files/omb/assets/ egov_docs/fea_v2.pdf
[42] View an example for architecture descriptions: www.iso-architecture.org/42010/.
[43] www.iso.org/home.html
[44] https://iec.ch/homepage
[45] www.ieee.org/
[46] www.iso-architecture.org/42010/faq.html#wh42010

Organization for Standardization (ISO), International Electrotechnical Commission (IEC), and Institute of Electronics Engineers (IEEE) offer to software architecture practices?

- Name at least three object-oriented design principles.

- What is the chief contribution of the Generalized Enterprise Reference Architecture and Methodology[47] to enterprise architecture?

- You're being commissioned to develop a strategy plan for application and system security. What software architecture frameworks would you employ to fulfill this task?

- Which software architecture frameworks would you utilize to promote enterprise interoperability?

- What is the contribution of the Control Objectives for Information and Related Technologies (COBIT)[48] framework to management of IT?

- Why is the Sherwood Applied Business Security Architecture (SABSA)[49] framework advocating security measures driven by business requirements?

- Why are the Twelve-Factor App[50] principles important to application architecture practices?

- What is the contribution of the Federal Enterprise Architecture Framework (FEAF) to the commercial industry's best practices, standards, and policies?

- What is the contribution of the Unified Architecture Framework (UAF) to enterprise architecture?

---

[47] P. Bernus, and L. Nemes, A Framework to Define a Generic Enterprise Reference Architecture and Methodology, CSIRO publishing, 1994 (download this paper from research-repository .griffith.edu.au/bitstream/handle/10072/176131/Bernus105429-Accepted .pdf)

[48] www.isaca.org/resources/cobit

[49] sabsa.org/sabsa-executive-summary/

[50] www.redhat.com/architect/12-factor-app

Index